Intersections between Mental Health and Law among Veterans

Jack Tsai • Evan R. Seamone
Editors

Intersections between Mental Health and Law among Veterans

Springer

Editors
Jack Tsai
Veterans Affairs National Center on Homelessness Among Veterans
Tampa, FL, USA

Department of Psychiatry
Yale University School of Medicine
New Haven, CT, USA

Evan R. Seamone
Veterans Benefits Attorney, Loxley Services, and Major
U.S. Army Reserve
Gainesville, FL, USA

ISBN 978-3-030-31663-1 ISBN 978-3-030-31664-8 (eBook)
https://doi.org/10.1007/978-3-030-31664-8

This Springer imprint is published by the registered company Springer Nature Switzerland AG
The registered company address is: Gewerbestrasse 11, 6330 Cham, Switzerland

Acknowledgments

Freedom, justice, and health are difficult but fundamental components of a thriving society. We must be careful in maintaining a balance among these components. We are privileged to live in a free and wealthy United States because of those who have come before us and their dedication to founding principles. This book is dedicated to the men and women who have served in the U.S. Armed Forces, their loved ones, and those who have served them.

Jack Tsai

Contents

Chapter 1
Introduction

Jack Tsai

What wounded veterans don't need is sympathy. They need to be treated like the men [and women] they are: equals, heroes, and people who still have tremendous value for society.

—Chris Kyle

Throughout human history, military forces have been essential to the preservation, protection, and operations of societies. In modern time, the United States military consists of five branches, including the Army, Air Force, and Navy, Marine Corps, and Coast Guard, each with different functions. Collectively, these military branches serve to ensure the security of the country; in turn, the country and its citizens have taken on the responsibility of creating systems of care to serve the healthcare needs of military personnel after their service and to help them transition back to civilian life. For that purpose, the U.S. Department of Veterans Affairs (VA) was created and is now the second largest federal department in the U.S. The VA consists of three entities: the Veterans Health Administration, the Veterans Benefit Administration, and the National Cemetery Administration. As part of the Veterans Health Administration, there are currently over 130 VA medical centers and over 1000 community-based outpatient clinics throughout the country. Although oft overlooked, the VA regularly serves veterans who are involved in the criminal justice system and/or who have civil legal problems. The VA can and does treat convicted felons and even sex offenders at their facilities since VA healthcare eligibility and compensation after military discharge is not a basis for denial of service. In addition to VA resources, there are countless regional and national veterans service organizations, and other privately and publicly funded institutions serving veterans and their healthcare needs.

J. Tsai (✉)
Veteran Affairs National Center on Homelessness among Veterans, Tampa, FL, USA

Department of Psychiatry, Yale University School of Medicine, New Haven, CT, USA
e-mail: Jack.Tsai@yale.edu

J. Tsai, E. R. Seamone (eds.), *Intersections between Mental Health and Law among Veterans*, https://doi.org/10.1007/978-3-030-31664-8_1

Major advances in science and medicine in the past few decades have led to substantial progress in improving veterans' health and well-being. For example, considerable progress has been made in addressing various medical and psychosocial problems that have plagued the veteran population, such as combat injuries (Sigford, 2008), chronic medical problems (Lew, Tun, & Cifu, 2009), mental illness (Karlin et al., 2010), unemployment (Resnick & Rosenheck, 2007), and homelessness (Tsai, O'Toole, & Kearney, 2017). However, many veterans continue to struggle with these problems. U.S. involvement with conflicts in Iraq and Afghanistan have also resulted in whole new generations of recent veterans with new problems and who need assistance with readjusting to life after their service (Hoge et al., 2004; Seal et al., 2009). While it would be stereotypical, mythological, and inaccurate to assume that war-traumatized veterans are prone to commit acts of violence or are like "ticking time bombs" (Horton, 2012), some "invisible wounds" sustained during the Global War on Terror place some veterans at greater risk of experiencing reactions that involve violence, misperception of threats, and impulsive behavior (Galovski & Lyons, 2004; Tanielian & Jaycox, 2008). When these reactions do occur, they often place veterans in conflict with the law.

There has been a continual gradual shift in our understanding and approach to health care. The current leading causes of mortality in the U.S., like heart disease, stroke, cancer, diabetes, and suicide, are known to be closely related to lifestyle, diet, stress management, and other psychosocial factors (Danaei et al., 2009; Jemal, Ward, Hao, & Thun, 2005). Health and well-being is now viewed in terms of not only disease and biological etiology, but the social context and the influence of environmental factors are importantly being considered. Social determinants of health can include cultural values, individual backgrounds, socioeconomic status, and other psychosocial problems like homelessness, incarceration, and legal problems (Jemal et al., 2005; Marmot et al., 2008; Marmot & Wilkinson, 2005). We have also increased our understanding of certain behavioral problems, such as addiction, as diseases or conditions that can be treated (Dole & Nyswander, 1967; Leshner, 1997; Wollschlaeger, 2007). There has been a movement towards rehabilitation and focus on functioning and quality of life rather than symptomatology (Anthony, 1993; Bond, Drake, Becker, & Mueser, 1999). This movement has been transmitted to approaches to addressing criminal justice problems and the high rates of mental illness and substance use disorders among those involved in the criminal justice system.

This book will focus on various important ways in which mental health and law intersect. The U.S. justice system is complex but can be separated into criminal and civil law. As already alluded to, there are many ways in which mental health and criminal law intersect but there are also ways in which mental health intersects with civil law. The circumstances of modern wars have at times transformed attorneys, judges, corrections professionals, and others into "first-responders" for untreated, invisible war wounds (Seamone, 2009). In this book, we try to delve into several important ways these intersections affect veterans, healthcare, and society at large.

What This Book Is About

This book is intended for a broad audience of academics, policymakers, program administrators, clinicians, researchers, and students who are interested in programs, services, and research on veterans with mental health problems involved in legal systems. The purpose of the book is to provide a comprehensive overview of these issues and highlight the innovative work in this area. The book contains a series of chapters that showcase and delve into the burgeoning areas in which mental health and law intersect. We focus on the U.S. veteran population given wide public support for their well-being and the range of mental health and social problems they encounter after their service. Since the intersection between mental health and law is a relatively nascent area, many of the chapters of the book also describe where the gaps in knowledge currently lay.

On the criminal law side, the U.S. criminal justice system is in a crisis and faces many major challenges with overcrowding in jails and prisons, correctional facilities serving as de-facto mental health institutions, and high recidivism rates among offenders released from these facilities (Fitzgerald & Vance, 2015; Pitts, Griffin III, & Johnson, 2014; Slate, Buffington-Vollum, & Johnson, 2013). New solutions and alternative approaches are needed.

Historically, the nation has had to content with the problem of veterans in the criminal justice system for many decades now and the government has recognized this since the early 20th century. For example, as early as the 1920s, the Veterans Bureau and chapters of the American Legion were concerned and conducted surveys of the nation's prisons and jails to determine how many veterans traumatized by World War I could be freed to receive the treatment they needed instead of having to be incarcerated where there was limited access to treatment (Seamone, 2013). These activities represent an impetus to recognize the connection between untreated mental health conditions from prior service and criminal offending and has long suggested that alternative approaches may be needed for criminal justice-involved veterans, particularly for criminal offending that can be tied to military service.

A review of recent historical trends in the incarceration of veterans shows that the proportion of veterans in state and federal prisons steadily rose for two decades between 1985 and 2000. But beginning in the year 2000, the number of veterans in state and federal prisons began to decline and has continued to decline for more than a decade according to the Bureau of Justice Statistics (Bronson, Carson, Noonan, & Berzofsky, 2015). For example, in 1986, 20% of state prisoners were veterans which fell to 10% in 2004. Overall, the most recent estimate from the Bureau of Justice Statistics states that an estimated 181,500 veterans were in state and federal prisons in 2011–12, down from 206,500 in 2004. This decline has occurred during a time period when the total state and federal prisoner population has grown dramatically. The decline in the proportion and number of veteran prisoners is likely due to several factors. For one, the decline coincides with the shrinking proportion of veterans in the overall U.S. population. For example, in 1985, veterans constituted 16% of the adult U.S. population but only 9% by 2012 (Bronson et al., 2015). Additionally, the veteran population is disproportionally older than other U.S. male adults in the population and this gap is increasing. In 2004, about 40% of veterans were 65 or older compared to less than 8% of the U.S. adult population that was in the age range (Noonan & Mumola, 2007).

Nonetheless, veterans involved in the criminal justice system have problems. In their most recent report, the Bureau of Justice Statistics found that veterans were more likely to be serving time for a violent offense as compared to non-veterans (64% versus 48%) and more likely to be in prison for a sexual offenses (35% versus 23%), presumably some of which was domestic violence (Bronson et al., 2015). Compared to non-veterans, veterans tended to have fewer prior arrests and had shorter criminal histories than non-veterans, but had longer average sentences, regardless of offense type. Notably, veterans in prison were twice as likely as non-veterans to report that a mental health professional has told them they have post-traumatic stress disorder (23% versus 11%). Thus, there are various opportunities for primary and secondary prevention and various points to intervene as conceptualized in the sequential intercept model (Blue-Howells, Clark, van den Berk-Clark, & McGuire, 2013) which is discussed further in Chap. 3.

Beyond criminal law, many veterans also experience civil legal issues like evictions, divorce, custody, applying for disability, access to healthcare, etc. In fact, the annual CHALENG survey of homeless veterans has consistently found that the top unmet needs of homeless veterans are related to legal assistance for eviction and foreclosure, child support, and outstanding warrants and fines (Tsai, Blue-Howells, & Nakashima, 2019). Recognition of these issues has led to the proliferation of medical-legal partnerships and special issues that veterans face in family court, which we discuss in this book. Unlike with criminal law, defendants who cannot afford an attorney are not assigned one by the court and must self-represent or seek legal aid. Legal aid offices are often inundated and under-staffed so they cannot serve the many clients that need their services. Thus, many low-income veterans do not receive the legal assistance they need which can affect their sense of procedural and distributive justice. Whereas distribute justice is concerned with fairness of the actual outcome of a case, procedural justice is the idea of fairness in the processes to resolve the case. Both forms of justice may be important to veterans and affect their mental health and other outcomes (Tsai et al., 2017).

Timeline of Major Events

Table 1.1 details major historical events in the past century and a half that pertain to veterans' health, benefits, legislation, and other aspects of law. Beginning in the mid-1800s, the U.S. engaged in its deadliest war resulting in the most American deaths since. The American Civil War (1861–1865) which resulted in an estimated 750,000 Americans dead. The post-war Reconstruction which lasted from the end of the war until 1877 also resulted in significant challenges that divided the nation as the South tried to maintain control of the labor and behavior of African Americans

Table 1.1 Historical timeline of major events related to veterans' health and law

• 1861–1865: American Civil War
The American Civil War involved more than 3 million soldiers and over 600,000 deaths. The war displaced many Veterans, broke up families, and caused rifts in communities. After the war, the country entered an economic recession for several years.
• 1912: Sherwood Act
The Sherwood Act extends military pensions to all Veterans. Union, Mexican, and Civil War Veterans now automatically receive pensions until the age of 62, regardless of injury or disability. Before this act, military pensions were only available to soldiers discharged due to illness or disability inflicted during service.
• 1914–1918: World War I
World War I involved nearly 5 million U.S. soldiers with more than 100,000 dead and 200,000 wounded.
• 1929–1939: The Great Depression
The Great Depression was the longest, deepest, and most widespread depression of the twentieth century. It has been estimated that nearly 25% of America's work force were in severe poverty during this time period.
• 1930: Veterans Administration Established
President Herbert Hoover signs an Executive Order to create the Veterans Administration to "consolidate and coordinate government activities affecting war Veterans," which later became the Department of Veterans Affairs.
• 1939–1945: World War II
Over 16 million U.S. soldiers served during World War II, which led to over 400,000 deaths during service and 600,000 wounded.
• 1944: G.I. Bill passed
The Servicemen's Readjustment Act, known as the G.I. bill provided returning Veterans with unemployment compensation and financial resources for education to help them re-integrate after military service.
• 1950–1953: Korean War
Over 1.5 million U.S. soldiers served during the Korean War, with over 30,000 deaths and 100,000 wounded.
• 1963: Gideon v. Wainright
The U.S. Supreme Court unanimously ruled that states are required under the Sixth Amendment to provide an attorney to defendants in criminal cases who are unable to afford their own attorneys.
• 1964: Civil Rights Act
This landmark act outlawed discrimination on the basis of race, color, religion, sex, or national origin, and required equal access to public places and employment.
• 1955–1975: Vietnam War
Over 3 million U.S. solders served during the Vietnam War, with over 50,000 deaths and 100,000 wounded. During the war and its aftermath, it is estimated there were over 50,000 homeless Veterans in a given night.
• 1971–present: President Nixon declares the "War on Drugs"
The federal government began a campaign to reduce the illegal drug trade, by using military intervention, enacting federal and state policies to specially penalize drug offenders, and imposing collateral consequences on drug offenders.

(continued)

Table 1.1 (continued)

• 1990–1991: Persian Gulf War
Over half a million U.S. soldiers served during the Gulf War, with over 300 deaths and 400 wounded.
• 2001–2014: Operations Enduring Freedom/Iraqi Freedom/New Dawn
Over 2.5 million U.S. soldiers served during the conflicts in Iraq and Afghanistan with over 6000 deaths and 900,000 wounded.
• 2007: Veterans Health Administration begins creating programs for criminal justice-involved veterans.
The Health Care for Re-entry Veterans (HCRV) program was created to assist Veterans with their community re-entry upon release from incarceration. The Veterans Justice Outreach (VJO) program was created to help criminal justice-involved Veterans connect to VA healthcare and social services.
• 2008: First Veterans treatment court created in Buffalo, New York
Judge Robert Russell creates the first Veterans treatment court in New York after noticing the number of veterans on his drug and mental health court dockets
• 2011: Veterans Affairs General Counsel Office issues Directive 2011-034
This Directive entitled "Homeless Veterans Legal Referral Process" supports development of medical-legal partnerships in Veterans Affairs medical centers and encourages referral and space for legal service providers.
• 2014–Present: Operation Inherent Resolve
Military intervention against the Islamic State of Iraq and Syria including campaigns in Iraq and Syria. Various airstrikes have been conducted on enemy forces, leading to limited U.S. casualties and substantial enemy and civilian casualties.

and reactionary forces in the North consisting of the Radical Republicans who emphasized civil rights and voting rights for newly enfranchised African Americans.

The U.S. was not involved in another war until 50 years later which was World War I, the Great War (1914–1918), a global war that the U.S. did not enter until 1917 on the part of the Allied Forces. When the U.S. entered World War I, Congress established a system of veteran benefits that included programs for disability compensation, and vocational rehabilitation. A few years later, in 1930 under President Herbert Hoover, the U.S. Department of Veterans Affairs was created, although at the time it had not yet become a federal department and was known as the Veterans Administration with Brigadier General Frank T. Hines as its first Administrator.

Unresolved conflicts of the World War I led to a second World War 21 years later (1939–1945). During the period of World War II, the veteran population increased dramatically as World War I veterans were aging and large number of men were sent to fight in the second world war. Congress enacted various benefits for war veterans during this time and began to consolidate services for veterans. The Serviceman's Readjustment Act, also known as the G.I., bill was signed into law in 1944 by President Franklin D. Roosevelt and offered a range of benefits for returning World War II veterans including accessible hospitals, low-interest home mortgages, and stipends covering tuition and expenses for veterans attending college or trade schools.

U.S. entered the Vietnam War nearly a decade later (1955–1975) and the Vietnam War was the longest war the U.S. had been involved in at the time. American involvement in the war stirred controversy within the country and many Americans opposed the war demonstrating in protests. Consequently, there was resentment and hostile feelings expressed by some segments of the public towards U.S. troops. Some veterans who were deployed and returned stateside described an "uneasy homecoming" (Faulkner & McGaw, 1977).

Near the end of the Vietnam War, the U.S. also began establishing an All-Volunteer Force. In 1973, the military draft was eliminated and the U.S. moved to a military that consisted of volunteers who enlisted. The military implemented a comprehensive plan to attract volunteers, including raising the pay of enlisted individuals, expanded recruiting structures, and improved the tasks and living conditions of military personnel.

Around the same time in the 1970s, in the civilian world, President Nixon declared a "war on drugs" which resulted in the incarceration of hundreds of thousands of Americans over several subsequent decades. In present day, some drug enforcement policies have changed while various other policies have stayed the same. Because many veterans have substance use disorders (Seal et al., 2011; Tsai, Kasprow, & Rosenheck, 2014), many drug enforcement policies enacted in the 1970s continue to affect the lives and incarceration of veterans and their loved ones.

On September 11, 2001, there were a series of four coordinated terrorist attacks by the Islamic terrorist group Al-Qaeda on major U.S. institutions including the World Trade Center complex and the Pentagon. The U.S. responded by launching the War on Terror, invading Afghanistan in 2001 and subsequently invading Iraq in 2002. These conflicts deployed a whole new generation of soldiers for Operations Enduring Freedom/Iraqi Freedom/New Dawn which have officially ended, and Operation Inherent Resolve was begun in 2014 in Syria and Iraq. Many veterans continue to serve in the Middle East and the country is continuing to receive veterans who have returned from these conflicts. There is widespread public support for these troops and much attention on the social readjustment of this recent generation of veterans. The VA and various public and private organizations have funded initiatives to promote the health and well-being of these veterans.

Case in point, beginning in 2007, the VA began developing two major programs to address criminal justice involvement among veterans—the Health Care for Re-entry Veterans (HCRV) program to help Veterans with community re-entry after incarceration (Tsai, Rosenheck, Kasprow, & McGuire, 2013) and the Veterans Justice Outreach (VJO) program to help divert criminal justice-involved Veterans away from incarceration and to VA healthcare and social services (Blue-Howells et al., 2013). In 2008, an initiative had begun outside the VA to create veterans treatment courts, which were modeled after drug and mental health courts but exclusively focused on veterans. A county court judge in New York named Robert Russell created the first veterans treatment court and there are now hundreds of veterans treatment courts throughout the country. While these veterans treatment courts may be controversial to some, these courts seek to address public health and public safety challenges and should not be viewed as a show of gratitude to veterans for their service. Rather, veterans treatment courts represent an alternative approach to addressing untreated mental health and substance abuse problems and reflect a greater need for new solutions amidst the larger crisis in the U.S. prison system.

In addition to criminal justice problems, in 2011, the VA General Counsel began to support the development of medical-legal partnerships to help veterans with their civil legal problems by issuing a new VA directive. Several medical-legal partnerships had already existed before this time (Tsai et al., 2017), but this VA directive formally encourage referral and space for community legal service providers in VA medical centers. Various VA medical-legal partnerships have since sprouted around the country with the support of VA General Counsel and various state bar associations, law schools, and non-profit organizations.

We hope this brief review of historical events provides some backdrop for America's current situation with veterans and the criminal justice system. We end this chapter with a review of the contents of the rest of the book.

Contents of the Book

After this introductory chapter, the book starts with Chap. 2 focused on the complex problem of criminal justice involvement among veterans written by VA researchers Daniel Blonigen, Ph.D. and Christine Timko, Ph.D. They discuss the prevalence, types, and models of understanding criminal behavior among veterans as well as the characteristics and needs of criminal justice-involved veterans. Chapter 3 then details the various criminal justice programs that have been created by the VA and the chapter is written by the national coordinator of VA's veterans justice outreach program Sean Clark, J.D. and VA data analyst Bessie Flatley, Ph.D.

In Chap. 4, a new emerging service model is introduced and described that focuses on civil law. Legal providers have begun partnering with many VA medical centers to help veterans address civil legal problems through medical-legal partnerships. The chapter is written by lawyers Krista Selnau, J.D. and Rose Goldberg, J.D. who operate such partnerships with the VA. After Chap. 4, the book begins to discuss programs and services outside of the VA.

Chapter 5 is dedicated to veterans treatment courts, which is a rapidly growing rehabilitative model for veterans involved in the criminal justice system. Veterans treatment courts, are modeled after mental health and drug courts, aiming to divert individuals to treatment rather than incarceration. This chapter is written by social work researcher Janice McCall, Ph.D. and Benjamin Pomerance, J.D. who helps direct the Division of Veterans' Services for New York State. Chapter 6 focuses on a different kind of court that veterans often become involved in, family courts. Family law is relevant to many veterans and their family members involved in conflicts with familial and domestic relationships, including divorce, child custody and support, and estate issues. There is also concern about "secondary trauma" experienced by spouses and children when a veteran with mental health issues does not receive treatment because of a criminal label or discharge characterization (Ahmadi,

Azampoor-Afshar, Karami, & Mokhtari, 2011). This chapter is authored by Judge Janice Rosa, J.D., whose wide-ranging experience includes initiating a docket devoted to military families in her family court in Buffalo, New York.

In Chap. 7, VA social workers Elizabeth Goggin, M.A., L.C.S.W. and Michele Roberts, L.C.S.W. describe the development and operations of all-veterans service units. All-veterans service units are specialized units in jails, prisons, and other correctional facilities that house only veterans and incorporate rehabilitation principles for incarcerated veterans.

Chapter 8 is written by the book's co-editor and Judge Advocate General officer Evan Seamone, LL.M., J.D., who describes the often complicated and lesser known aspects of military law as they relate to courts-martial, administrative separation proceedings, and the stigmatizing military discharges that result from these fora. The process of determining military discharges and how they affect eligibility of veterans for various VA benefits are also discussed.

In Chap. 9, VA psychologist Shoba Sreenivasan and other academics focus on the important challenges of assisting veterans with sexual offenses, reviewing both the scope of the problem as well as the current literature and where gaps in knowledge and services remain.

In the last chapter, Chap. 10, former Army psychiatrist and recognized expert on combat mental health issues Elspeth Ritchie, M.D. presents information about the needs of special veteran populations that need to be considered in research and treatment, such as female veterans, veterans with "bad paper" discharges," and differences between veterans of different service eras.

References

Ahmadi, K., Azampoor-Afshar, S., Karami, G., & Mokhtari, A. (2011). The association of veterans' PTSD with secondary trauma stress among veterans' spouses. *Journal of Aggression, Maltreatment & Trauma, 20*(6), 636–644.

Anthony, W. A. (1993). Recovery from mental illness: The guiding vision of the mental health service system in the 1990s. *Psychosocial Rehabilitation Journal, 16*, 11–23.

Blue-Howells, J. H., Clark, S. C., van den Berk-Clark, C., & McGuire, J. F. (2013). The US Department of Veterans Affairs Veterans Justice Programs and the sequential intercept model: Case examples in national dissemination of intervention for justice-involved veterans. *Psychological Services, 10*(1), 48.

Bond, G. R., Drake, R. E., Becker, D. R., & Mueser, K. T. (1999). Effectiveness of psychiatric rehabilitation approaches for employment of people with severe mental illness. *Journal of Disability Policy Studies, 10*(1), 18–52.

Bronson, J., Carson, A., Noonan, M., & Berzofsky, M. (2015). *Veterans in prison and jail, 2011–12*. Washington, DC: US Department of Justice, Office of Justice Programs, Bureau of Justice Statistics.

Danaei, G., Ding, E. L., Mozaffarian, D., Taylor, B., Rehm, J., Murray, C. J. L., & Ezzati, M. (2009). The preventable causes of death in the United States: Comparative risk assessment of dietary, lifestyle, and metabolic risk factors. *PLoS Medicine, 6*(4), e1000058.

Dole, V. P., & Nyswander, M. E. (1967). Heroin addiction—A metabolic disease. *Archives of Internal Medicine, 120*(1), 19–24.

Faulkner, R. R., & McGaw, D. B. (1977). Uneasy homecoming: Stages in the reentry transition of Vietnam veterans. *Urban Life, 6*(3), 303–328.

Fitzgerald, J., & Vance, S. E. (2015). How today's prison crisis is shaping tomorrow's federal criminal justice system. *Federal Probation, 79*(2), 24–28.

Galovski, T., & Lyons, J. A. (2004). Psychological sequelae of combat violence: A review of the impact of PTSD on the veteran's family and possible interventions. *Aggression and Violent Behavior, 9*(5), 477–501.

Hoge, C. W., Castro, C. A., Messer, S. C., McGurk, D., Cotting, D. I., & Koffman, R. L. (2004). Combat duty in Iraq and Afghanistan, mental health problems, and barriers to care. *New England Journal of Medicine, 351*(1), 13–22.

Horton, A. (2012). *Perpetuating the erroneous "Ticking Bomb" view of veterans*. Retrieved from https://www.blogs.va.gov/VAntage/5813/usa-today-perpetuates-erroneous-"ticking-bomb"-view-of-veterans/

Jemal, A., Ward, E., Hao, Y., & Thun, M. (2005). Trends in the leading causes of death in the United States, 1970–2002. *JAMA, 294*(10), 1255–1259.

Karlin, B. E., Ruzek, J. I., Chard, K. M., Eftekhari, A., Monson, C. M., Hembree, E. A., … Foa, E. B. (2010). Dissemination of evidence-based psychological treatments for posttraumatic stress disorder in the Veterans Health Administration. *Journal of Traumatic Stress, 23*(6), 663–673.

Leshner, A. I. (1997). Addiction is a brain disease, and it matters. *Science, 278*(5335), 45–47.

Lew, H. L., Tun, C., & Cifu, D. X. (2009). Prevalence of chronic pain, posttraumatic stress disorder, and persistent postconcussive symptoms in OIF/OEF veterans: Polytrauma clinical triad. *Journal of Rehabilitation Research and Development, 46*(6), 697–702.

Marmot, M., Friel, S., Bell, R., Houweling, T. A. J., Taylor, S., & Commission on Social Determinants of Health. (2008). Closing the gap in a generation: Health equity through action on the social determinants of health. *Lancet, 372*(9650), 1661–1669.

Marmot, M., & Wilkinson, R. (Eds.). (2005). *Social determinants of health*. Oxford: Oxford University Press.

Noonan, M. E., & Mumola, C. J. (2007). *Veterans in state and federal prison, 2004*. Retrieved from https://bjs.gov/content/pub/pdf/vsfp04.pdf

Pitts, J. M. A., Griffin, O. H., III, & Johnson, W. W. (2014). Contemporary prison overcrowding: Short-term fixes to a perpetual problem. *Contemporary Justice Review, 17*(1), 124–139.

Resnick, S. G., & Rosenheck, R. (2007). Dissemination of supported employment in Department of Veterans Affairs. *Journal of Rehabilitation Research and Development, 44*(6), 867–878.

Seal, K. H., Cohen, G., Waldrop, A., Cohen, B. E., Maguen, S., & Ren, L. (2011). Substance use disorders in Iraq and Afghanistan veterans in VA healthcare, 2001–2010: Implications for screening, diagnosis and treatment. *Drug and Alcohol Dependence, 116*(1), 93–101.

Seal, K. H., Metzler, T. J., Gima, K. S., Bertenthal, D., Maguen, S., & Marmar, C. R. (2009). Trends and risk factors for mental health diagnoses among Iraq and Afghanistan veterans using Department of Veterans Affairs Health Care, 2002–2008. *American Journal of Public Health, 99*(9), 1651–1658.

Seamone, E. R. (2009). Attorneys as first-responders: Recognizing the destructive nature of posttraumatic stress disorder on the combat veteran's legal decision-making process. *Military Law Review, 202*, 144–184.

Seamone, E. R. (2013). A historical touchstone for Nebraska in the mission to divert criminally-involved veterans from confinement. *Nebraska Lawyer, Nov/Dec*, 5–13.

Sigford, B. J. (2008). "To care for him who shall have borne the battle and for his widow and his orphan"(Abraham Lincoln): The Department of Veterans Affairs Polytrauma System of Care. *Archives of Physical Medicine and Rehabilitation, 89*(1), 160–162.

Slate, R. N., Buffington-Vollum, J. K., & Johnson, W. W. (2013). *The criminalization of mental illness: Crisis and opportunity for the justice system*. Durham, NC: Carolina Academic Press.

Tanielian, T., & Jaycox, L. H. (Eds.). (2008). *Invisible wounds of war: Psychological and cognitive injuries, their consequences, and services to assist recovery*. Santa Monica, CA: RAND Corporation.

Tsai, J., Blue-Howells, J., & Nakashima, J. (2019). Needs of homeless veterans: Five years of the CHALENG Survey 2012–2016. *Journal of Public Health, 41*(1), e16–e24.

Tsai, J., Kasprow, W. J., & Rosenheck, R. A. (2014). Alcohol and drug use disorders among homeless veterans: Prevalence and association with supported housing outcomes. *Addictive Behaviors, 39*(2), 455–460.

Tsai, J., Middleton, M., Retkin, R., Johnson, C., Kenneally, K., Sherman, S., & Rosenheck, R. A. (2017). Partnerships between healthcare and legal providers in the Veterans Health Administration. *Psychiatric Services, 68*(4), 321–323.

Tsai, J., Middleton, M., Villegas, J., Johnson, C., Retkin, R., Seidman, A., … Rosenheck, R. A. (2017). Medical-legal partnerships at Veterans Affairs medical centers improved housing and psychosocial outcomes for vets. *Health Affairs, 36*(12), 2195–2203.

Tsai, J., O'Toole, T., & Kearney, L. K. (2017). Homelessness as a public mental health and social problem: New knowledge and solutions. *Psychological Services, 14*(2), 113–117.

Tsai, J., Rosenheck, R. A., Kasprow, W. J., & McGuire, J. F. (2013). Risk of incarceration and other characteristics of Iraq and Afghanistan Era Veterans in State and Federal Prisons. *Psychiatric Services, 64*(1), 36–43.

Wollschlaeger, B. (2007). The science of addiction: From neurobiology to treatment. *JAMA, 298*(7), 807–812.

Chapter 2
Criminal Justice Involvement Among Veterans

Daniel M. Blonigen, Christopher M. King, and Christine Timko

Readiness to react instantly and violently when surprised, a learned skill in training and combat, often comes to haunt and impair veterans in civilian life.

—Jonathan Shay (Achilles in Vietnam, 1995)

Being arrested is the first way of getting help. (Marine combat veteran in a Veterans Treatment Court. Retrieved from http://www.msnbc.com/jansing-co/now-vets-can-get-help-instead-jail-time)

Abbreviations

BJS	Bureau of Justice Statistics
HUD-VASH	Housing and Urban Development-Veterans Affairs Supportive Housing
MRT	Moral Reconation Therapy

D. M. Blonigen (✉)
HSR&D Center for Innovation to Implementation, VA Palo Alto Health Care System, Menlo Park, CA, USA

Clinical Psychology PhD Program, Palo Alto University, Palo Alto, CA, USA

Department of Psychiatry and Behavioral Sciences, Stanford University School of Medicine, Palo Alto, CA, USA
e-mail: Daniel.Blonigen@va.gov

C. M. King
Department of Psychology, Montclair State University, Montclair, NJ, USA
e-mail: kingch@montclair.edu

C. Timko
HSR&D Center for Innovation to Implementation, VA Palo Alto Health Care System, Menlo Park, CA, USA

Department of Psychiatry and Behavioral Sciences, Stanford University School of Medicine, Palo Alto, CA, USA
e-mail: Christine.Timko@va.gov

J. Tsai, E. R. Seamone (eds.), *Intersections between Mental Health and Law among Veterans*, https://doi.org/10.1007/978-3-030-31664-8_2

OEF/OIF/OND	Operation Enduring Freedom/Operation Iraqi Freedom/Operation New Dawn
PTSD	Posttraumatic stress disorder
R&R	Reasoning and Rehabilitation
RNR	Risk-Need-Responsivity
T4C	Thinking for a Change
TBI	Traumatic brain injury
US	United States
VHA	Veterans Health Administration
VIO-SCAN	Violence Screening and Assessment of Needs

Shay's (1995) observations of the impact of combat trauma aligns with a common archetype of a military veteran in criminal justice system—a "wounded warrior" programmed for violence and exposed to trauma and other moral injury during his or her service, who now carries the scars of battle into a civilian life marked by recklessness and illegal activity. Certainly, this scenario is applicable to some veterans who become involved in the criminal justice system and is one that is commonly used in media reports of veterans who act out violently. However, this archetype fails to acknowledge the resiliency demonstrated by most veterans who successfully readjust to civilian life. Further, as illustrated by the second quote, involvement in the criminal justice system can serve as the impetus for rehabilitation for many veterans who struggle with addiction and other mental health issues. To facilitate such efforts, relevant stakeholders (e.g., policymakers, criminal justice personnel, treatment providers) should be aware of the unique criminogenic risks and needs that characterize veterans in the criminal justice system.

The most current estimates indicate that approximately 181,500 veterans are housed in jails and prisons, which represents 8% of the total incarcerated population in the United States (US; Bronson, Carson, Noonan, & Berzofsky, 2015). Importantly, nearly 70% of the US correctional population is supervised in the community on parole or probation (Kaeble & Glaze, 2016); thus, estimates on the number of incarcerated veterans are a fraction of the total number of veterans who are involved in some stage of the criminal justice system (i.e., arrest and initial detention, courts, community supervision, jails, prisons). We use the term *justice-involved veterans* to denote this larger population.

The past decade has seen a surge of empirical research on criminal justice involvement among veterans. The goal of this chapter is to provide an overview of this literature and highlight what is known, and what gaps in knowledge remain, regarding criminal justice involvement among veterans of the US military. First, we describe the most current data on the rate of criminal justice involvement in veterans and the types of offenses that are most common in this population. When available, we focus on the evidence of characteristics that distinguish veterans from their civilian counterparts in the criminal justice system. Second, we review studies that have examined associations between mental health problems (including substance use and trauma) and criminal justice involvement among veterans using a range of approaches. Here, the prevalence of mental health problems among veterans involved in the criminal justice system is highlighted, as are differences in the rate and type of these problems between justice-involved veterans and non-veterans. Third, we review research relevant to criminal recidivism among justice-involved veterans and use a leading model of offender rehabilitation—the Risk-Need-Responsivity (RNR) model—to frame the discussion. Fourth, we summarize research examining the impact of criminal justice involvement on veterans' housing and employment statuses. Finally, we end by highlighting directions for future research to address gaps in knowledge regarding criminal justice involvement among veterans.

Prevalence and Type of Criminal Behavior Among Veterans

Incarcerated Veterans

Some of the most comprehensive data on the prevalence and type of criminal behavior among justice-involved veterans are for those incarcerated in jails and prisons. Such data are based on the National Inmate Survey, which is administered by the Bureau of Justice Statistics (BJS), most recently in 2011–2012 (Bronson et al., 2015). BJS data are reported separately for inmates of jails and prisons, given that these populations differ in conviction status, offense distribution, and average length of stay. The estimated 181,500 veterans (8% of all incarcerated adults) in 2011–2012 is a decrease from the estimates reported by the BJS in 2004 (206,500; 9% of all incarcerated adults) and 1998 (225,700; 12% of all incarcerated adults).

In terms of their military history, most incarcerated veterans reported receiving an honorable military discharge, with only 5% receiving a dishonorable or bad conduct discharge. A little less than half of all incarcerated veterans served less than three years in a military branch, most commonly in the Army. The majority of incarcerated veterans in both jail (66%) and prison (67%) were discharged from the military after the Vietnam era but prior to conflicts in Iraq and Afghanistan (i.e., between 1974 and 2000). Veterans who were discharged during the most recent military era (Operation Enduring Freedom/Operation Iraqi Freedom/Operation New Dawn; OEF/OIF/OND) accounted for only 25% and 13% of inmates in jails and prisons, respectively. This accords with other research indicating that, across multiple age groups and within different race/ethnic groups, OEF/OIF/OND veterans are less than half as likely as veterans from other service eras to be incarcerated (Tsai, Rosenheck, Kasprow, & McGuire, 2013). However, compared to other incarcerated veterans, OEF/OIF/OND veterans are more likely to report combat exposure and have a diagnosis of posttraumatic stress disorder (PTSD; Tsai et al., 2013). While differences in trauma exposure between incarcerated veterans of different service eras are notable, only 31% and 25% of veterans in jails and prisons, respectively, report combat exposure during military service (Bronson et al., 2015). These rates are slightly lower than the rate of combat exposure in a nationally representative survey of US military veterans (e.g., 38%; Campbell, Wisco, Marx, & Pietrzak, 2017). Further, it suggests that difficulties coping with combat trauma may not be the most common pathway to criminal justice involvement for most incarcerated veterans.

Comparisons Between Veterans and Non-Veterans

Demographic Characteristics

The BJS data also afford comparisons between veteran and non-veteran inmates in prevalence of justice involvement and other characteristics. Among their differences, the rate of incarceration for veterans (855 per 100,000 veterans in the US, or 0.86%) is lower than the rate of incarceration for non-veterans (968 per 100,000 US residents, or 0.97%). One factor that may explain this difference is that incarcerated veterans are older than non-veterans, and risk of crime decreases with age (Sweeten, Piquero, & Steinberg, 2013). On average, veterans incarcerated in jail were 11 years older than non-veterans (43 years vs. 32 years), and veterans incarcerated in prison were 12 years older than non-veterans (49 years vs. 37 years). In terms of other demographics, incarcerated veterans comprise a smaller proportion of Black (non-Hispanic) and Hispanic inmates (44% in jails, 38% in prisons) relative to incarcerated non-veterans (59% in jails; 63% in prisons). A significantly smaller proportion of incarcerated veterans have never been married (32% in jails; 24% in prisons) compared to non-veteran inmates (61% in jails; 57% in prisons). Incarcerated veterans are also more educated than their non-veteran counterparts. For example, at the time of the survey, fewer incarcerated veterans in jail (22%) and prisons (28%) had not yet received their high school diploma or GED, relative to non-veteran inmates of jails (56%) and prisons (61%).

Offense Profiles

Incarcerated veterans can also be distinguished from their non-veteran counterparts with respect to offense profiles (Bronson et al., 2015). For example, veterans in prisons are less likely than non-veterans to have been convicted of property, drug, or driving under the influence/driving while intoxicated offenses. These differences are also observed for property and drug offenses among jail inmates. In addition, prison sentence lengths are longer for incarcerated veterans than non-veterans. In jails, the proportion of those not sentenced is nearly equivalent for veterans (53%) and non-veterans (52%), and among those serving sentences, the length of the sentence is not significantly different between the two groups. One of the most robust differences between incarcerated veterans and non-veterans is their likelihood of committing a violent offense. In both jails and prisons, incarcerated veterans are more likely to have committed a violent offense than non-veteran inmates; after adjusting for differences in age and race/ethnicity, 64% of veterans incarcerated in prisons had been sentenced for a violent offense, compared to 52% of non-veterans. A similar offense profile has been observed for justice-involved veterans from the OEF/OIF/OND era. Among a national sample of OEF/OIF/OND veterans who had a contact with re-entry services from the Veterans Health Administration (VHA), the most common offense was a violent offense (35%), followed by property (25%) and drug (24%) offenses (Tsai et al., 2013). Notably, among justice-involved veterans contacted by VHA in jails or courts, public order offenses (e.g., weapons offense, public intoxication) were most common (29%), followed by violent (25%) and drug offenses (22%) (Department of Veterans Affairs, 2012). These latter figures suggest that the higher rate of violent offending among incarcerated veterans (vs. non-veterans) in the BJS survey could reflect the fact that veterans who are non-violent offenders may have been diverted from prison.

Within the category of violent offenses, two types of offenses have been highlighted as driving this difference between veterans and non-veterans: sexual offenses and intimate partner violence. In the BJS data, differences in the rate of violent offending are due to a higher proportion of veteran inmates convicted of a violent sexual offense (35% vs. 23% for non-veterans). Regarding intimate partner violence, through deployments and reintegration, military service often puts stress on the family unit. When combined with other sequalae associated with military service (e.g., head trauma, PTSD, substance use), such stress can increase risk for physical conflicts between veterans and their partners (Gierisch et al., 2013). In accordance with this, a review of studies on intimate partner violence among veterans found the prevalence of this offense type to range from 14% to 58%, with rates highest among veterans with mental health problems (Marshall, Panuzio, & Taft, 2005). These rates are up to three times higher than those found among non-veterans (16%; Straus & Gelles, 1990).

Although comprehensive, the BJS only provides data on the prevalence and type of criminal behavior among incarcerated veterans. Population-based data can also be used to compare the rate of criminal justice involvement among civilians and veterans in the general population. For example, data from the National Study on Drug Use and Health from 2002 to 2014 suggests that military service members and veterans have higher lifetime rates of arrests than their civilian counterparts (Snowden, Oh, Salas-Wright, Vaughn, & King, 2017). However, the effects were driven largely by individuals who were only in the military briefly, rather than those with more extensive military careers. This aligns with the BJS data (Bronson et al., 2015), which indicates that nearly half of all incarcerated veterans served in the military less than three years. By comparison, an estimated 28% of active duty soldiers from 2004 to 2009 had less than three years of military service (Ursano et al., 2015). Thus, to the extent that veterans are at increased risk of criminal justice involvement relative to civilians, this may be driven by those who did not "fit" in the military culture and discharged early via self-selection or were removed administratively.

Mental Health Problems Among Justice-Involved Veterans

Associations between mental health problems and criminal involvement among veterans have been examined using several different approaches and sample types. The 2011–2012 data from the BJS provides estimates of mental health problems for incarcerated veterans. Approximately one-half of all veterans in prison (48%) or jail (55%) reported that they had been told by a mental health professional that they had a mental health disorder. These prevalence rates were significantly higher than those for non-veterans in prison (36%) or jail (43%). Among veterans in prison who were told they had a mental health disorder, the most common disorder was depression (27% vs. 24% for non-veterans), followed by PTSD (23% vs. 11%), bipolar disorder (17% vs. 16%), personality disorder (16% vs. 13%), anxiety disorder (12% vs. 11%), and schizophrenia or another psychotic disorder (10% vs. 9%). Among prison inmates who had a mental health disorder, veterans were significantly more likely to have PTSD or a personality disorder; all other disorder prevalence differences between veteran and non-veteran prisoners were not statistically significant. Similarly, among veterans in jail who were told they had a mental health disorder, the most common was also depression (34% vs. 30% for non-veterans), followed by PTSD (31% vs. 15%), bipolar disorder (27% vs. 23%), personality disorder (17% vs. 15%), anxiety disorder (19% vs. 17%), and schizophrenia or another psychotic disorder (13% vs. 14%). As was observed for prison inmates, among jail inmates who had a mental health disorder, veterans were significantly more likely to have PTSD or a personality disorder. In addition, jail inmates who were veterans were also significantly more likely to have depression, bipolar disorder, or anxiety disorder compared to their non-veteran counterparts.

Among prison inmates, no significant difference was found between veterans and non-veterans on serious psychological distress in the past 30 days (14% veterans, 15% non-veterans). However, veterans were more likely to be in treatment for a mental health problem (18% vs. 15% for non-veterans), taking prescription medication (14% vs. 12%), and receiving counseling or therapy from a trained professional (13% vs. 11%). Veterans were also more likely than non-veterans to have ever stayed in a hospital overnight for a mental health problem (26% vs. 22%). Among jailed inmates, there was similarly no significant difference between veterans and non-veterans on past 30-day serious psychological distress (28% veterans, 26% non-veterans). However, jailed veterans were more likely than jailed non-veterans to be in treatment for a mental health problem (26% vs. 19%), taking prescription medication (22% vs. 17%), and receiving counseling or therapy from a trained professional (11% vs. 8%). Jailed veterans were more likely than jailed non-veterans to have ever stayed in a hospital overnight for a mental health problem (35% vs. 28%).

The BJS data also provide associations between combat experience and mental health indicators among incarcerated veterans (Bronson et al., 2015). Understanding the relation between combat trauma and criminal offending is a unique concern among justice-involved veterans (Blodgett et al., 2015). Among veterans in prison, those with combat experience were more likely to have an indicator of a mental health problem (64% vs. 49% of those without combat experience), equally likely to have had serious psychological distress in the past 30 days (16% vs. 13%), and more likely to have been told by a mental health professional that they had a mental health disorder (59% vs. 44%). Among veterans in jail, those with combat experience were also less likely to have no indicator of a mental health problem (27% vs. 41% of those without combat experience), more likely to have past 30-day serious psychological distress (31% vs. 27%), and more likely to have been told by a mental health professional that they had a mental health disorder (67% vs. 49%).

Associations between mental health problems and criminal involvement among veterans is further informed by a systematic review of the research literature in this area (Blodgett et al., 2015). Across 13 samples that reported a general rate of mental health problems among justice-involved veterans in either incarcerated or community settings, 13–62% of veterans had some mental health problems. Rates at the lower end of the range were based on more strict measures (e.g., a veteran reporting that a mental health professional had diagnosed them with a specific condition), whereas rates on the higher end were based on less strict measures (e.g., a veteran reporting any symptoms of a mental health disorder). Regarding specific mental health disorders, the prevalence of PTSD in general ranged from 4% to 39% (five samples), and the prevalence of combat-related PTSD ranged from 5% to 27% (four samples). Diagnostic rates at the higher end of these ranges were based on a formal assessment instrument. The prevalence of anxiety ranged from 10% to 51% (six samples), depression from 14% to 51% (nine samples), bipolar disorder from 3% to 11% (four samples), and adjustment disorder from 8% to 61% (four samples). In contrast to the wide ranges for these specific disorders, the diagnostic rate for the broader category of mood disorders ranged from 19% to 29% (5 samples). The prevalence of psychotic disorders ranged from 4% to 14% (four samples). Only two samples examined suicide in justice-involved veterans, with reports of 7% and 16% prevalence of suicidal ideation, and 0% and 1% prevalence of suicide attempts. In terms of substance use disorders, 21–71% of justice-involved veterans had an alcohol use disorder (15 samples), 26–65% had a drug use disorder (11 samples), and 57–61% had an alcohol use disorder, a drug use disorder, or both (two samples). Co-occurring mental health and substance use disorders were found for 23% and 53% of justice-involved veterans, respectively, in the latter two samples.

Four studies specifically compared justice-involved veterans to other justice-involved adults (i.e., non-veterans) on rates of mental health and substance use problems (Blodgett et al., 2015). Findings across these studies were mixed: in contrast to differences in the rate of mental health problems that were observed in the BJS data (Bronson et al., 2015), few significant differences were found in other studies identified in the systematic review. In addition, five studies compared justice-involved veterans to other veterans (Blodgett et al., 2015). Despite differences in how these studies were designed and how they defined the justice-involved and comparison groups, justice-involved veterans were consistently found to have more mental health problems, including substance misuse and co-occurring mental health and substance use disorders, than other veterans. For example, currently incarcerated veterans were more likely than veterans living in the community to report having had prior treatment for, or diagnosis of, a mental health disorder (13% vs. 8%; Greenberg & Rosenheck, 2009). Regarding alcohol use disorders, comparisons between justice-involved veterans and other veterans found rates of 44% versus 13% (Erickson, Rosenheck, Trestman, Ford, & Desai, 2008), 29% versus 13% (Black et al., 2005), and 48% versus 42% (McGuire, Rosenheck, & Kasprow, 2003), respectively. Regarding drug use disorders, comparisons yielded rates of 49% versus 7% (Erickson et al., 2008), and 62% versus 39% (McGuire et al., 2003) for justice-involved veterans versus other veterans, respectively.

Yet another approach to estimating the prevalence of mental health problems among justice-involved veterans has been to examine data for veterans served by VHA's Veterans Justice Programs. One of these programs—Health Care for Reentry Veterans—links veterans to VHA and community services upon reentry from state and federal prisons. Among veterans with an outreach visit from a Reentry Specialist who subsequently received VHA care, 69% were diagnosed with at least one mental health or substance use disorder (57% with at least one mental health disorder, and 49% with at least one substance use disorder; Finlay et al., 2017). The most common mental health disorders were depression, PTSD, and anxiety. The most common substance use disorders were alcohol, other drug, and cocaine use disorders. Thirty-five percent of justice-involved veterans seen in VHA were diagnosed with co-occurring mental health and substance use disorders.

The prevalence of mental health and substance use disorders has also been reported for veterans in treatment courts or jails who received an outreach visit from a Specialist from VHA's Veterans Justice Outreach program (Finlay et al., 2015). This study also provides insight into gender differences. Among women, the prevalence of mental health and substance use disorders was 88% and 58%, respectively, compared to 76% and 72% among men. Women had higher odds than men of being diagnosed with any mental health disorder, depression, PTSD, anxiety, bipolar disorder, and personality disorders. Conversely, women had lower odds than men of being diagnosed with any substance use disorder, and with an alcohol, cocaine, cannabis, or other drug use disorder, specifically. Women also had lower odds than men of being diagnosed with co-occurring mental health and substance use disorders.

Gender differences in mental health indicators among justice-involved veterans have also been examined using data from the Jail Diversion and Trauma Recovery Program, which was initiated in 2008 by the Substance Abuse and Mental Health Services Administration (Stainbrook, Hartwell, & James, 2016). The goal of this program was to support the implementation of jail diversion in 13 states for persons with PTSD and other trauma-related disorders, with a priority emphasis on veterans. The rates of mental health and substance use problems were high for both women and men in this sample, but female veterans reported higher rates of mental health problems, whereas male veterans reported higher rates of alcohol use problems. Specifically, more female veterans had a history of mental health treatment, met criteria for PTSD, and had moderate or extreme difficulty related to global mental health and depression. Female veterans also had higher PTSD symptom severity scores. In contrast, male veterans were more likely than women to report heavy alcohol use in the past 30 days. There were no differences between women and men for illegal drug use, which was reported by slightly over one-third of the full sample. Overall, these findings are similar to those obtained with a different sample and definition of justice involvement (Finlay et al., 2015).

The studies reviewed thus far in this section have examined rates of mental health disorders among justice-involved veterans. Another approach to establishing links between mental health and criminal involvement among veterans is to examine the criminal histories of veterans in treatment for mental health problems. For instance, one study investigated the prevalence of specific types of criminal arrests among a large nationally representative sample of male patients in VHA addiction treatment programs, all of whom served in the military before September 11, 2001 (Weaver, Trafton, Kimerling, Timko, & Moos, 2013). Among these patients, 85% had at least one lifetime criminal charge, and 58% had at least three such charges. These charges were categorized as specific to drugs (25% of patients), driving under the influence (52%), not related to drugs or alcohol and non-violent (69%), or violent (25%). In addition, 46% of patients had at least one lifetime conviction, and 17% had at least three such convictions. Several comparisons were made between patients with comorbid alcohol and drug use disorders versus those with discrete alcohol or drug use disorders. The former group had greater odds of lifetime criminal charges (any and repeated), and of being on parole or probation at the time of treatment admission, than those with discrete alcohol- or drug-related diagnoses. Similarly, those with comorbid alcohol and drug use disorders had more than double the odds of convictions relative to those with just alcohol use disorders, whereas there was no reliable difference in odds in comparison to those with drug use disorders only. Patients with comorbid alcohol and drug use disorders had the greatest odds of reporting prior arrests for nonviolent crimes compared to both substance-specific groups. They also evidenced increased odds of having any prior violent charge relative to patients with discrete alcohol use disorders.

Another study of criminal involvement among veterans in VHA addiction treatment found that patients clustered into three profiles based on their criminal history, which was assessed by type of offense, number of convictions, and number of months incarcerated (Schultz, Blonigen, Finlay, & Timko, 2015). The three types of criminal history profiles identified were *mild* (low numbers of criminal offenses, convictions, and months incarcerated; 79% of patients); *moderate* (high number of public order offenses, repeated convictions, and >3 years incarcerated; 14% of patients); and *severe* (violent criminal offenses, repeated convictions, and >10 years incarcerated; 7% of patients). Patients with mild criminal histories had more severe alcohol problems than patients with severe criminal histories, whereas patients with moderate and severe criminal histories were more likely to report having had trouble controlling violent behavior in the 30 days before treatment. However, all groups improved during treatment such that they did not differ on alcohol or drug use severity or violent behavior one year after entering treatment.

A third study investigated veterans in addiction or mental health treatment who reported any lifetime history of military or non-military trauma exposure (Bennett, Morris, Sexton, Bonar, & Chermack, 2017). Overall, 46% reported a history of any violent or nonviolent legal charge. More specifically, 22% endorsed a history of any violent offense, most commonly for assault (20%), and 39% endorsed a history of any non-violent offense, most commonly forgery (34%) or violation of probation or parole (24%). Fifteen percent of the sample endorsed having had both a violent and nonviolent legal charge.

In summary, across both incarcerated and community settings, justice-involved veterans appear to have higher rates of mental health disorders than other veterans, with substance use disorders and PTSD among the most prevalent conditions. Based on several indicators, mental health problems appear to be more common for incarcerated veterans than non-veterans. PTSD and personality disorders, in particular, are consistently more prevalent among veterans in jails and prisons. Similar to gender differences in the general population, male justice-involved veterans tend to be at higher risk for substance use disorders, whereas female justice-involved veterans are at higher risk for other mental health conditions. Among veterans in treatment for substance use or mental health problems, a history of criminal justice involvement is the norm rather than the exception. A history of criminal justice involvement is also more common among those with co-occurring mental health and substance use disorders and those with polysubstance use disorders.

Criminal Recidivism Among Justice-Involved Veterans

Critical to the rehabilitation of justice-involved veterans and other adults is knowledge of the factors that drive risk for criminal behavior. Knowledge of these factors can guide assessment and treatment planning efforts with justice-involved adults to minimize risk for future run-ins with the legal system. At the heart of this issue is managing risk for *recidivism*, defined as rearrest, reconviction, or reincarceration for a new offense or violation of the terms of conditional release. For justice-involved adults generally, recidivism is the norm rather than the exception. For example, based on data compiled by the BJS on adult prisoners released from 30 states in 2005, 68% were rearrested within three years of release, and 77% were rearrested within five years of release (Durose, Cooper, & Snyder, 2014).

Comparisons Between Veterans and Non-Veterans

Whether the rate of recidivism is similar or different for incarcerated veterans and non-veterans following correctional release has, to date, not been directly estimated. However, some insights into this issue can be gleaned from the 2011–2012 National Inmate Survey, which examined differences between incarcerated veterans and non-veterans in their criminal justice histories (Bronson et al., 2015). In both jails and prisons, veterans are more likely than non-veterans to report being first-time offenders. Specifically, after adjusting for differences in age and race/ethnicity, 32% of veterans in jails (vs. 25% of non-veterans) and 27% of veterans in prisons (compared to 23% of non-veterans) had no prior history of incarceration. Further, 43% of veterans in prison (vs. 55% of non-veterans) and 62% of veterans in jails (vs. 68% of non-veterans) reported four or more prior arrests. Although firm conclusions cannot be drawn from these figures alone, they suggest that the rate of recidivism may be lower for incarcerated veterans than non-veterans. Nonetheless, these figures also illustrate that recidivism is still the norm among justice-involved veterans, given that 68% of veterans in jails and 73% of veterans in prisons had at least one prior episode of incarceration. Consistent with this, data from VHA's Veterans Justice Program indicates that veterans served by these programs have an average of eight arrests in their lifetime (Department of Veterans Affairs, 2012). Together, these data suggest that many justice-involved veterans, like their non-veteran counterparts, are caught in a cycle of contact with the criminal justice system.

The Risk-Need-Responsivity Model: Application to Research on Recidivism Risk Among Justice-Involved Veterans

The Risk-Need-Responsivity (RNR) model is one of the leading frameworks for effective correctional rehabilitation (Andrews & Bonta, 2010a, 2010b). This model outlines the concepts and practices that have the strongest empirical support for reducing risk for recidivism among offenders. As reflected in its name, *risk*, *need*, and *responsivity* represent the model's core principles. Several studies and meta-analyses have shown that interventions and services that adhere to these principles have the most evidence for reducing criminal recidivism among offenders (Andrews & Bonta, 2010a, 2010b; Lipsey & Cullen, 2007). This is particularly true for services that attend to program integrity in terms of selecting skilled staff, providing appropriate training and ongoing supervision, and using structured and manualized approaches (Bonta & Andrews, 2017). In the following sections, we review these core principles and discuss their potential application and relevance to efforts to study recidivism risk among justice-involved veterans (see Table 2.1 for a summary of this literature).

The Risk Principle and Veterans

The risk principle refers to *who* should be treated. Specifically, this principle emphasizes the importance of matching service intensity to offenders' level of risk for recidivism, and prioritizing resources and intensive services for offenders who are at moderate to high risk of criminal recidivism. Accordingly, offenders who are estimated to be at low risk for recidivism would not be referred to more intensive programming and would not be assigned to programs with high-risk offenders. Indeed, some evidence suggests that low-risk offenders who are assigned to inten-

Table 2.1 Risk-Need-Responsivity (RNR) model principles and crime prevention initiatives for veterans

RNR principles	Relevance to veteran correctional diversion and rehabilitation
Risk	• Need more research (cf. Douds et al., 2017; Hartley & Baldwin, 2016; Rodriguez et al., 2017) about whether VJP are working with moderate and higher risk cases (e.g., there is a possibility that higher risk cases are systematically screened out of veterans treatment courts based on offense severity, VA eligibility, or other admission criteria; e.g., Erickson, 2016); matching service intensity to risk level; and avoiding mixing cases of different risk levels (cf. Timko et al., 2016). • Criminogenic risk assessment tools (such as fourth-generation tools that facilitate comprehensive RNR services plans) are not typically employed in current correctional diversion and rehabilitation services for veterans (Rodriguez et al., 2017; but see Hartley & Baldwin, 2016). • There is a pressing need for more research on structured criminogenic risk assessment with veterans (Elbogen et al., 2010). • There currently exists a violence risk screener tool for use with veterans: the VIOSCAN (Elbogen et al., 2014).
Need	• Traditional clinical assessment tends to involve use of valid assessment tools for some criminogenic needs (e.g., substance use), yet VJOs have expressed limitations of traditional clinical measures for some veteran-specific issues (Douds et al., 2017). • Although no studies of the validity of general criminal risk–need assessment tools have yet been reported, there is other evidence of the generalizability of many of the Central Eight risk factors to veterans, as well as some veterans-specific risk factors (Blonigen et al., 2016; King & Wade, 2017). • Depending on the individual, posttraumatic stress may function as a direct risk factor (e.g., intrusive symptoms increasing the risk for violent offending; Bennett et al., 2017), indirect risk factor (distress increasing the risk for substance misuse), non-criminogenic need (no direct or indirect relationship with offending in the individual case), or responsivity factor (mood symptoms decreasing treatment motivation). • There are gaps in VHA services for treating individual criminogenic needs, and in the availability of evidence-based correctional rehabilitation programs within VHA (Blonigen et al., 2017). • Research is needed to ensure that veteran diversionary efforts are predominantly targeting criminogenic needs (versus non-criminogenic needs), and doing so efficaciously (see Tsai et al., 2018).
General responsivity	• Initiatives have disseminated evidence-based, cognitive behavioral, treatments throughout VHA (e.g., Karlin & Cross, 2014), including those that address criminogenic needs (Blonigen et al., 2017). • Cognitive-behavioral treatments for criminal thinking are currently being piloted within the VHA (Blonigen et al., 2018).
Specific responsivity	• Military culture has been incorporated into diversion efforts (e.g., crisis intervention team training, veterans treatment courts) as a relevant demographic factor (Douds et al., 2017; Vaughan et al., 2016). • One intervention for criminogenic thinking has been modified to incorporate veteran culture: Moral Reconation Therapy (Little & Robinson, 2013). • Other candidate treatment-tailoring factors for justice-involved veterans include interpersonal trust and stigma (Timko et al., 2014).

sive programs or monitored frequently may have a higher likelihood of negative outcomes (Andrews & Dowden, 2006). This may be due to affiliation with high-risk offenders in such programs or disruption of low-risk offenders' prosocial networks and resources (Andrews & Dowden, 2006). At present, research to determine whether services for justice-involved veterans are adhering to these aspects of the risk principle is limited. For example, there is some evidence that veteran treatment courts are effective in reducing recidivism in this population (e.g., Hartley & Baldwin, 2016). However, it has also been suggested that higher-risk cases are systematically screened out of admission to these courts based on veterans' offense severity or eligibility for VHA services (Erickson, 2016).

Adherence to the risk principle of the RNR model also goes along with the *assessment* principle, which directs the use of structured recidivism risk assessments that validly differentiate low-risk from high-risk cases (Bonta & Andrews, 2007). Actuarial and structured professional judgment approaches to recidivism risk assessment have consistently shown predictive superiority to unstructured professional judgment (Fazel, Singh, Doll, & Grann, 2012; Grove, Zald, Lebow, Snitz, & Nelson, 2000; Hanson & Morton-Bourgon, 2009). Structured assessments of recidivism risk, particularly fourth-generation tools that facilitate comprehensive RNR treatment planning and services delivery (e.g., Level of Service/Case Management Inventory; Andrews, Bonta, & Wormith, 2004) are not typically employed in diversion and rehabilitation services for veterans (Rodriguez et al., 2017). Thus, the implementation of tools that facilitate adherence to the risk principle may not be widely implemented in crime prevention services for justice-involved veterans.

In terms of the development and validation of criminogenic risk assessment tools for the veteran population, such work to date has been limited to the prediction of violence risk. A five-item violence risk screening tool, the "*Vio*lence *Sc*reening and *A*ssessment of *N*eeds" (VIO-SCAN), was derived using two veteran samples—a random national sample of post-9/11 veterans, and a self-selected regional sample of veterans from the same service era (Elbogen et al., 2014). The violence risk factors measured by the VIO-SCAN are financial instability, combat experience, alcohol misuse, history of violence or arrests, and comorbid anger and probable PTSD. Items are scored dichotomously and added together to yield a total score ranging from 0 to 5. In the samples noted above, the VIO-SCAN total score was modestly to strongly predictive of any violence or aggression over the course of 1 year. Although these findings provide preliminary support for use of the VIO-SCAN to predict risk for violence among veterans, the screener is not regarded as an actuarial tool per se. Consequently, total scores on the VIO-SCAN should not be used to assign veterans into probabilistic risk categories (e.g., low, moderate, or high risk). Rather, the screener should be used to identify which veterans should be referred for a more comprehensive risk assessment. Although no structured violence risk assessment tools exist for such a follow-up assessment, evidence-based guidance is available (Elbogen et al., 2010).

The Need Principle and Veterans

The need principle refers to *what* should be treated. Specifically, this principle emphasizes that rehabilitation efforts should primarily target "criminogenic needs"—i.e., factors that are robust predictors of criminal recidivism and are changeable. Research to identify the criminogenic needs of justice-involved adults has been led by Andrews and Bonta (2010b), who highlighted the "Central Eight" risk factors for recidivism. These risk factors, derived from multiple meta-analyses (Andrews & Bonta, 2006), consist of the following: (1) *history of antisocial behavior*—particularly early, frequent, and varied antisocial activities; (2) *antisocial personality pattern*—traits such as impulsivity, hostility, sensation-seeking, and callous disregard for others; (3) *antisocial cognitions*—attitudes and beliefs that support a criminal identity and rationalization of criminal acts; (4) *antisocial associates*—close relationships with individuals who engage in or are supportive of criminal behavior; (5) *family or marital dysfunction*; (6) *lack of positive involvement in school or work*; (7) *lack of positive involvement in prosocial activities,* such as leisure and recreation; and (8) *substance use*.

The Central Eight represent intermediate targets for rehabilitation due to their theorized functional relationship to criminal behavior. By contrast, factors such as low self-esteem, low intelligence, emotional distress, or diagnoses of major depression or serious mental illness are generally weak predictors of recidivism and are thus categorized as non-criminogenic needs (Andrews & Bonta, 2006). Targeting such needs alone—which may need to be addressed for humanitarian, motivational, or other reasons—without a substantial focus on concomitant criminogenic needs is likely to be insufficient in reducing risk of recidivism among most criminal offenders. Further, the need principle also goes along with a *breadth* principle for treatment planning, which involves targeting multiple criminogenic needs when working with high-risk individuals. With a higher risk level comes a greater number of criminogenic needs. Thus, when working with high-risk individuals it is best to target the full range of criminogenic needs rather than focus treatment planning solely or predominantly on one or two risk factors or on non-criminogenic needs (e.g., a mental illness that does not have a case-specific connection to an individual's offending behavior).

The Need Principle and Veterans: The Central Eight

The validity of the Central Eight in the prediction of criminal recidivism among civilians has been well established; however, the extent to which these risk factors apply to justice-involved veterans has received less empirical attention. The importance of conducting this research is underscored by the fact there are differences between justice-involved veterans and non-veterans in various demographics linked to recidivism (e.g., age, marital status, education, and employment), as well as differences between these groups in the prevalence of mental health conditions such as substance use disorders and PTSD that may suggest a relationship to criminal involvement (Bronson et al., 2015).

In response to this gap, Blonigen et al. (2016) reviewed the literature to identify studies examining one or more of the Central Eight risk factors for criminal justice involvement or criminal recidivism in samples that were exclusively or predominantly veterans. Thirteen studies were identified; however, due to the relatively small number of studies, Blonigen and colleagues conducted a narrative review rather than synthesizing the data through meta-analytic techniques. Notably, no studies were identified that systematically tested the Central Eight risk factors as predictors of criminal recidivism in veterans, which represents a significant gap in the extant literature.

Regarding antisocial history, cognitions, peers, and personality, each risk factor had at least one study that found a significant link with criminal justice involvement among veterans. As for the other Central Eight risk factors, substance use was consistently linked to higher risk for criminal justice involvement in veteran samples, with findings robust across different measurements of substance use and across different service eras (e.g., Vietnam, OEF/OIF/OND). Among all of the Central Eight risk factors, substance use was most commonly examined as a correlate or predictor of criminal involvement among veterans. Evidence for an association between the remaining three risk factors of the Central Eight and criminal involvement in veterans was either mixed (family/marital dysfunction; school/work involvement) or no studies were identified (prosocial activities). Not included in the review by Blonigen et al. (2016) was a more recent longitudinal study, which found that family problems were a significant predictor of future legal problems among veterans in mental health treatment (Timko, Finlay, Schultz, & Blonigen, 2016).

The Need Principle and Veterans: Beyond the Central Eight

In addition to the Central Eight, there may be other criminogenic needs that are more common among, or unique to, veterans. Specifically, trauma exposure and PTSD, traumatic brain injury (TBI), and homelessness are all more prevalent among veterans than non-veterans, particularly those with a history of criminal involvement (Tsai, Rosenheck, Kasprow, & McGuire, 2014). We turn our attention to these additional needs in the sections below.

Trauma and PTSD

In the review by Blonigen et al. (2016), several studies were identified that observed a significant link between combat exposure and PTSD and risk for violent behavior. For example, multiple studies have found significant associations between combat exposure with PTSD and both general aggression and intimate partner violence

(Elbogen et al., 2010). Other work suggests that links between PTSD and violence in the veteran population may not be direct and may depend on other intervening variables. For instance, in a large sample of OEF/OIF/OND veterans, PTSD was found to be a significant predictor of post-deployment arrests among individuals reporting high levels of anger or irritability (Elbogen, Johnson, Newton, et al., 2012). Notably, this combination of PTSD and anger/irritability was significant after controlling for history of prior arrests and substance use problems. PTSD has also been found to be more strongly linked to violent behavior among individuals with comorbid substance use disorders (Greenberg & Rosenheck, 2009). For example, recent work examining predictors of criminal justice involvement among substance-using veterans seeking specialty mental health care in VHA found that, after controlling for various demographic factors and cocaine use, PTSD symptom severity was associated with violent, but not non-violent, criminal charges (Bennett et al., 2017). Additional analyses suggested that this effect may have been particularly driven by intrusive symptoms (e.g., recurrent, involuntary distressing memories of the trauma). Collectively, these studies suggest that PTSD may be a specific pathway to criminal justice involvement, but that (a) the significance of this risk factor may be augmented by the presence of other criminogenic needs, and (b) the link between PTSD and criminal involvement in this population is more strongly related to violent offending.

TBI

The relationship between TBI and criminal justice involvement is often described as a function of the behavioral changes associated with TBI, such as increased impulsivity, aggression, and low frustration tolerance. Accordingly, TBI has been linked to increased risk of violent criminal offenses in the general population (Farrer, Frost, & Hedges, 2012), particularly in the presence of co-occurring mental health problems (Trudel, Nidiffer, & Barth, 2007). TBI has been highlighted as a specific mental health concern among incarcerated veterans (Pinals, 2010; Rosenthal & McGuire, 2013), and is linked to a higher risk of violent behavior in this population (Elbogen et al., 2010). The relevance of this issue is often raised for veterans who served in combat during the Iraq and Afghanistan eras, due to the common use of intermittent explosive devices in these conflicts (Hoge et al., 2008). However, whether TBI is uniquely related to criminal justice involvement in veterans above and beyond PTSD is difficult to determine, given that the two are marked by similar symptoms, behavioral changes, and often caused by the same event. In a study of Iraq and Afghanistan returnees, TBI in combination with anger/irritability was not significantly linked to an increased risk of post-deployment arrests after accounting for the effects of PTSD and substance use problems (Elbogen, Johnson, Newton, et al., 2012). Thus, the extent to which TBI is linked to criminal involvement among veterans may be a function of other comorbid mental health problems (Sreenivasan et al., 2013).

Homelessness

Some evidence suggests that the link with criminal involvement may be more common among veterans than non-veterans. For example, a BJS report indicated that among state prisoners, a higher proportion of veteran than non-veteran inmates were homeless prior to incarceration (12% vs. 10%; Mumola, 2000). Other data from VHA indicates that 30% of incarcerated veterans have a history of homelessness (Tsai et al., 2013), compared to a rate of 18% among a nationally representative sample of adults in the US with a history of incarceration (Greenberg & Rosenheck, 2013).

Outside of studies reporting differences in prevalence, there is limited research that has directly examined whether homelessness is a unique risk factor for criminal involvement in the veteran population. However, the link between financial stability and post-deployment adjustment has been examined in a large sample of OEF/OIF/OND veterans (Elbogen, Johnson, Wagner, Newton, & Beckham, 2012). In this study, across mental health diagnoses, greater financial stability was significantly associated with lower likelihood of arrests or aggression. Considered in reverse, financial instability, which may be conceptualized as a correlate of or precursor to homelessness, may be linked to criminal involvement among OEF/OIF/OND veterans.

The Need Principle and Veterans: Synthesizing the Literature

Subsequent to Blonigen et al.' (2016) narrative review of RNR and veteran-specific risk factors for criminal justice involvement among veterans, King and Wade (2017) conducted a meta-analysis of the same studies. They broadly conceptualized the outcomes for 12 of the studies as justice involvement, and the outcome for the 13th study as violence. The 13 studies were coded for all indicators of the Central Eight as well as for PTSD, TBI, and homelessness/severe financial problems. Although more studies are being added to the meta-analysis, preliminary results (see Table 2.2) are that the number of studies per risk factor ranged from none (leisure–recreation) to 9 (substance use), with a mode of two studies (antisocial cognitions, homelessness or severe financial problems, and TBI). Most of the Central Eight risk factors—all but education and employment problems—were reliably associated with justice involvement among veterans. The magnitude of these effects was small and roughly consistent with that which is observed with offenders in general (Bonta & Andrews, 2017). Evidence in support of Blonigen et al.'s (2016) suggested veterans-specific risk factors was strongest for TBI.

Although King and Wade's (2017) findings are notable, it must be acknowledged that there was substantial heterogeneity for most risk factors examined in this meta-analysis, which was likely due to the high degree of measurement variability for both predictors and outcomes in the observed studies. Nonetheless, these preliminary meta-analytic results concur with the conclusions of the narrative review of

Table 2.2 Preliminary meta-analysis of central eight risk factors and veteran-specific risk factors for justice involvement among veterans

Central Eight risk factors	k	N	Q	I^2	Fail-safe n	r Random	Fixed	95% CI Random	Fixed
Antisocial history	4	3176	133.30***	97.75%	392	.26*	.38***	[.09, .42]	[.36, .41]
Antisocial thinking	2	2150	1.16	13.59%	2	.06*	.06**	[.02, .10]	[.03, .10]
Antisocial associates	4	1605	6.37	52.90%	21	.11*	.14***	[.04, .17]	[.10, .18]
Antisocial pattern/ personality	5	2672	5.11	21.74%	103	.16***	.15***	[.12, .21]	[.12, .18]
Substance use	9	45,927	50.89***	84.28%	737	.13***	.09***	[.08, .17]	[.08, .10]
Education/ employment problems	8	59,507	110.13***	93.64%	28	.06	−.01	[.01, .12]	[−.01, .0]
Family/marital problems	7	22,238	72.17***	91.69%	585	.12**	.20***	[.06, .18]	[.19, .21]
Leisure/recreation deficits	0	–	–	–	–	–	–	–	–
Traumatic stress	6	59,202	20.97**	76.16%	102	.04*	.04***	[.01, .08]	[.03, .04]
Homelessness/ severe financial problems	2	2998	22.35***	95.53%	12	.09	.07***	[−.06, .23]	[.04, .10]
Traumatic brain injury	2	2998	4.97*	79.87%	32	.12**	.13***	[.05, .19]	[.10, .16]

Note. One study involved violence or aggression as the outcome variable—conduct that could potentially give rise to a justice system contact. Also, one study contributed effect size information to both the antisocial thinking and antisocial pattern/personality domains based on partially overlapping variables (i.e., one item was used as a measure of antisocial thinking, and that same item alongside two other items was used as a measure of antisocial pattern/personality). Given the small number of primary studies identified by Blonigen et al. (2016), what was considered a measure of a risk factor was sometimes quite broad (e.g., in one study, at least 50–100% disabled—relative to 0–49% disabled—was treated as an education/employment deficit, among other more straightforward education/employment problem indicators reported in that same study). Outcomes also ranged from retrospective to cross-sectional to prospective. Some primary reports were not entirely clear as to the direction of effect sizes; in these instances, educated judgments were made about the direction of effects, with final resort to the hypothesized direction of the effect based on prior theory and data about the Central Eight with general offenders. Some studies did not specify non-significant results; 0 was imputed for the effect size in these instances. Multivariable results were used when bivariable results were not available. Likewise, standardized regression (beta) coefficients were used as an estimate of the correlation coefficient when no other effect sizes could be extracted. The reported results used the average effect size across several measures of a single risk factor or outcome within single studies or samples (i.e., if multiple studies utilized the same sample); note, however, that a single effect size for each study could have been selected instead—using the single most theoretically relevant effect, for instance. Significant Q values and I^2 values greater than 50% or 75%, respectively, indicate noteworthy statistical heterogeneity among primary studies, which may be due to clinical, methodological, or other/unknown differences among those studies. When statistical heterogeneity is present, the random effects results are likely the preferable effect size estimates. Rosenthal's fail-safe n is also reported, which is the estimated number of studies with null results (e.g., unpublished research) that would be needed to make the aggregate effect size non-significant

*$p < .05$

**$p < .01$

***$p < .001$

this literature (Blonigen et al., 2016) and justify more research on the Central Eight risk factors in veterans. A useful future direction would be prospective, multi-wave validation studies of either general offender criminogenic risk assessment tools, or veteran-specific criminogenic risk assessment tools, in samples of justice-involved veterans.

The Responsivity Principle and Veterans

The responsivity principle refers to *how* justice-involved individuals should be treated and consists of two components—general responsivity and specific responsivity. General responsivity emphasizes the importance of using structured treatments with a cognitive-behavioral orientation to reduce risk for recidivism among offenders. In support of this principle, meta-analyses of cognitive-behavioral treatments for reducing recidivism, which generally focus on restructuring maladaptive cognitions and behaviors, indicate significant reductions in the rate of recidivism (ranging from 8% to 25%) relative to comparison treatments (Aos, Miller, & Drake, 2006; Landenberger & Lipsey, 2005; Wilson, Bouffard, & MacKenzie, 2005). These reductions have been observed across a range of offender types.

The cognitive-behavioral interventions that have shown the most promise in reducing risk of recidivism are ones that focus on restructuring antisocial thinking (Blodgett, Fuh, Maisel, & Midboe, 2013). The most commonly studied treatments of this kind are Moral Reconation Therapy (MRT; Little & Robinson, 1988), Thinking for a Change (T4C; Bush, Glick, & Taymans, 2011), and Reasoning and Rehabilitation (R&R; Ross, Fabiano, & Ross, 1986). Each intervention is manualized, delivered in a group format, and uses exercises and homework assignments to modify antisocial personality patterns, cognitions, and affiliations. In so doing, these interventions were designed to directly address the criminogenic needs from the RNR model that are associated with the highest risk of recidivism (Andrews & Bonta, 2010b). In terms of their evidence, meta-analyses of MRT (Aos et al., 2006; Ferguson & Wormith, 2013; Little, 2005) and R&R (Aos et al., 2006; Tong & Farrington, 2006; Wilson et al., 2005) have found that justice-involved adults receiving these treatments have significantly lower rates of recidivism relative to participants receiving other interventions or no treatment. For example, compared to participants from control conditions, the rate of recidivism is reduced by one-third among justice-involved adults receiving MRT (Ferguson & Wormith, 2013). However, none of these studies was a randomized controlled trial. The research base for T4C is much less extensive than MRT or R&R; however, multiple studies have also reported positive effects on recidivism (Lee et al., 2012; Lipsey & Cullen, 2007) and social and interpersonal functioning (Golden, 2002).

For justice-involved veterans, particularly those who are eligible for and linked to VHA services (Blue-Howells, Clark, van den Berk-Clark, & McGuire, 2013), adherence to the principle of general responsivity is demonstrated by VHA's commitment to providing evidence-based, cognitive-behavioral interventions for veterans with substance use and other mental health disorders (Karlin & Cross, 2014).

Such interventions often include relapse prevention and social skills training, which do not directly target antisocial thinking but have nonetheless been found to be effective for improving outcomes among justice-involved adults (Milkman & Wanberg, 2007). Further, among veterans with co-occurring substance use and mental health disorders, one study found a 33% decrease in criminal recidivism among veterans who received services in VHA, but a 48% increase among veterans who received services from the state (Pandiani, Ochs, & Pomerantz, 2010).

Cognitive-behavioral interventions that more directly target antisocial thinking (MRT, T4C, and R&R) have not yet been implemented systematically within VHA or other offender rehabilitation settings for veterans. Interviews with Specialists from VHA's Veterans Justice Programs found that, by and large, justice-involved veterans have access to services that address most risk factors of the Central Eight, but access to services and cognitive-behavioral interventions that directly target antisocial thinking are limited (Blonigen et al., 2016). Indeed, no trials to date have examined the efficacy or effectiveness of MRT, T4C, or R&R with justice-involved veterans. However, a multisite randomized controlled trial of MRT for justice-involved veterans in VHA mental health residential treatment programs is currently underway (Blonigen et al., 2018). The results will provide the first test of the effectiveness and potential widespread implementation in VHA of a cognitive-behavioral treatment for antisocial thinking to reduce recidivism and improve health outcomes among justice-involved veterans.

The *specific responsivity* principle emphasizes the importance of tailoring or adapting services or interventions to recipients' unique strengths and characteristics (e.g., learning styles, intellectual abilities; demographic or cultural factors) to facilitate their full engagement and participation in treatment. A review of evidence-based treatments for criminal recidivism, including MRT, T4C, and R&R, noted that during reintegration (i.e., entering civilian life after military service), veterans often feel isolated and disconnected from loved ones and other civilians and, in general, struggle with interpersonal relationships (Timko et al., 2016). Such struggles can lower tolerance for frustration, increase suspicion of others' intentions, and ultimately increase risk for criminal involvement (Brown, 2008; Halvorson, 2010). Thus, treatments for recidivism for veterans may need to incorporate more trust-building activities and emphasize the formation of healthy interpersonal relationships. Self-stigma regarding substance use, mental health issues, and associated problems such as criminal justice involvement is also common among veterans (Glynn et al., 2014). To mitigate this stigma, treatments for recidivism could be adapted for veterans by framing the treatment as a "class" or "education" rather than therapy per se.

Specific responsivity often includes consideration of cultural factors. In this vein, treatments for recidivism could incorporate veteran culture into their curricula, similar to how military service is emphasized as a relevant demographic factor in veteran treatment courts (Douds, Ahlin, Howard, & Stigerwalt, 2017; Vaughan, Holleran, & Brooks, 2016). Among the three main treatments for antisocial thinking, only the materials for MRT have been adapted for veterans (Little & Robinson, 2013). These adaptations entailed revisions to the workbook, titled "Winning the

Invisible War," which includes veteran-centric examples and stories rather than changes to the content of the MRT steps or exercises. The ongoing trial of MRT in VHA (Blonigen et al., 2018) is using the new veteran-specific curriculum.

Impact of Criminal Records on Employment and Housing Among Veterans

Critical to breaking the cycle of recidivism and promoting long-term recovery among justice-involved veterans is identifying and addressing the barriers to employment and stable housing for these veterans following release from correctional settings. Those with a criminal history may face a range of barriers to finding employment or housing (Pager, 2003; Western, Kling, & Weiman, 2001). In this section, we review extant research examining the impact of a criminal record on the employment and housing statuses of formerly incarcerated veterans.

Employment

As for many justice-involved adults, unemployment is a significant issue among justice-involved veterans. The most recent BJS data indicate that approximately one-quarter of veterans incarcerated in jails and prisons were unemployed in the month prior to their arrest (Mumola, 2002). For these and other justice-involved veterans, a key question concerns the major barriers to employment in this population. This question was the focus of a narrative review that sought to identify the most salient barriers to employment faced by justice-involved adults and examine their generalizability to justice-involved veterans (McDonough, Blodgett, Midboe, & Blonigen, 2015). Thirty-two studies were reviewed and eight barriers were identified using qualitative methods. The study concluded that most of the employment barriers that justice-involved veterans likely face—i.e., lack of education and vocational skills; lack of job-readiness skills and criminogenic thinking; competing needs (e.g., mental health and other substance use problems); homelessness; legal restrictions; and employer stigma and criminal background checks—are barriers faced by justice-involved adults more generally. However, some important nuances to these findings were highlighted. For example, regarding lack of education and vocational skills, incarcerated veterans tend be more highly educated than their non-veteran counterparts (Bronson et al., 2015). In addition, veteran inmates are more likely to have held a job in the month prior to arrest (e.g., 78% vs. 67% in state prisons; 72% vs. 63% in jails; Mumola, 2000). Thus, a lack of education or vocational skills may not be as prominent of a barrier to employment for justice-involved veterans as other justice-involved adults.

In terms of competing needs and homelessness, compared to non-veterans in the criminal justice system, veterans have higher rates of substance use and other mental health disorders (Bronson et al., 2015) and homelessness (Fargo et al., 2012). Thus, it may be critical for employment interventions for justice-involved veterans to be integrated with treatment for substance use, other mental health problems, and housing assistance. Finally, in terms of legal restrictions, denying employment to applicants solely because of their criminal records may violate Title VII of the Civil Rights Act of 1964 (Equality Employment Opportunity Commission, 2012). However, such applicants can, in certain circumstances, be disqualified from employment in jobs that would put them in contact with vulnerable groups such as children or the elderly (Equality Employment Opportunity Commission, 2012). The offense profile of justice-involved veterans is marked by greater prevalence of violent criminal charges, particularly sexual offenses, than non-veterans, which may preclude more veterans from employment in positions that put them in contact with vulnerable groups.

Two unique barriers to employment for justice-involved veterans have also been identified (McDonough et al., 2015). First, employers can receive information on the military discharge status of applicants, and they may be reluctant to hire individuals with a less than honorable discharge. Less than a quarter of incarcerated veterans in jails and prisons received such a discharge from the military (Bronson et al., 2015); however, those who did tended to have lengthier and more serious criminal histories, as well as higher levels of prior substance use problems (Noonan & Mumola, 2007). Another unique barrier to employment for justice-involved veterans is entitlements and financial disincentives (e.g., VA disability compensation), which may reduce motivation to find formal or full-time employment (Tsai & Rosenheck, 2013, 2016). For example, most justice-involved adults face a host of financial obligations that may subject them to wage garnishment following release from prison (i.e., having a certain amount of one's paycheck automatically withheld and sent directly to another institution or individual to pay off a debt; Visher, LaVigne, & Travis, 2004). Among service-connected veterans, a concern that employment would reduce receipt of benefits has been linked to an increased willingness to turn down a job (Meshberg-Cohen, Reid-Quinones, Black, & Rosen, 2014). Similarly, a national study of Veterans Treatment Court participants observed that those receiving VA or non-VA benefits were less likely to be employed (Tsai, Finlay, Flatley, Kasprow, & Clark, 2018). Thus, through efforts such as expanding vocational rehabilitation services, or offering benefits counseling at the time of benefits application to address potential misconceptions (Tsai & Rosenheck, 2013), there may be value in helping justice-involved veterans overcome disincentives to seeking or obtaining employment.

Few studies have directly examined the impact of a criminal record on employment among veterans (see McDonough et al., 2015). A recent study examined whether history of criminal justice involvement and other factors were associated with employment among homeless veterans across 19 sites in the Housing and Urban Development-Veterans Affairs Supportive Housing (HUD-VASH) program from 1992 to 2003 (Tsai & Rosenheck, 2016). A history of criminal justice involvement was not significantly associated with job attainment or earnings, whereas a diagnosis of a psychotic disorder and reliance on public-support income were negatively associated with these outcomes. In contrast, a secondary analysis of data from a randomized trial comparing supported employment with treatment as usual among job-seeking veterans with spinal cord injuries found that participants with felony convictions were generally less likely to find employment regardless of study condition (LePage, Ottomanelli, Barnett, & Njoh, 2014).

Taken together, the reviewed findings are mixed in terms of whether a criminal record directly impacts the employment prospects of justice-involved veterans. Nonetheless, barriers to work such as financial disincentives and competing needs (e.g., psychiatric problems; McDonough et al., 2015) may serve as indirect pathways that impact homeless veterans with a history of justice involvement. Such effects may also hamper the impact of evidence-based work-related interventions, such as supported employment. Further, as previously discussed, employment deficits have been associated with justice involvement among veterans, and thus may constitute a criminogenic risk factor for justice-related outcomes.

Housing

Homelessness and criminal justice involvement are closely intertwined (Greenberg & Rosenheck, 2008), and arrest history predicts longer duration of homelessness (Caton et al., 2005). It may be asked whether a history of incarceration has an impact on veterans' housing status following reentry from a correctional setting. Release from a correctional setting is a high-risk period for many individuals and can lead to returns to homelessness for those who lack sufficient assistance or support (Metraux, Byrne, & Culhane, 2009). Studies have examined the role of criminal history on the housing status of veterans participating in permanent supportive housing programs, which combine permanent housing subsidies with supportive services such as case management to assist veterans with obtaining and maintaining their housing. The HUD-VASH program is the largest supported housing program in the country for homeless veterans. Among veterans in HUD-VASH from 1992 to 2003, neither having a substance use problem nor a more extensive criminal history were associated with how quickly veterans became housed (Tsai, O'Connell, Kasprow, & Rosenheck, 2011). Another study compared the outcomes of veterans enrolled in HUD-VASH with different criminal histories over a one-year period (Tsai & Rosenheck, 2013). At time of entry into HUD-VASH, most participants had at least one criminal charge (79%) and those with more extensive criminal histories had poorer housing status. However, after enrollment into the housing program, extent of criminal history was not associated with housing status and all groups showed substantial improvement on housing.

More recent research on veteran participants from the HUD-VASH program has examined factors affecting premature exit from this program, including the impact of criminal justice history. Among veterans who enrolled in HUD-VASH, several psychosocial factors have been linked to premature program exits (i.e., before being placed in permanent community housing), including a diagnosis of SUD and criminal justice involvement (Gabrielian et al., 2016). Data from a multisite study of the HUD-VASH program has also been used to identify factors associated with exiting the program due to incarceration and returning to homelessness (Cusack & Montgomery, 2017). While only 6.6% of exits were due to incarceration, veterans with a previous incarceration were 13 times more likely to exit the program because of reincarceration. A drug use disorder diagnosis also increased risk of this outcome more than two-fold, and a decrease in outpatient visits for substance use prior to exit increased risk for the outcome nearly four-fold. Finally, a history of incarceration, either prior to program entry or at the time of exit, was a significant predictor of experiencing another period of homelessness after program exit. Collectively, these findings highlight the vicious cycle of homelessness and incarceration that occurs among many veterans, and the need for housing and reentry services (i.e., services to assist persons with reintegration into the community from correctional custody) to assess for this risk and intervene to break the cycle. It is noteworthy that the receipt of service-connected income reduced the risk of exiting the HUD-VASH program due to incarceration by half (Cusack & Montgomery, 2017). Thus, services that provide employment training to assist veterans with obtaining a stable income during reentry from jail or prison may be beneficial in helping veterans break the cycle of homelessness and incarceration.

Directions for Future Research

The available literature on justice-involved veterans highlights the unique pathways to criminal justice involvement in this population and the range of characteristics and risk factors that characterize this distinct yet heterogeneous group. Importantly, while veterans make up a significant sub-population of adults incarcerated in jails and prisons in the US, most veterans never become involved in the criminal justice system. However, for those who do, substance use and mental health problems are common, with the available evidence suggesting that these issues are more common among veterans than non-veterans in correctional settings.

Although veterans who become involved in the criminal justice system appear to have lower rates of criminal recidivism than non-veterans, reoffending is still the norm among justice-involved veterans. Nevertheless, there remains an absence of studies directly estimating the rate of criminal recidivism among justice-involved veterans, relative to that of their non-veteran counterparts. Further, research focused on the development and validation of criminogenic risk assessment tools for the veteran population may be needed. The development of a violence risk screening instrument for use with veterans is promising, but there are as of yet no validated comprehensive risk assessment tools for general, violent, or sexual recidivism among veterans. As such veteran-specific tools are developed, it will be critical to verify whether they provide more accurate predictions of recidivism risk among justice-involved veterans than other established risk assessment tools for the general offender population.

The RNR model can serve as a useful framework for studying risk assessment and management with justice-involved veterans. In accordance with the need principle, prospective, multi-wave studies are needed to systematically identify the dynamic risk factors that predict recidivism in this population. Ideally, such studies would determine whether there are different risk factors, or differences in the effect size for these factors in the prediction of criminal recidivism, between veterans and non-veterans, and whether promoting change in these risk factors reduces risk for future criminal justice involvement in veterans. In this vein, the extent to which trauma/PTSD, TBI, and homelessness/financial instability may be veteran-specific risk factors for recidivism—exerting effects beyond the generally applicable Central Eight criminogenic needs from the RNR model—should be clarified. Future research exploring factors that moderate and mediate associations between risk factors and criminal involvement and recidivism among veterans will be beneficial. More research is also needed to understand the types of interventions that are most effective for reducing risk for criminal recidivism among veterans, and if and how treatments for criminal recidivism that were developed and validated with non-veterans need to be adapted to meet the needs of justice-involved veterans.

In terms of employment status among formerly incarcerated veterans, future studies should directly assess which barriers to employment for justice-involved adults are most relevant to the veteran population. At present, the available literature suggests that incorporating substance use or mental health treatment into employment training programs may be critical for justice-involved veterans. There is also value in further investigating how best to overcome the financial disincentives to seeking or obtaining employment among veterans who receive public benefits. Regarding housing status, formerly incarcerated veterans appear to benefit from supportive housing programs as much as veterans without a criminal history; however, formerly incarcerated veterans are at increased risk for dropout, particularly if they have a more extensive criminal history and do not stay engaged in addiction treatment services. Research examining how best to maintain veterans' engagement in employment training services may help to mitigate this criminogenic risk.

In conclusion, the available literature highlights a number of key differences between justice-involved veterans and their civilian counterparts and illustrates how consideration of an individual's military history can provide important context to understanding their pathway to criminal involvement. More research is needed to fully understand the unique criminogenic risks and needs of this group of justice-involved adults. A richer understanding of these issues will aid in the development and implementation of the highest quality correctional services for the men and women who served their country but are caught in a cycle of involvement with the criminal justice system.

References

Andrews, D. A. & Bonta, J. (2006). *The psychology of criminal conduct*. Cincinnati, OH: Anderson Publishing.

Andrews, D. A., & Bonta, J. (2010a). Rehabilitating criminal justice policy and practice. *Psychology, Public Policy and Law, 16*, 39–55.

Andrews, D. A., & Bonta, J. (2010b). *The psychology of criminal conduct* (5th ed.). Cincinnati, OH: LexisNexis/Anderson.

Andrews, D. A., Bonta, J. L. & Wormith, J. S. (2004). *Level of service/case management inventory (LS/CMI): An offender assessment system*. Toronto Multi-Health Systems.

Andrews, D. A., & Dowden, C. (2006). Risk principle of case classification in correctional treatment. A meta-analytic investigation. *International Journal of Offender Therapy and Comparative Criminology, 50*(1), 88–100.

Aos, S., Miller, M., & Drake, E. (2006). Evidence-based public policy options to reduce future prison constructions, criminal justice costs, and crime rates. *Federal Sentencing Reporter, 19*, 275.

Bennett, D. C., Morris, D. H., Sexton, M. B., Bonar, E. E., & Chermack, S. T. (2017). Association between posttraumatic stress and legal charges among substance using veterans. *Law and Human Behavior, 42*, 135–144. https://doi.org/10.1037/lhb0000268

Black, D. W., Carney, C. P., Peloso, P. M., Woolson, R. F., Letuchy, E., & Doebbeling, B. N. (2005). Incarceration and veterans of the first Gulf War. *Military Medicine, 170*, 612–618.

Blodgett, J. C., Avoundjian, T., Finlay, A. K., Rosenthal, J., Asch, S. M., Maisel, N. C., & Midboe, A. M. (2015). Prevalence of mental health disorders among justice-involved veterans. *Epidemiologic Reviews, 37*, 163–176. https://doi.org/10.1093/epirev/mxu003

Blodgett, J. C., Fuh, I. L., Maisel, N. C., & Midboe, A. M. (2013). *A structured evidence review to identify treatment needs of justice-involved veterans and associated psychological interventions*. Menlo Park: Department of Veterans Affairs.

Blonigen, D. M., Bui, L., Elbogen, E. B., Blodgett, J. C., Maisel, N. C., Midboe, A. M., … Timko, C. (2016). Risk of recidivism among justice-involved veterans. *Criminal Justice Policy Review, 27*(8), 812–837. https://doi.org/10.1177/0887403414562602

Blonigen, D. M., Cucciare, M. A., Timko, C., Smith, J. S., Harnish, A., Kemp, L., … Smelson, D. (2018). Study protocol: A hybrid effectiveness-implementation trial of Moral Reconation Therapy in the US Veterans Health Administration. *BMC Health Services Research, 18*, 164.

Blonigen, D. M., Rodriguez, A. L., Manfredi, L., Britt, J., Nevedal, A., Finlay, A. K., … Timko, C. (2017). The availability and utility of services to address risk factors for recidivism among justice-involved veterans. *Criminal Justice Policy Review, 28*(8), 790–813. https://doi.org/10.1177/0887403416628601

Blue-Howells, J. H., Clark, S. C., van den Berk-Clark, C., & McGuire, J. F. (2013). The U.S. Department of Veterans Affairs Veterans Justice programs and the sequential intercept model: case examples in national dissemination of intervention for justice-involved veterans. *Psychological Services, 10*(1), 48–53. https://doi.org/10.1037/a0029652

Bonta, J., & Andrews, D. A. (2017). *The psychology of criminal conduct* (6th ed.). New York, NY: Routledge.

Bronson, J., Carson, A. C., & Noonan, M. (2015). *Veterans in prison and jail, 2011–12*. Washington, DC: U.S. Department of Justice, Office of Justice Programs, Bureau of Justice Statistics.

Brown, W. B. (2008). Another emerging "storm": Iraq and Afghanistan Veterans with PTSD in the criminal justice system. *Justice Policy Journal, 5*, 1–37.

Bush, J., Glick, B., & Taymans, J. (2011). *Thinking for a change: Integrated cognitive behavior change program*. Washington, DC: National Institute of Corrections Academy.

Campbell, A. A., Wisco, B. E., Marx, B. P., & Pietrzak, R. H. (2017). Association between perceptions of military service and mental health problems in a nationally representative sample of United States military veterans. *Psychological Trauma, 10*, 482–489. [Epub on Nov 27, 2017]. https://doi.org/10.1037/tra0000337

Caton, C. L. M., Dominguez, B., Schanzer, B., Hasin, D. S., Shrout, P. E., Felix, A., … Hsu, E. (2005). Risk factors for long-term homelessness; Findings from a longitudinal study of first-time homeless single adults. *American Journal of Public Health, 95*(10), 1753–1759. https://doi.org/10.2105/AJPH

Cusack, M., & Montgomery, A. E. (2017). Examining the bidirectional association between veteran homelessness and incarceration within the context of permanent supportive housing. *Psychological Services, 14*(2), 250–256. https://doi.org/10.1037/ser0000110

Department of Veterans Affairs. (2012). *HOMES: Veterans justice outreach and health care for re-entry veterans summary data*. Washington, DC: Veterans Justice Program.

Douds, A. S., Ahlin, E. M., Howard, D., & Stigerwalt, S. (2017). Varieties of veterans' courts: A statewide assessment of veterans' treatment court components. *Criminal Justice Policy Review, 28*(8), 740–769.

Durose, M. R., Cooper, A. D., & Snyder, H. N. (2014). *Recidivism of prisoners released in 30 states in 2005: Patterns from 2005 to 2010*. Washington, DC: U.S. Department of Justice, Office of Justice Program, Bureau of Justice Statistics.

Elbogen, E. B., Cueva, M., Wagner, H. R., Sreenivasan, S., Bracu, M., Beckham, J. C., & Van Male, L. (2014). Screening for violence risk in military veterans: Predictive validity of a brief clinical tool. *American Journal of Psychiatry, 171*(7), 749–757.

Elbogen, E. B., Fuller, S., Johnson, S. C., Brooks, S., Kinneer, P., Calhoun, P. S., & Beckham, J. C. (2010). Improving risk assessment of violence among military veterans: An evidence-based approach for clinical decision-making. *Clinical Psychology Review, 30*(6), 595–607. https://doi.org/10.1016/j.cpr.2010.03.009

Elbogen, E. B., Johnson, S. C., Newton, V. M., Straits-Troster, K., Vasterling, J. J., Wagner, H. R., & Beckham, J. C. (2012). Criminal justice involvement, trauma, and negative affect in Iraq and Afghanistan war era veterans. *Journal of Consulting and Clinical Psychology, 80*(6), 1097–1102. https://doi.org/10.1037/a0029967

Elbogen, E. B., Johnson, S. C., Wagner, H. R., Newton, V. M., & Beckham, J. C. (2012). Financial well-being and post-deployment adjustment among Iraq and Afghanistan war veterans. *Military Medicine, 177*(6), 669–675.

Equal Employment Opportunity Commission. (2012). *Annual report on the Federal work force part I*, EEO complaints processing: Office of Federal Operations.

Erickson, J. W. (2016). Veterans treatment courts: A case study of their efficacy for veterans' needs. *International Journal of Law and Psychiatry, 49*, 221–225.

Erickson, S. K., Rosenheck, R. A., Trestman, R. L., Ford, J. D., & Desai, R. A. (2008). Risk of incarceration between cohorts of veterans with and without mental illness discharged from inpatient units. *Psychiatric Services, 59*(2), 178–183.

Fargo, J., Metraux, S., Byrne, T., Munley, E., Montgomery, A. E., & Jones, H. (2012). Prevalence and risk of homelessness among US veterans. *Preventing Chronic Disease, 9*, e45. https://doi.org/10.5888/pcd9.110112

Farrer, T. J., Frost, R. B., & Hedges, D. W. (2012). Prevalence of traumatic brain injury in intimate partner violence offenders compared to the general population: A meta-analysis. *Trauma, Violence, & Abuse, 13*(2), 77–82. https://doi.org/10.1177/1524838012440338

Fazel, S., Singh, J. P., Doll, H., & Grann, M. (2012). Use of risk assessment instruments to predict violence and antisocial behaviour in 73 samples involving 24 827 people: Systematic review and meta-analysis. *BMJ, 345*, e4692. https://doi.org/10.1136/bmj.e4692

Ferguson, L. M., & Wormith, J. S. (2013). A meta-analysis of moral reconation therapy. *International Journal of Offender Therapy and Comparative Criminology, 57*(9), 1076–1106. https://doi.org/10.1177/0306624X12447771

Finlay, A. K., Binswanger, I. A., Smelson, D., Sawh, L., McGuire, J., Rosenthal, J., … Frayne, S. (2015). Sex differences in mental health and substance use disorders and treatment entry among justice-involved veterans in the Veterans Health Administration. *Medical Care, 53*(4), S105–S111.

Finlay, A. K., Stimmel, M., Blue-Howells, J., Rosenthal, J., McGuire, J., Binswanger, I., … Timko, C. (2017). Use of Veterans Health Administration mental health and substance use disorder treatment after exiting prison: The Health Care for Reentry Veterans Program. *Administration and Policy in Mental Health and Mental Health Services Research, 44*(2), 177–187.

Gabrielian, S., Burns, A. V., Nanda, N., Hellemann, G., Kane, V., & Young, A. S. (2016). Factors associated with premature exits from supported housing. *Psychiatric Services, 67*(1), 86–93. https://doi.org/10.1176/appi.ps.201400311

Gierisch, J. M., Shapiro, A., Grant, N. N., King, H. A., McDuffie, J. R. & Williams, Jr., J. W. (2013). *Intimate partner violence: Prevalence among U.S. military veterans and active duty servicemembers and a review of intervention approaches*. Washington, DC: Department of Veterans Affairs.

Glynn, L. H., Kendra, M. S., Timko, C., Finlay, A. K., Blodgett, J. C., Maisel, N. C., … Blonigen, D. M. (2014). Facilitating treatment access and engagement for justice-involved veterans with substance use disorders. *Criminal Justice Policy Review, 27*(2), 138–163. https://doi.org/10.1177/0887403414560884

Golden, L. S. (2002). *Evaluation of the efficacy of a cognitive behavioral program for offenders on probation: Thinking for a change*. University of Texas Southwestern Medical Center at Dallas.

Greenberg, G. A., & Rosenheck, R. A. (2008). Jail incarceration, homelessness, and mental health: A national study. *Psychiatric Services, 59*(2), 170–177.

Greenberg, G. A., & Rosenheck, R. A. (2009). Mental health and other risk factors for jail incarceration among male veterans. *The Psychiatric Quarterly, 80*(1), 41–53. https://doi.org/10.1007/s11126-009-9092-8

Greenberg, G. A., & Rosenheck, R. A. (2013). Psychiatric correlates of past incarceration in the national co-morbidity study replication. *Criminal Behaviour and Mental Health, 24*, 18–35.

Grove, W. M., Zald, D. H., Lebow, B. S., Snitz, B. E., & Nelson, C. (2000). Clinical versus mechanical prediction: A meta-analysis. *Psychological Assessment, 12*(1), 19–30.

Halvorson, A. (2010). *Understanding the military: The institution, the culture and the people*. (Substance Abuse and Mental Health Services Administration, Trans.).

Hanson, R., & Morton-Bourgon, K. E. (2009). The accuracy of recidivism risk assessments for sexual offenders: A meta-analysis of 118 prediction studies. *Psychological Assessment, 21*(1), 1–21.

Hartley, R. D., & Baldwin, J. M. (2016). Waging war on recidivism among justice-involved veterans. An impact evaluation of a large urban veterans treatment court. *Criminal Justice Policy Review, 30*, 52–78.

Hoge, C. W., McGurk, D., Thomas, J. L., Cox, A. L., Engel, C. C., & Castro, C. A. (2008). Mild traumatic brain injury in U.S. soldiers returning from Iraq. *The New England Journal of Medicine, 358*, 453–463. https://doi.org/10.1056/NEJMoa072972

Kaeble, D., & Glaze, L. (2016). *Correctional populations in the United States, 2015*. U.S. Department of Justice, Office of Justice Programs, Bureau of Justice Statistics.

Karlin, B. E., & Cross, G. (2014). From the laboratory to the therapy room: National dissemination and implementation of evidence-based psychotherapies in the U.S. Department of Veterans Affairs Health Care System. *The American Psychologist, 69*(1), 19–33. https://doi.org/10.1037/a0033888

King, C., & Wade, N. (2017). *A meta-analysis of risk factors for justice involvement among military veterans*. Paper presented at the 125th Annual Convention of the American Psychological Association, Washington, D.C.

Landenberger, N. A., & Lipsey, M. W. (2005). The positive effects of cognitive-behavioral programs for offenders: A meta-analysis of factors associated with effective treatment. *Journal of Experimental Criminology, 1*(4), 451–476.

Lee, S., Aos, S., Drake, E., Pennucci, A., Miller, M., & Anderson, L. (2012). *Return on investment: Evidence-based options to improve statewide outcomes*. Olympia: Washington State Institute for Public Policy.

LePage, J., Ottomanelli, L., Barnett, S. D., & Njoh, E. N. (2014). Spinal cord injury combined with felony history: Effect on supported employment for Veterans. *Journal of Rehabilitation Research and Development, 51*(10), 1497–1504. https://doi.org/10.1682/JRRD.2014.02.0045

Lipsey, M. W., & Cullen, F. T. (2007). The effectiveness of correctional rehabilitation: A review of systematic reviews. *Annual Review of Law and Social Science, 3*, 297–320.

Little, G. L. (2005). Meta-analysis of moral reconation therapy, recidivism results from probation and parole implementations. *Cognitive-Behavioral Treatment Review, 14*(1/2), 14–16.

Little, G. L., & Robinson, K. D. (1988). Moral reconation therapy: A systematic step-by-step treatment system for treatment resistant clients. *Psychological Reports, 62*, 135–151.

Little, G. L., & Robinson, K. D. (2013). *Winning the invisible war: An MRT workbook for veterans*. Memphis, TN: Eagle Wing Books.

Marshall, A. D., Panuzio, J., & Taft, C. T. (2005). Intimate partner violence among military veterans and active duty servicemen. *Clinical Psychology Review, 25*(7), 862–876. https://doi.org/10.1016/j.cpr.2005.05.009

McDonough, D. E., Blodgett, J. C., Midboe, A. M., & Blonigen, D. M. (2015). *Justice-involved veterans and employment: A systematic review of barriers and promising strategies and interventions (Center for Innovation to Implementation)*. Menlo Park: VA Palo Alto Health Care System.

McGuire, J., Rosenheck, R. A., & Kasprow, W. J. (2003). Health status, service use, and costs among veterans receiving outreach services in jail or community settings. *Psychiatric Services, 54*(2), 201–207.

Meshberg-Cohen, S., Reid-Quinones, K., Black, A. C., & Rosen, M. I. (2014). Veterans' attitudes toward work and disability compensation: Associations with substance abuse. *Addictive Behaviors, 39*(2), 445–448.

Metraux, S., Byrne, T., & Culhane, D. P. (2009). Institutional discharges and subsequent shelter use among unaccompanied adults in New York City. *Journal of Community Psychology, 38*(1), 28–38.

Milkman, H., & Wanberg, K. (2007). *Cognitive behavioral treatment*. Washington, DC: U.S. Department of Justice, National Institute of Corrections.

Mumola, C. J. (2000). *Veterans in prison or jail*. Washington, DC: U.S. Department of Justice, Office of Justice Programs, Bureau of Justice Statistics.

Mumola, C. J. (2002). Survey of inmates in state and federal correctional facilities. *2001 Annual Survey of Jails, and the 2001 National Prisoners Statistics Program.*

Noonan, M. E., & Mumola, C. J. (2007). *Veterans in state and federal prison, 2004*. Washington, DC: U.S. Department of Justice, Office of Justice Programs, Bureau of Justice Statistics.

Pager, D. (2003). The mark of a criminal record. *American Journal of Sociology, 108*(5), 937–975.

Pandiani, J. A., Ochs, W. R., & Pomerantz, A. S. (2010). Criminal justice involvement of armed forces veterans in two systems of care. *Psychiatric Services, 61*(8), 835–837.

Pinals, D. A. (2010). Veterans and the justice system: The next forensic frontier. *Journal of the American Academy of Psychiatry and the Law, 38*, 163–167.

Rodriguez, A. L., Manfredi, L., Wong, A. C., Nevedal, A., Timko, C., Rosenthal, J., & Blonigen, D. M. (2017). Implementation potential of structured risk assessments for criminal recidivism in the Veterans Health Administration: Qualitative perspectives from providers. *Criminal Justice Policy Review, 30*, 819–839. [E-pub, Aug 14, 2017]. https://doi.org/10.1177/0887403417725567

Rosenthal, J., & McGuire, J. (2013). Incarcerated veterans. In L. Gideon (Ed.), *Special needs offenders in correctional institutions*. Thousand Oaks, CA: Sage.

Ross, R., Fabiano, E. A., & Ross R. (1986). *Reasoning and rehabilitation: A handbook for teaching cognitive skills: Volumes 1 & 2, handbook & supplements*. Ottawa: T3 Associates.

Schultz, N. R., Blonigen, D., Finlay, A., & Timko, C. (2015). Criminal typology of veterans entering substance abuse treatment. *Journal of Substance Abuse Treatment, 54*, 56–62. https://doi.org/10.1016/j.jsat.2015.01.007

Shay, J. (1995). *Achilles in Vietnam: Combat trauma and the undoing of character*. New York: Scribner.

Snowden, D. L., Oh, S., Salas-Wright, C. P., Vaughn, M. G., & King, E. (2017). Military service and crime: New evidence. *Social Psychiatry and Psychiatric Epidemiology, 52*(5), 605–615. https://doi.org/10.1007/s00127-017-1342-8

Sreenivasan, S., Garrick, T., McGuire, J., Smee, D. E., Dow, D., & Woehl, D. (2013). Critical concerns in Iraq/Afghanistan war veteran-forensic interface: Combat-related postdeployment criminal violence. *Journal of the American Academy of Psychiatry and the Law, 41*, 263–273.

Stainbrook, K., Hartwell, S., & James, A. (2016). Female veterans in jail diversion programs: Differences from and similarities to their male peers. *Psychiatric Services, 67*(1), 133–136.

Straus, M. A., & Gelles, R. J. (1990). How violent are American families? Estimates from the National Family Violence Resurvey and other studies. In M. A. Straus & R. J. Gelles (Eds.), *Physical violence in American families* (pp. 95–112). New Brunswick, NJ: Transaction.

Sweeten, G., Piquero, A. R., & Steinberg, L. (2013). Age and the explanation of crime, revisited. *Journal of Youth and Adolescence, 42*(6), 921–938. https://doi.org/10.1007/s10964-013-9926-4

Timko, C., Finlay, A., Schultz, N. R., & Blonigen, D. M. (2016). Dually diagnosed patients with arrests for violent and nonviolent offenses: Two-year treatment outcomes. *Journal of Addiction, 2016*, 6793907. https://doi.org/10.1155/2016/6793907

Timko, C., Midboe, A. M., Maisel, N. C., Blodgett, J. C., Asch, S. M., Rosenthal, J., & Blonigen, D. M. (2014). Treatments for recidivism risk among justice-involved Veterans. *Journal of Offender Rehabilitation, 53*, 620–640.

Tong, L. S. J., & Farrington, D. P. (2006). How effective is the "reasoning and rehabilitation" programme in reducing reoffending? A meta-analysis of evaluations in four countries. *Psychology, Crime & Law, 12*(1), 3–24.

Trudel, T. M., Nidiffer, F. D., & Barth, J. T. (2007). Community-integrated brain injury rehabilitation: Treatment models and challenges for civilian, military, and veteran populations. *Journal of Rehabilitation Research and Development, 44*(7), 1007–1016. https://doi.org/10.1682/jrrd.2006.12.0167

Tsai, J., Finlay, A., Flatley, B., Kasprow, W. J., & Clark, S. (2018). A national study of veterans treatment court Participants: Who benefits and who recidivates? *Administration and Policy in Mental Health, 45*(2), 236–244. https://doi.org/10.1007/s10488-017-0816-z

Tsai, J., O'Connell, M., Kasprow, W. J., & Rosenheck, R. A. (2011). Factors related to rapidity of housing placement in Housing and Urban Development-Department of Veterans Affairs Supportive Housing program of 1990s. *Journal of Rehabilitation Research and Development, 48*, 755–762.

Tsai, J., & Rosenheck, R. A. (2013). Examination of Veterans Affairs disability compensation as a disincentive for employment in a population-based sample of Veterans under age 65. *Journal of Occupational Rehabilitation, 23*(4), 504–512. https://doi.org/10.1007/s10926-013-9419-z

Tsai, J., & Rosenheck, R. A. (2016). Psychosis, lack of job skills, and criminal history: Associations with employment in two samples of homeless men. *Psychiatric Services, 67*(6), 671–675. https://doi.org/10.1176/appi.ps.201500145

Tsai, J., Rosenheck, R. A., Kasprow, W. J., & McGuire, J. F. (2013). Risk of incarceration and other characteristics of Iraq and Afghanistan era veterans in state and federal prisons. *Psychiatric Services, 64*(1), 36–43.

Tsai, J., Rosenheck, R. A., Kasprow, W. J., & McGuire, J. F. (2014). Homelessness in a national sample of incarcerated veterans in state and federal prisons. *Administration and Policy in Mental Health, 41*(3), 360–367. https://doi.org/10.1007/s10488-013-0483-7

Ursano, R. J., Kessler, R. C., Stein, M. B., Naifeh, J. A., Aliaga, P. A., Fullerton, C. S., … Army Study to Assess Risk and Resilience in Servicemembers Collaborators. (2015). Suicide attempts in the US army during the wars in Afghanistan and Iraq, 2004 to 2009. *JAMA Psychiatry, 72*(9), 917–926.

Vaughan, T. J., Holleran, L. B., & Brooks, R. (2016). Exploring therapeutic and militaristic contexts in a veteran treatment court. *Criminal Justice Policy Review, 30*, 79–101.

Visher, C., LaVigne, N., & Travis, J. (2004). *Returning home: Understanding the challenges of reentry*. Washington, DC: Urban Institute.

Weaver, C. M., Trafton, J. A., Kimerling, R., Timko, C., & Moos, R. (2013). Prevalence and nature of criminal offending in a national sample of veterans in VA substance use treatment prior to the Operation Enduring Freedom/Operation Iraqi Freedom conflicts. *Psychological Services, 10*(1), 54–65. https://doi.org/10.1037/a0030504

Western, B., Kling, J. R., & Weiman, D. F. (2001). The labor market consequences of incarceration. *Crime & Delinquency, 47*(3), 410–427.

Wilson, D. B., Bouffard, L. A., & Mackenzie, D. L. (2005). A quantitative review of structured, group-oriented, cognitive-behavioral programs for offenders. *Criminal Justice and Behavior, 32*(2), 172–204. https://doi.org/10.1177/0093854804272889

Chapter 3
VA Programs for Justice-Involved Veterans

Sean Clark and Bessie Flatley

> *To identify justice-involved Veterans and contact them through outreach, in order to facilitate access to VA services at the earliest possible point. Veterans Justice Programs accomplish this by building and maintaining partnerships between VA and key elements of the criminal justice system.*
>
> —Mission Statement, Veterans Justice Programs

Abbreviations

BJS	Bureau of Justice Statistics
CHALENG	Community Homelessness Assessment, Local Education and Networking Groups
FY	Fiscal Year
HCRV	Health Care for Reentry Veterans
MLP	Medical-Legal Partnership
VA	U.S. Department of Veterans Affairs
VHA	Veterans Health Administration
VJO	Veterans Justice Outreach
VJP	Veterans Justice Programs
VTC	Veterans Treatment Court

S. Clark (✉)
Veterans Justice Programs, U.S. Department of Veterans Affairs,
Lexington VA Medical Center (122-HP-LD), Lexington, KY, USA
e-mail: Sean.Clark2@va.gov

B. Flatley
Clinical Operations, VHA Homeless Programs, U.S. Department of Veterans Affairs,
Philadelphia, PA, USA
e-mail: Elizabeth.Flatley2@va.gov

J. Tsai, E. R. Seamone (eds.), *Intersections between Mental Health and Law among Veterans*, https://doi.org/10.1007/978-3-030-31664-8_3

Introduction

The U.S. Department of Veterans Affairs operates two national programs—Health Care for Reentry Veterans and Veterans Justice Outreach—focused specifically on veterans who are involved with the criminal justice system. Although these programs are active in thousands of criminal justice settings across the country, they are relatively unknown outside VA and criminal justice circles. This chapter introduces the work of these programs, and situates them both within their historical context as outreach programs operated by the federal government, and within the current context of justice involvement among U.S. Veterans. First, we examine veterans' prevalence among the overall U.S inmate population, as well as trends in the rates at which they are incarcerated. Next, we consider some examples of Federal efforts to serve justice-involved veterans over the past century. Following this review is a brief history of the creation and development of the U.S. Department of Veterans Affairs' Veterans Justice Programs, which we track alongside the rapid expansion of the Veterans Treatment Court model. Next, we describe the two Veterans Justice Programs as they exist today. We also review available data on outcomes for veterans served by these VA programs. Finally, we conclude by examining an area of current growth for the Veterans Justice Programs.

Veterans' Presence in the Criminal Justice System

The U.S. Department of Justice's Bureau of Justice Statistics has collected data on incarcerated veterans since the late 1970s, as part of its broader mandate to study U.S. prison and jail populations as a whole (see Blonigen & Timko, elsewhere in this volume, for a more detailed assessment of criminal justice involvement among veterans). Its periodic assessments over this period reveal a significant change in the prevalence of veterans among these inmate populations: although veterans were over-represented in inmate populations when BJS began this work in the post-Vietnam era, their share of the overall prison and jail populations has steadily declined. As a result, veterans are now under-represented in prisons and jails, compared to their numbers in the U.S. adult population. Figure 3.1 charts this decline over the course of five BJS surveys conducted between 1978 and 2011–12.

These data reflect veterans' decreasing presence in correctional settings, but they also contextualize this decline in terms of a parallel trend: over the same period, veterans' share of the overall U.S. population has declined as well. Bronson and colleagues draw this connection explicitly in summarizing their findings: "In 1978, 19% of U.S. adult residents, 24% of prisoners, and 25% of jail inmates were military veterans. By 2011–12, veterans accounted for 9% of the general population, 8% of state and federal prisoners, and 7% of jail inmates." (Bronson, Carson, Noonan, & Berzofsky, 2015). Over this same period, the rates at which veterans are incarcerated have also declined, and veterans remain less likely to be incarcerated

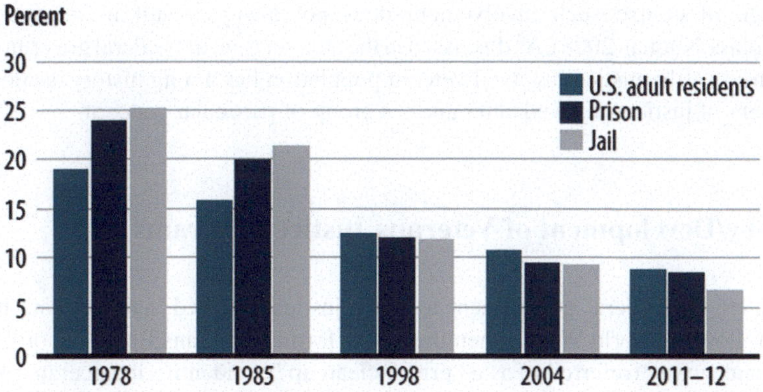

Fig 3.1 Estimated percent of veterans in the U.S. resident population in prison and jail, 1978, 1985, 1998, 2004, and 2011–12 (Source: BJS)

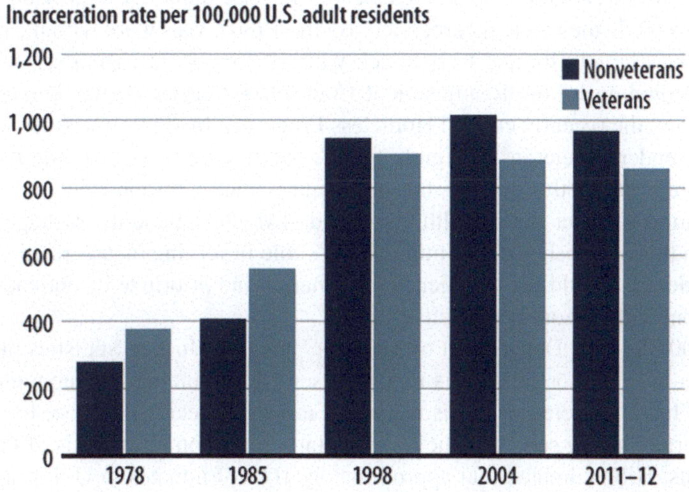

Fig. 3.2 Incarceration rate of veterans in prison and jail, 1978, 1985, 1998, 2004, and 2011–12 (Source: BJS)

than their non-veteran counterparts in the U.S. adult population. Figure 3.2 depicts rates of incarceration among veterans and non-veterans, as estimated by BJS.

Although veterans' declining share of U.S. inmate populations is at first glance a cause for celebration among those concerned about this group, the fact that this decline mirrors a broader trend in the U.S. must temper this enthusiasm. Veterans no longer occupy a disproportionately high number of prison and jail cells, but the number of veterans in such facilities is still high in absolute terms (181,500 in 2011–12, according to BJS). An estimated 1.1 million veteran arrests each year also indicates a substantial amount of involvement with the criminal justice system, although of course such involvement does not always result in incarceration (Mumola & Noonan 2008). As discussed in the next section, the Federal government's awareness of the justice-involved veteran population has a long history, as does its treatment of justice-involved veterans as a group of particular concern.

History/Development of Veterans Justice Programs

Efforts by the Federal government to serve justice-involved veterans date to the years following World War I, when the newly formed Veterans Bureau coordinated a national survey (referred to as a "prison clean up") to identify incarcerated veterans and connect them with needed treatment and benefits (Seamone, 2013). That initiative by the Veterans Bureau, an institutional forerunner of today's U.S. Department of Veterans Affairs (VA), did not lead to sustained programming for justice-involved veterans at the national level. This lack of continuity reflected, in part, a shift in VA's position on the extent of its legal authority to provide services to veterans while they were incarcerated. By the 1980s, VA's work with incarcerated veterans was largely limited to outreach with a focus on accessing services post-release, including by the Readjustment Counseling Service (better known as Vet Centers) and the recently created Homeless Programs. In 1999, VA issued a regulation that rendered veterans ineligible for VA health care services while they were incarcerated, citing the duty of the government entity responsible for veterans' incarceration to meet their health care needs (Medical Benefits Package, 1999). Although this established clear limits on VA's role in serving incarcerated veterans, the next decade would see the agency systematize and prioritize its outreach to this population, within those new limits.

In 2000, the U.S. Department of Justice's Bureau of Justice Statistics published "Veterans in Prison or Jail." This report presented the findings of anonymous surveys BJS had conducted with prison and jail inmates, specifically those for inmates who reported having served in the U.S. military. Based on its analysis of these survey results, BJS estimated that approximately 10% of inmates in U.S. prisons and jails were veterans (Mumola, 2000). The following year, the President signed into law the Homeless Veterans Comprehensive Assistance Act of 2001 (2012). This directed VA to work with the Department of Labor, the Bureau of Prisons, and state correctional authorities to identify incarcerated veterans and contact them through outreach, in order to provide information and assistance with accessing services upon release, particularly regarding health care, benefits, and employment.

In 2004, the VA Office of Mental Health Services adopted a new strategic plan that called for outreach to incarcerated Veterans nationwide. In 2006, VA's Under Secretary for Health issued guidance to VHA facilities on conducting prison outreach, establishing the policy framework and operational parameters that would define the agency's future work in the area, and creating the program that would come to be known as Health Care for Reentry Veterans (HCRV). In 2006 and 2007, VHA hired 38 new staff (initially called Incarcerated Veterans Outreach Specialists) to conduct outreach to veterans in prison.

Once hired and trained, these new staff quickly began gaining access to prison facilities across the U.S. By Fiscal Year 2009, HCRV Specialists were conducting outreach in 877 (68%) of the 1294 state and Federal prisons operating at the time. Maintaining this large geographic footprint required Specialists to travel extensively between prison facilities in their assigned coverage areas, and a rigorous travel schedule remains a defining characteristic of the program today.

VHA expanded its justice-focused efforts in 2009, when it required that every VA medical center provide outreach to veterans at earlier stages of the criminal justice process. Each facility was tasked with designating a member of its existing outreach staff as a Veterans Justice Outreach Specialist, with the understanding that this individual would provide outreach in criminal justice settings as a collateral duty. VHA began hiring full-time VJO Specialists in 2010, adding new positions each year as demand for VJO services increased; as of Fiscal Year 2018, VA funded 314 such positions nationally.

A significant factor driving this increase in demand for VJO services has been the rapid expansion of the Veterans Treatment Court model throughout the U.S. (see Baldwin, elsewhere in this volume, regarding Veterans Treatment Courts). The first treatment court to focus on the needs of veteran defendants was the Alaska Veterans Court, which started in 2004. In February 2008, after extensive consultation and planning with veterans' organizations, the local VA medical center, and others, Judge Robert Russell launched the Buffalo Veterans Treatment Court (Russell, 2009). With its inclusion of local veterans volunteering as mentors for court participants, the Buffalo VTC established the model on which most courts that followed it would base themselves (Holbrook & Anderson, 2011).

The number of VTCs operating across the nation has been rapidly increasing since the launch in 2008 of Judge Russell's Buffalo Veterans Treatment Court. A total of five VTCs were operating by the end of that year, and an additional 20 courts opened in 2009. By 2011, there were 128 such courts. That number more than doubled over the following 2 years, and 2013 saw 271 courts in operation across the country. As of June 30, 2016, there were 461 VTCs and other veteran-focused courts, spread across 47 states.

Utilizing an interdisciplinary court team approach, VTCs provide the opportunity for treatment and rehabilitation as an alternative to incarceration by addressing the mental health and substance use treatment needs of justice involved veterans (Clark, McGuire, & Blue-Howells, 2010; Smee et al., 2013). They also attend to psychosocial problems court participants may experience, such as homelessness and unemployment.

Justice for Vets, the VTC-focused element of the National Association of Drug Court Professionals (NADCP), includes access to VA health care as one of the "Ten Key Components" of a VTC (Russell, 2009), and in their role as essential members of the court team, VJO Specialists serve as liaisons between the courts and VA Medical Centers to help ensure VA health care access for court participants. In this role, VJO Specialists help determine whether court participants are eligible for VA health care, and for those who are and elect to engage with VA treatment, VJO Specialists facilitate access to VA programs in response to each veteran's clinically assessed needs.

VJO Specialists participate as court team members of VTCs that meet the definition of a Veterans Treatment Court as defined by NADCP, as well as other veteran-focused courts and courts with separately designated dockets for veterans. According to the VJP National Program Office inventory on VJO Specialist court involvement in VTCs and other veteran-focused court programs (Flatley, Clark, Rosenthal, & Blue-Howells, 2017), as of the end of June 2016, a total of 241 VJO Specialists were responsible for covering 461 operational VTCs and other veteran-focused courts or veterans dockets. More than two-thirds of these courts accept veterans ineligible for VA health care services. For those veterans who are ineligible for VA health care, the VJO Specialist's role is limited to connecting them with the community services most appropriate to their treatment needs. This function may also be performed by the court coordinator or other court staff, instead of the VJO Specialist. For veterans who are engaged in VA and/or community treatment programs, with the veteran's permission, VJO Specialists provide regular updates to the treatment team on his/her progress in treatment, providing the judge with critical information which is used to determine how a veteran's case will proceed.

The means by which VJO Specialists participate as court team members varies according to the needs of the court and VJO Specialist availability—for example, more than half of Specialists are responsible for the coverage of two or more courts. But overall, VJO Specialists are actively engaged in court participation; 75% always participate in court sessions in person, and spend an average of 18 h per month interacting with the court team in court sessions or staffings on non-court days. Court schedules vary considerably, but nearly 80% of the courts under the coverage of VJO Specialists meet at minimum two times a month, and some courts meet as often as twice a week.

These courts also vary in their criteria for participation, and in their structural complexity. In addition to allowing both VA-eligible and ineligible veterans to participate in court, most courts accept participants charged with offenses of varying severity. Nearly two-thirds of the courts VJO Specialists work in accept both felony and misdemeanor cases. Over 60% of courts will consider all violent offenses, including domestic violence, when determining whether a veteran is eligible to participate in court (in many jurisdictions, veterans facing violent charges are admitted only with the consent of the alleged victim).

Functions

Today, VA's Veterans Justice Programs provide outreach, and facilitate access to needed VA services, to veterans across the full spectrum of the criminal justice system. Demographic information is available for 12,343 Veterans served by the Veterans Justice Programs (3388 served by HCRV and 8955 served by VJO) during Fiscal Year 2017 (October 2016 to September 2017) (Northeast Program Evaluation Center (NEPEC), 2017a, 2017b). The majority of veterans who entered both programs in FY17 were white/non-Hispanic, and male; however, HCRV veterans were slightly older on average with a mean age of 52 as compared to 44 for VJO veterans. Because of the demonstrated nexus between incarceration and homelessness, especially for the adult males who constitute the majority of the Veteran population, both programs are components of VA's Homeless Programs (Burt, Aron, & Lee, 2001; see also Ritchie, elsewhere in this volume, regarding the link between incarceration and homelessness). During the twelve months prior to the arrest associated with entry into Veterans Justice Programs in FY 2017, 26% of veterans who entered the HCRV Program and 37% of veterans who entered the VJO Program were living on the street or in a shelter. At program entry, 38% of veterans entering VJO and 40% of veterans entering HCRV were literally homeless, at imminent risk of losing housing, or unstably housed (NEPEC, 2017a, 2017b). Most veterans served by these programs reported several prior encounters with the criminal justice system: in VJO, while 8% of veterans reported no prior arrests, 25% reported 1–3 prior arrests, and 20% reported having been arrested 10 or more times. Among veterans served by HCRV, 10% reported no prior arrests, 32% reported 1–3 prior arrests, and 21% reported 10 or more arrests. The Veterans Justice Programs are intended to provide a pathway into VA treatment for justice-involved veterans throughout the criminal justice process, as illustrated in Fig. 3.3, which imposes these VA programs' areas of coverage over the major stages of the criminal justice process, as depicted in the Sequential Intercept Model (Munetz & Griffin, 2006).

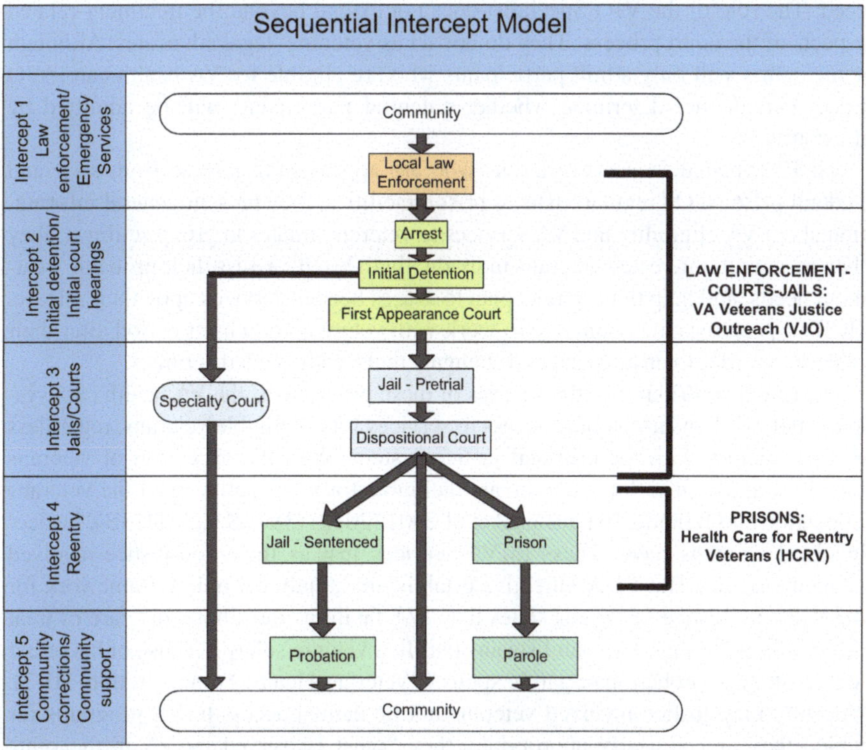

Fig. 3.3 Outreach provided by VA Veterans Justice Programs, by criminal justice setting, as depicted in the Sequential Intercept Model (Munetz & Griffin, 2006)

VJO Specialists focus on the earlier stages of a Veteran's progress through the criminal justice system. They serve as a resource for community law enforcement agencies, providing education about locally-available VA resources, and in some cases, delivering formal training to officers, for example as part of Crisis Intervention Team programming. VJO Specialists also conduct outreach in local jails, with the goal of assessing veteran inmates' service needs, and helping to facilitate their access to responsive VA services upon release (Blue-Howells, Clark, van den Berk-Clark, & McGuire, 2013).

Although most of the veterans they serve do not participate in Veterans Treatment Courts or other veteran-focused courts (Tsai, Flatley, Kasprow, Clark, & Finlay, 2017), VJO Specialists' work in these settings is by far the best-known aspect of the program. The participation of VA staff in order to facilitate access to VA health care for participants is one of the "Ten Key Components" of a VTC (Russell, 2009). VJO Specialists serve as members of VTC treatment teams, acting as liaisons between the courts and the VA medical centers where they are based, and so helping to ensure such access for court participants. For VTC participants who are eligible and elect to engage with VA treatment, VJO Specialists facilitate access to programs in response to each veteran's clinically assessed needs. With the Veteran's permission, they provide regular updates to the treatment team on his/her progress in treatment—critical information judges use to decide how the veteran's case will proceed. The role of the VJO Specialist does not extend beyond the treatment-related aspects of the court process. They do not act as veterans' legal advocates. Although some courts will only admit participants who are eligible for VA health care, VJO Specialists do not determine whether potential participants will be admitted by the courts.

HCRV Specialists serve veterans who are approaching release from state and Federal prisons. On regular visits to prison facilities, they present general information about VA eligibility and VA services to veteran inmates in group settings. They then meet with interested veterans individually to briefly assess their probable treatment needs, and help the veterans plan to access needed services upon their release. HCRV Specialists may continue to work with veterans for a brief period after their release, in order to ensure successful engagement with needed services.

A critical contributor to the success of these programs is the VA health care system's policy of ensuring equal access to services for all eligible veterans, regardless of their history with the criminal justice system. With the exception of veterans identified as "fugitive felons," who are ineligible for VA benefits under the Veterans Education and Benefits Expansion Act of 2001 (2012) (38 U.S.C. § 5313B), justice-involved veterans have access to VA services just as their non-justice-involved counterparts do. The VHA Directive establishing a national policy framework for the Veterans Justice Programs states that "VA facilities must not deny care or treat differently with regard to wait lists any enrolled veteran solely because of his or her legal history or probation or parole status." (Veterans Health Administration, 2017). Not only may justice-involved veterans not be denied access to VA programs for which they are clinically appropriate, they "must be served by VA in the same patient-centered manner as other Veterans in VA medical and mental health settings."

Important as this policy is, VA's ability to serve justice-involved veterans through the VJO and HCRV programs still depends entirely on partnerships with the criminal justice entities that operate the facilities where this outreach takes place. Prisons and jails are, of course, highly controlled environments, and VA outreach staff must apply for and secure access to them just as other external service providers do (see Goggin and Roberts, elsewhere in this volume, regarding prisons' and jails' development of veteran-specific housing units, which can increase the efficiency of outreach to incarcerated veterans by VA and non-VA service providers). Treatment court sessions may be open to the public, but for VA staff to participate in the pre-court staffing meetings where defendants' clinical progress and compliance with requirements is reviewed, they must be members of the courts' treatment teams. None of the core functions of the VJO and HCRV programs could be performed without the active cooperation of criminal justice partners.

Accurately identifying veterans in criminal justice settings is a challenge shared by VJP staff and their criminal justice partners. Many prisons, jails, and court systems do not have longstanding methods of identifying veterans among their inmates or defendants. Those that do have typically had to rely on individuals' willingness to self-report their Veteran status when asked, for example as part of a facility's intake questionnaire. Because veterans may perceive a variety of disincentives to self-identify (e.g., the reduction or loss of VA financial benefits), the effectiveness of these methods can be limited. To address this issue, VA developed a web-based tool that allows prison, jail, and court staff to identify inmates or defendants who have served in the military, using military service records (U.S. Department of Veterans Affairs, 2015). The Veterans Reentry Search Service provides a secure platform where justice system staff upload basic demographic information on their facility or system's population. After comparing this information against the VA/DoD Identity Repository, VRSS notifies the user of the individuals for whom it found a record of military service. At the same time, VRSS generates results for the VJP staff who conduct outreach in the user's geographic area. More than half of all state prison systems, and several hundred local jails, have used VRSS, and generally report identifying more veterans using the system than by relying on self-report methods.

Several additional limiting factors shape VA's work with this population. First, VA cannot provide health care services to veterans while they are incarcerated, due to a regulation that renders veterans ineligible for VA care while a "or inmate in an institution of another government agency, if that agency has a duty to give the care or services." (Medical Benefits Package, 1999). Because governments generally have a duty, arising from the Eighth Amendment's prohibition of cruel and unusual punishment, to provide medical care for inmates in their custody (Estelle v. Gamble, 1976), VA cannot provide such care for veterans while they are held in prison or jail facilities. Second, VA cannot take custody of Veterans from criminal justice entities, or hold Veterans in its facilities against their wishes. VA health care services are provided on a voluntary basis, so VA residential or inpatient treatment programs are not a similarly-restrictive alternative to incarceration. Third, the VA health care system was not designed to reflect the needs and priorities of criminal justice practitioners. This fact is highlighted most often in the context of VA's work with courts.

Treatment courts, including VTCs, generally require participants to submit to regular drug testing conducted by their jurisdictions' probation or pretrial services agencies. About 80% of VTC participants with a substance use disorder diagnosis who are eligible for VA health care receive at least some VA substance use disorder treatment during their court participation (Finlay, 2016). These VA programs generally conduct drug testing themselves, but this testing is intended to inform treatment rather than monitor subjects' compliance with court requirements. It may not satisfy the evidentiary and procedural requirements that probation-based drug testing systems are built around, due to being unobserved or comparatively infrequent (American University, School of Public Affairs, Justice Programs Office, 2016). Treatment courts may understandably want to rely on the results of drug testing conducted by VA in order to save government resources and streamline participants' testing-related obligations, but the fact that VA services were not designed to meet the needs of the criminal justice system often frustrates such expectations.

Finally, VA's ability to provide outreach to justice-involved veterans is limited by the capacity of the staff who work in the Veterans Justice Programs. The number of VJP staff—approximately 350 full-time employees—has grown considerably over the past decade. However, the continual expansion of the Veterans Treatment Court model, along with growing interest in identifying justice-involved veterans in other criminal justice settings (e.g., veteran-specific housing units in prisons and jails), means that VA's capacity often lags behind the demand for its services in this area. Each of these limiting factors can be a source of frustration, both for VA staff and their criminal justice partners, but frank communication and collaborative problem-solving have proven to be the best means of keeping these partnerships productive and effective.

Needs and Outcomes: Access to Treatment and Other VA Services

Significant levels of clinical need, most notably for mental health and substance use disorders, are a well-documented feature of the U.S. justice-involved population generally, and the justice-involved veteran population in particular. The Bureau of Justice Statistics estimates that 48% of veterans in prison, and 55% of Veterans in jail, have been diagnosed with a mental health disorder. (Bronson et al., 2015).

The prevalence of these conditions among the justice-involved veterans served by VJP outreach staff exceeds those BJS estimates. Most veterans seen in the VJO program receive a mental health (77%) diagnosis, a substance use disorder diagnosis (71%), or both (58%) (Finlay et al., 2014). Among veterans seen in the HCRV program, 57% receive a mental health diagnosis, 47% receive a substance use disorder diagnosis, and 35% receive both (Finlay et al., 2015). For comparison, these diagnoses appear in the VHA patient population as a whole at rates of 28%, 9%, and 6%, respectively. Together, these figures describe a population with significant, and often complex, clinical needs.

Data on the rates at which these veterans access VA services responsive to their needs suggest that the VJO and HCRV programs are fulfilling their mission by linking veterans to those services at high rates. Within 1 year of their initial contact with a VJO Specialist, 97% of veterans with a mental health diagnosis had had at least one VHA mental health visit, and 78% had had at least six visits (Finlay et al., 2014). Within 1 year of first seeing an HCRV Specialist, 93% of veterans with a mental health diagnosis had had at least one VHA mental health visit, and 52% had had at least six (Finlay et al., 2015). Among veterans who received a substance use disorder diagnosis following contact with a VJO Specialist, 72% accessed VHA substance use disorder treatment at least once within the following year. Among those who received such a diagnosis after seeing an HCRV Specialist, 57% accessed VHA substance use disorder treatment at least once within the same period. Veterans served by the VJO program while participating in Veterans Treatment Courts also saw significant improvements in their housing status and receipt of VA benefits (Tsai, Finlay, Flatley, Kasprow, & Clark, 2018).

New Directions: Legal Services

By definition, all veterans served by VJO and HCRV Specialists have, or have had, legal needs related to their criminal justice involvement. For some, these needs do not extend beyond representation by a defense attorney in a pending criminal case. However, many veterans seen in VJO, HCRV, and the other VA Homeless Programs have unmet needs for civil legal services, as well. Each year, VA conducts a national survey known as CHALENG (Community Homelessness Assessment—Local Education and Networking Groups) to evaluate the adequacy of its services in response to the perceived needs of homeless and at-risk veterans. VA solicits responses to this survey from homeless and formerly homeless veterans, as well as from VA and community homeless service providers.

In 2016, veterans' top 10 reported unmet needs included four that were explicitly legal: legal assistance to prevent eviction/foreclosure (ranked #5 for male veterans, #8 for female veterans), legal assistance for child support issues (#4 for male veterans, #7 for female veterans), legal assistance to help restore a driver's license (#7 for male veterans, #9 for female veterans) and legal assistance for outstanding warrants/fines (#8 for male veterans). A fifth reported unmet need, for discharge upgrades (ranked #10 for female veterans), is one veterans often address with the assistance of an attorney (VA Office of Public Affairs, 2017). Unmet legal needs have been similarly prominent in the CHALENG top 10 for several years.

The risk of homelessness posed by eviction and foreclosure proceedings is obvious and direct, but other unmet legal needs in the CHALENG top 10 appear to relate to veterans' homelessness, as well. The inability to obtain a driver's license may render a veteran unemployable, particularly in communities with few or nonexistent public transportation options. If employed, a veteran with unpaid child support obligations may receive wages garnished at a rate that threatens his or her ability to retain housing (see Rosa and Seamone, elsewhere in this volume, regarding family law issues among veterans). Child support arrearages can also generate arrest warrants, and as noted above, incarceration, even for a brief period, has been shown to be the most powerful predictor of homelessness among adult men.

VA does not have statutory authority to provide legal services to veterans directly, or to fund such services for veterans who are not being served by a grantee of the Supportive Services for Veteran Families, one of VA's Homeless Programs. As a result, VA must work with external partners to facilitate veterans' access to legal services. Specifically, VA staff members may provide veterans with information about local legal service providers, and VA medical centers may allow non-VA legal service providers to use office space to serve veterans. VA facilities currently host over 165 free legal clinics. These are operated by a diverse group of legal service providers, including legal aid organizations, law school clinical programs, state or local bar associations' pro bono initiatives, and private law firms. The nature of VJO Specialists' work in local justice system settings makes them particularly well-positioned to assist with the establishment of these on-site legal clinics, and VJO Specialists work closely with many of the clinics currently operating in VA facilities.

More than 20 of these clinics follow the Medical-Legal Partnership model, in which clinicians and attorneys collaborate to identify and address patients' needs in a holistic way (see Goldberg and Selnau, elsewhere in this volume, on Medical-Legal Partnerships for veterans). The MLP model is still relatively new to the VA system, but it has a longer history in non-VA health care settings in the U.S., where it has been found to improve clinical outcomes (Weintraub et al., 2010). Recently, the first formal evaluation of MLPs in VA facilities found that they had significant positive impacts on veterans' housing, income, and mental health status (Tsai et al., 2017).

Although VA's ability to help veterans address their unmet civil legal needs is limited, VJO Specialists continue to help build partnerships with community legal service providers to facilitate Veterans' access to these services. As described above, both the VJO and HCRV programs are built around community partnerships. The growing number of legal clinics, including MLPs, operating in VA facilities represents the extension of this collaborative approach into a new area in which veterans have needs that VA cannot fully address on its own.

Conclusion

Veterans are not over-represented in the criminal justice system, but the incarcerated veteran population is large in absolute terms, as is the estimated number of Veterans arrested each year. Because of the strong link between incarceration and homelessness, the two VA outreach programs that serve justice-involved veterans form part of VA's broader effort addressing Veteran homelessness. The Veterans Justice Outreach and Health Care for Reentry Veterans programs are intended to locate veterans through outreach in criminal justice settings, and to facilitate their access to needed VA treatment. The justice-involved veterans served by these programs have extensive clinical needs, receiving diagnoses of mental health and substance use disorders at rates greatly exceeding those seen in the VHA patient population as a whole. After being seen by VJO and HCRV outreach specialists, justice-involved veterans do go on to access treatment responsive to their needs. As the number of Veterans Treatment Courts and other veteran-specific criminal justice interventions continues to grow, the demand for VJO and HCRV services grows as well. As VA's work with justice-involved veterans continues to develop, the agency is also partnering with legal service providers to help veterans address their unmet civil legal needs—including through partnerships where clinical and legal providers collaborate to address veterans' needs holistically.

References

American University, School of Public Affairs, Justice Programs Office. (2016). Veterans treatment courts: 2015 survey results.

Blue-Howells, J. H., Clark, S. C., van den Berk-Clark, C., & McGuire, J. F. (2013). The U.S. Department of Veterans Affairs Veterans Justice Programs and the sequential intercept model: Case examples in national dissemination of intervention for justice-involved veterans. *Psychological Services, 10*(1), 48–53. https://doi.org/10.1037/a00296522016

Bronson, J., Carson, E. A., Noonan, M., & Berzofsky, M. (2015). *Veterans in prison and jail, 2011–12 (NCJ 249144)*. Washington, DC: U.S. Department of Justice Office of Justice Programs.

Burt, M., Aron, L. Y., & Lee, E. (2001). *Helping Americas' homeless: Emergency shelter or affordable housing?* Washington, DC: The Urban Institute.

Clark, S., Blue-Howells, J., & McGuire, J. (2010). Development of veterans treatment court: Local and legislative initiatives. *Drug Court Review, 7*(1), 171–208.

Estelle v. Gamble (1976). 429 U.S. 97.

Finlay, A. K. (2016). *Veterans treatment court participants: Mental health and substance use disorder diagnoses and treatment use*. Paper presented at the National Association of Drug Court Professionals Annual Conference, Anaheim, CA.

Finlay, A. K., Smelson, D., Sawh, L., McGuire, J., Rosenthal, J., Blue-Howells, J., … Harris, A. H. S. (2014). U.S. Department of Veterans Affairs Veterans Justice Outreach program: Connecting justice-involved veterans with mental health and substance use disorder treatment. *Criminal Justice Policy Review, 27*, 1–20.

Finlay, A. K., Stimmel, M., Blue-Howells, J., Rosenthal, J., McGuire, J., Binswanger, I., & Timko, C. (2015). Use of Veterans Health Administration mental health and substance use disorder treatment after exiting prison: The Health Care for Reentry Veterans program. *Administration and Policy in Mental Health and Mental Health Services Research, 44*, 177–187. https://doi.org/10.1007/s10488-015-0708-z

Flatley, B., Clark, S., Rosenthal, J., & Blue-Howells, J. (2017). *Veterans Court Inventory 2016 update: Characteristics of and VA involvement in Veterans Treatment Courts and other Veteran-focused court programs from the Veterans Justice Outreach Specialist Perspective*. Washington, DC: US Department of Veterans Affairs, Veterans Health Administration.

Holbrook, J., & Anderson, S. (2011). Veterans courts: Early outcomes and key indicators for success. *Widener Law School Legal Studies Research Paper Series, 11*, 25), 1–25),52.

Homeless Veterans Comprehensive Assistance Act of 2001 (2012). 38 U.S.C. §§ 2001–2066.
Medical Benefits Package (1999). 38 C.F.R. § 17.38(c)(5).
Mumola, C. J. (2000). *Veterans in prison or jail (NCJ 178888)*. Washington, DC: U.S. Department of Justice Office of Justice Programs.
Mumola, C. J., & Noonan, M. E. (2008). *Justice-involved veterans: National estimates and research resources*. Paper presented at the VHA National Veterans Justice Outreach Planning Conference, Baltimore, MD.
Munetz, M. R., & Griffin, P. A. (2006). Use of the sequential intercept model as an approach to decriminalization of people with serious mental illness. *Psychiatric Services, 57*, 544–549.
Northeast Program Evaluation Center (NEPEC). (2017a). *Health care for re-entry veterans (HCRV) FY 2017 fourth quarter report*. Washington, DC: US Department of Veterans Affairs, Veterans Health Administration.
Northeast Program Evaluation Center (NEPEC). (2017b). *Veterans justice outreach (VJO) FY 2017 fourth quarter report*. Washington, DC: US Department of Veterans Affairs, Veterans Health Administration.
Russell, R. T. (2009). Veterans treatment court: A proactive approach. *New England Journal of Civil and Criminal Confinement, 35*, 357–372.
Seamone, E. R. (2013). A historical touchstone for Nebraska in the mission to divert criminally-involved veterans from confinement. *The Nebraska Lawyer, 16*(6), 7–15.
Smee, D. E., McGuire, J., Garrick, T., Sreenivasan, S., Dow, D., & Woehl, D. (2013). Critical concerns in Iraq/Afghanistan war veteran-forensic interface: Veterans treatment court as diversion in rural communities. *Journal of the American Academy of Psychiatry and the Law Online, 41*(2), 256–262.
Tsai, J., Finlay, A., Flatley, B., Kasprow, W. J., & Clark, S. (2018). A national study of veterans treatment court participants: Who benefits and who recidivates. *Administration and Policy in Mental Health and Mental Health Services Research, 45*, 236–244. https://doi.org/10.1007/s10488-017-0816-z
Tsai, J., Flatley, B., Kasprow, W. J., Clark, S., & Finlay, A. (2017). Diversion of veterans with criminal justice involvement to treatment courts: Participant characteristics and outcomes. *Psychiatric Services, 68*(4), 375–383. https://doi.org/10.1176/appi.ps.201600233
Tsai, J., Middleton, M., Villegas, J., Johnson, C., Retkin, R., Seidman, A., … Rosenheck, R. (2017). Medical-legal partnerships at veterans affairs medical centers improved housing and psychosocial outcomes for vets. *Health Affairs, 36*(12), 2195–2203. https://doi.org/10.1377/hlthaff.2017.0759
U.S. Department of Veterans Affairs. (2015). *Veterans Reentry Search Service (VRSS) user guide: Correctional Facility (CF) and Court System (CS) users*. Retrieved from https://vrss.va.gov/guides/VRSS_CFCS_UserGuide.pdf.
VA Office of Public Affairs. (2017). *Community homelessness assessment, local education and networking groups*. Washington, DC: U.S. Department of Veterans Affairs.
Veterans Education and Benefits Expansion Act of 2001 (2012). 38 U.S.C. § 5313B.
Veterans Health Administration. (2017). *VHA directive 1162.06: Veterans justice programs*. Washington, DC: U.S. Department of Veterans Affairs.
Weintraub, D., Rodgers, M., Botcheva, L., Loeb, A., Knight, R., Ortega, K., … Huffman, L. (2010). Pilot study of medical-legal partnership to address social and legal needs of patients. *Journal of Health Care for the Poor and Underserved, 21*(2), 157–168.

Chapter 4
Medical-Legal Partnerships in the VA

Krista Selnau and Rose Carmen Goldberg

> *As a physician who treats veterans, I've seen up close that many of the factors contributing to homelessness can't be fixed without a lawyer's help. To fully address health, we have to address the social conditions that affect it. Working with lawyers in our clinic every day is one of the best upstream solutions to some of these intractable problems our veterans face (Manchanda, Murphy, Lawton, & Middleton, 2016, p. 11).*
>
> Dr. Rishi Manchanda

Abbreviations

CBOC	Community Based Outpatient Clinic
CHALENG	Community Homelessness Assessment, Local Education and Networking Groups
COD	Character of discharge
CVLC	Connecticut Veterans Legal Center
MLP	Medical-legal partnership
MOU	Memorandum of understanding
MST	Military sexual trauma
NCMLP	National Center for Medical-Legal Partnership
OGC	Office of General Counsel
OVC	Oakland Vet Center
Pine Tree	Pine Tree Legal Assistance
PTSD	Post-traumatic stress disorder
Swords	Swords to Plowshares

K. Selnau (✉)
Pine Tree Legal Assistance, Augusta, ME, USA
e-mail: kselnau@suffolk.edu

R. C. Goldberg
Swords to Plowshares, San Francisco, CA, USA
e-mail: rose.carmen.goldberg@aya.yale.edu

J. Tsai, E. R. Seamone (eds.), *Intersections between Mental Health and Law among Veterans*, https://doi.org/10.1007/978-3-030-31664-8_4

Togus	Togus Department of Veterans Affairs Medical Center
VA	United States Department of Veterans Affairs
VAMC	United States Department of Veterans Affairs Medical Center
VBA	Veterans Benefits Administration
VHA	Veterans Health Administration
VLSI	Veterans Legal Services Initiative

Overview of Chapter

In this chapter, we discuss an innovative service model that is helping veterans rebuild their lives as civilians: MLPs. We focus on MLPs that partner lawyers and VA healthcare sites. The chapter proceeds in seven parts. First, we provide a general introduction to the MLP framework and give an overview of the current state of MLPs at VA facilities (VA MLPs). Second, we discuss common legal problems that veterans face upon returning to civilian life that can be addressed through VA MLPs. Third, we provide windows into the inner workings of four prominent VA MLPs that serve different segments of the veteran population at different types of VA healthcare sites. Fourth, we present new data on the characteristics of veterans that participate in MLPs and on the health benefits that flow from this interdisciplinary service model. Fifth, we share the story of a veteran who participated in a VA MLP, describing how the medical-legal intervention changed his life. Sixth, we discuss funding mechanisms for VA MLPs, including recent congressional momentum for federal government funding for VA MLPs. Finally, we conclude with closing thoughts about the need for additional data gathering and outcome measurement to further assess and refine this powerful service model.

Part I: Introduction to MLPs

In this section, we begin with a general overview of the MLP model. We then home in on VA MLPs in particular, describing the current landscape of VA MLPs across the country and discussing the VA's role in encouraging implementation of MLPs at its healthcare facilities.

What is a Medical-Legal Partnership?

MLPs are an interdisciplinary model of care that recognize that some health problems cannot easily be resolved without legal intervention (National Center for Medical-Legal Partnership [NCMLP], FAQ, n.d.-b). Clinicians and lawyers in MLPs work as members of the same team. Lawyers offer aid at healthcare facilities, and clinicians refer their patients to these lawyers for help with the legal issues contributing to or acting as major casual factors in to their health problems.

Through this coordinated approach, clinicians and lawyers are able to address individuals' "social determinants of health" more effectively than each profession can on its own. These social factors, such as housing conditions and income for basic necessities, can impact health. For instance, an oft-cited example of how MLPs address the social determinants of health considers the intersection of childhood asthma and housing conditions (Kremer, Lowell, & Zolezzi-Wyndham, 2015). A child might visit his doctor repeatedly for help with chronic asthma. On her own, the doctor is generally limited to managing the child's health condition: the doctor may prescribe a new medication or increase the dosage of an existing one when the child's asthma worsens. However, if the doctor is part of an MLP, she will be trained to identify potential legal issues underlying the child's asthma, such as mold in the home. Also because of the MLP, the doctor can refer her patient to a lawyer onsite, who can pursue legal remedies for the housing condition that is harming the child's health. By working together, the lawyer and doctor have the power to cure the child's asthma, instead of simply managing it.

The MLP model is relatively new. The first MLP launched in 1993 and several dozen additional partnerships followed in the early 2000s (Lawton, 2014). Today, MLPs have been established at 294 private and public healthcare facilities in 41 states, and these numbers are growing rapidly (NCMLP, n.d.-a). These MLPs serve a variety of populations, including children, Native Americans, veterans, and the elderly, and provide an array of legal services (NCMLP, n.d.-a). Despite these differences, MLPs tend to have three core features in common: (1) legal assistance onsite at a healthcare facility; (2) training by lawyers for healthcare providers on health-harming legal needs; and (3) referrals by healthcare providers to lawyers.

To support the growing MLP movement, in 2006 the National Center for Medical-Legal Partnership (NCMLP) took root. Initially hosted at Boston Medical Center, NCMLP began as a "technical assistance center, conducting site visits, phone calls and webinars to help [MLP] programs navigate the challenges that arose - everything from capacity and resources to training and service priorities" (Lawton, 2014). NCMLP now operates out of the Milken Institute School of Public Health at the George Washington University and functions primarily to mainstream and expand implementation of MLPs. To these ends, its main objectives are to build an evidence-base to support the MLP approach, and to redefine interdisciplinary education through trainings for healthcare, public health, and legal professionals (Lawton, 2014).

Starting a Medical-Legal Partnership

Before lawyers start providing legal services at a healthcare facility, the MLP legal and health partners generally enter into a memorandum of understanding (MOU). Such MOUs establish the parameters of the collaboration and terms of confidentiality (NCMLP, Toolkit Phase II, 2014). Once the MOU is in place, lawyers begin training clinical staff on how to identify the health-harming legal needs of their patients and how to refer patients for legal assistance. For example, an MLP legal training might include an overview of housing law as well as some magic words clinicians can listen for that might indicate their patient has a legal problem. Clinicians may also train MLP lawyers on a variety of topics, such as compassion fatigue or techniques for building strong working relationships with patients who have experienced trauma. For instance, mental health clinicians might provide lawyers with a list of legal words to avoid, such as 'proof,' when working with veterans who experienced Military Sexual Trauma (MST) to avoid exacerbating anxiety (L. Baggett, personal communication, March 8, 2018).

To streamline the referral process, some MLPs use a legal needs screener that help clinicians identify patients who could benefit from legal aid. It is also common for MLP lawyers to provide consults to clinical staff. These legal consults provide clinicians an opportunity to ask questions about potential legal issues they have spotted and to request referrals for legal assistance outside of the MLP lawyer's practice area.

Best practices for starting and sustaining an MLP include developing a joint mission statement (Marple, 2015), gaining health partner leadership support (R. Lilly, personal communication, February 9, 2018), and training frontline clinical staff on MLP services and legal issues (NCMLP, Toolkit Phase I, 2015). One MLP has established a formal advisory council consisting of leadership from both the health and legal side of the partnership to jointly develop best practices (L. Eilhardt, personal communication, March 12, 2018). The council also fosters health partner buy-in by encouraging administrative and frontline staff to actively participate in the MLP. To measure the impact of the partnership, some MLPs track legal and health outcomes in online case management systems (Curran, 2016) and electronic medical records (Gottlieb, Tirozzi, Manchanda, Burns, & Sandel, 2015). This data can be used to solicit funding to sustain the presence of lawyers at healthcare partners' sites, which can be critical to the longevity of an MLP: most healthcare partners do not fund the services of the lawyers at their sites.

Legal Clinics Vs. Medical-Legal Partnerships

MLPs are not the only service model that brings lawyers to healthcare sites. Some lawyers provide legal aid at healthcare facilities through legal clinics. A legal clinic, as opposed to an MLP, typically operates autonomously from the host healthcare facility. Notably, legal clinic lawyers often do not work closely with clinicians and bidirectional communication is limited. For instance, while MLP lawyers get client referrals from clinicians and may collaborate with clinicians on the client's case if it involves medical evidence, in a legal clinic lawyers often connect with clients simply by making themselves available onsite. Further, though clinicians may tell their patients about the legal clinic, they usually will not screen patients for legal issues or use a formal referral system. Legal clinics are also less likely to involve trainings for clinicians on how to identify legal issues since no formal referral system is in place

(Tobin Tyler, Lawton, Conroy, Sandel, & Zuckerman, 2011). In contrast, the level of integration between lawyers and clinicians in an MLP is more akin to how specialty providers operate within a healthcare setting. A patient may see their primary care physician for a general health check-up but they would not expect to receive specialized cardiology services from their primary care physician. Instead, the primary care physician refers the patient to the appropriate specialist. In MLPs, lawyers are another important specialty referral source (Tobin Tyler et al., 2011).

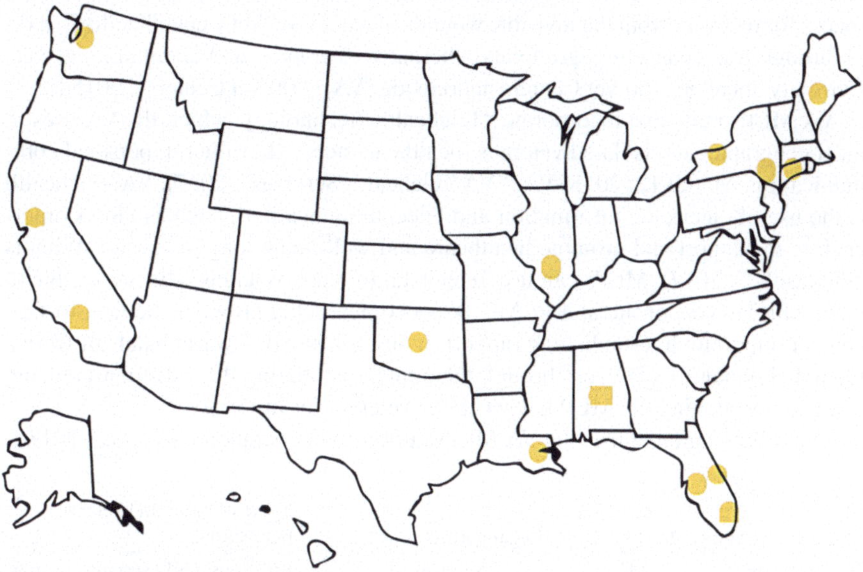

Map of VA medical-legal partnerships

VA Medical-Legal Partnerships

Today, there are 167 VA legal clinics, with 25 of these constituting full-fledged MLPs (United States Department of Veterans Affairs [VA] Office of General Counsel [OGC], 2018). VA MLPs exist at various types of VA healthcare sites, with most located at VA Medical Centers (VAMC). VAMCs are comprehensive healthcare sites, which provide a wide range of traditional hospital services, such as primary care and surgery, as well as specialized services, such as geriatrics and speech pathology (VA Veterans Health Administration [VHA], “About VHA”, 2018a). Currently, there are 168 VAMCs (VA VHA, “Where do I Get Care”, 2018b).

Several VA MLPs are located at Community Based Outpatient Clinics (CBOC). CBOCs were designed to make access to care easier than visiting a large medical center, and generally provide the most commonly sought outpatient services, such as wellness checkups (VA VHA, "About VHA", 2018a). The VA runs 1053 CBOCs that provide care of varying complexity (VA VHA, "Where do I Get Care", 2018b).

Vet Centers also host VA MLPs. Vet Centers exclusively provide mental healthcare, and operate somewhat distinctly from the rest of the VA healthcare system. Congress created Vet Centers in 1979 in response to veterans' desire for community-based alternatives to VAMCs for counseling (VA, "Vet Center Program", 2015e). True to Congress' intention, the atmosphere of Vet Centers stands in contrast to the clinical feel often associated with traditional health clinics. They provide welcoming spaces for recovery from the invisible wounds of war (VA, "Vet Center Facility", n.d.-c) through free counseling, group and alternative therapies, and community events. Currently, there are 300 Vet Centers nationwide (VA, "300 Vet Centers", 2015d).

VA MLPs may also incorporate "Telehealth" technology, which the VA uses to meet geographically isolated veterans' healthcare needs (L. Eilhardt, personal communication, March 12, 2018; VA, "VA Telehealth Services", 2017). VA Telehealth is the use of electronic information and telecommunications, such as videoconferencing, to support and promote healthcare and well-being long-distance ("What is Telehealth?", 2017). MLPs can use Telehealth to reach veterans who are unable to meet with lawyers onsite at a VAMC. Videoconferencing provides the face-to-face contact important to establishing rapport. It also allows for a warm hand-off from a trusted clinician to a lawyer, through the clinician initiating the videoconferencing call and introducing the MLP lawyer to the veteran, for instance.

The following table lists the VA MLPs currently in operation (VA OGC, 2018):

	State and city	Type of VA facility	Legal partner	Types of cases and veteran population
1	Alabama, Montgomery	VAMC	Legal Services of Alabama	Evictions, child support, payday loan abuse, domestic violence
2	Alabama, Tuskegee	VAMC	Legal Services of Alabama	Driver's license reinstatement, domestic violence divorces, protection orders, wage garnishment, bankruptcy, predatory lending, Power of Attorney (POA)
3	California, Long Beach	VAMC	Inner City Law Center	VA benefits and pension, discharge upgrades, traffic fines ***Women Veterans***
4	California, Los Angeles	VAMC	Inner City Law Center	VA benefits, discharge upgrades, social security, expungements, low level ticket clearing
5	California, Oakland	Vet Center	Swords to Plowshares	Discharge upgrades, VA Character of Discharge determinations and benefits
6	California, San Francisco	VAMC	U.C. Hastings College of Law	Estate planning, public benefits ***Senior Veterans***
7	Connecticut, West Haven	VA Community Center	Connecticut Veterans Legal Center	Family law, landlord/tenant, criminal, consumer, benefits, discharge upgrades

	State and city	Type of VA facility	Legal partner	Types of cases and veteran population
8	Florida, Bay Pines	VAMC	Stetson University, Bay Area Legal Services, Gulfcoast Legal Services	Elder law, family law, guardianship and fiduciary issues, benefits, landlord/tenant, child support, discharge upgrades
9	Florida, Miami	VAMC	Florida International University Law School, Dade County Legal Aid, Miami Legal Services, Dade County Bar	Benefits, discharge upgrades, guardianship and competency issues, permanency planning, employment, expungements, child support
10	Florida, Viera	CBOC	Community Legal Services of Mid-Florida	VA benefits, landlord/tenant
11	Illinois, Marion	VAMC	Land of Lincoln Legal Assistance	Family law, expungements, housing, consumer, public benefits, guardianships
12	Louisiana, New Orleans	VAMC	Southeast Louisiana Legal Services	Benefits, housing, consumer
13	Maine, Augusta	VAMC	Pine Tree Legal Assistance	VA benefits, student loans, housing, landlord/tenant, consumer, discharge upgrades, VA Character of Discharge determinations
14	New York, Jamaica	VA Community Center	Veterans Advocacy Project, Urban Justice Center	Benefits, discharge upgrades, landlord/tenant, VA Character of Discharge determinations
15	New York, Bronx	Vet Center	Veterans Advocacy Project, Urban Justice Center	Civil cases, discharge upgrades, benefits
16	New York, Bronx	VAMC	LegalHealth, New York Legal Assistance Group	Evictions, , benefits, family law, wills, POA ***Senior Veterans***
17	New York, Bronx	VAMC	LegalHealth, New York Legal Assistance Group	Benefits, discharge upgrades, evictions, student loans, family law, POA ***Women Veterans***
18	New York, Bronx	VAMC	LegalHealth, New York Legal Assistance Group	Evictions, federal student loans, benefits, family law, wills, POA
19	New York, Canandaigua	VAMC	Legal Assistance of Western New York	Civil cases, housing, benefits, family law, wills, POA, discharge upgrades, education law, consumer
20	New York, New York	VAMC	LegalHealth, New York Legal Assistance Group	Benefits, discharge upgrades, evictions, student loans, family law, POA ***Women Veterans***
21	New York, New York	VAMC	LegalHealth, New York Legal Assistance Group	Evictions, student loans, benefits, family law, wills, POA

	State and city	Type of VA facility	Legal partner	Types of cases and veteran population
22	New York, New York	VAMC	LegalHealth, New York Legal Assistance Group	Evictions, student loans, benefits, family law, wills, POA ***Senior Veterans***
23	New York, Northport	VAMC	LegalHealth, New York Legal Assistance Group	Evictions, student loans, benefits, family law, wills, POA
24	Oklahoma, Oklahoma City	VAMC	Legal Aid Services of Oklahoma	Family law, estate planning, VA benefits, housing law
25	Washington, Seattle	VAMC	Northwest Justice Project	Child support, protection orders, discharge upgrades, driver's license restoration

VA Support of Medical-Legal Partnerships

The VA supports implementation of the MLP model at its healthcare facilities, and has taken strides to increase the number of partnerships (VA VAntage Point, 2017). To encourage VA healthcare sites to open their doors to legal aid providers, in 2011 the VA issued Directive 2011-034, "Homeless Veterans Legal Referral Process" (VA, "Directive", 2011). The Directive encourages VA healthcare staff to refer veterans to legal service providers for assistance with legal issues, such as child support or outstanding warrants or fines, that can contribute to veterans' risk of homelessness. Furthermore, the Directive asks that VA staff provide space to legal service providers onsite whenever possible.

Soon after issuing the Directive, the VA issued a Memorandum, "Advising Clients on Working with Non-VA Legal Service Providers," to further clarify some of the parameters of legal providers setting up shop at VA sites (VA, "Memorandum", 2012). Of particular note, the Memorandum sets forth requirements for establishing an MOU, such as that MOUs must be reduced to writing. In addition, the VA healthcare facility should have the VA Regional Counsel review any proposed MOU prior to executing it. Furthermore, the Memorandum notes that when the legal provider will use VA space to provide services (as opposed to simply serving as an external referral source) an MOU is not sufficient. The VA site and legal provider must also enter into a Space-Sharing Agreement. The Memorandum also outlines privacy requirements, explaining that any disclosures by VA staff to legal providers must be done in accordance with the Privacy Act, Health Insurance Portability and Accountability Act, and any other applicable laws. Legal providers, in turn, must comply with these same laws when requesting information from the VA. For instance, requests for protected information must include a waiver agreement signed by the veteran prior to disclosure. Finally, the VA site must take steps to ensure that veterans understand that onsite legal providers are not a VA entity, and that a referral does not constitute a VA endorsement of the legal advice provided.

In 2016, the VA created an MLP Task Force composed of VA leadership from the OGC, the Veterans Health Administration (VHA), and the Veterans Justice Outreach program (L. Eilhardt, L. Jackson, S. Clark, personal communication, March 8, 2018). The ultimate goal of the Task Force is to establish an MLP at every VAMC, and then to increase the number of partnerships at CBOCs.

One of the Task Force's primary endeavors is to provide hands-on technical assistance to aspiring and new VA MLPs. To this end, the Task Force provides template documents such as MOUs and holds one-on-one calls with legal and/or VA partners to talk through any challenges. Through this work, the Task Force has identified several common barriers to the establishment of VA MLPs: space limitations at VHA sites, unfamiliarity with the MLP concept, lack of sustainable funding for legal services, and inadequate supply of lawyers near rural VA healthcare sites. However, the Task Force views the recent surge in number of VA MLPs as cause for optimism about the expansion of this important service delivery model (L. Eilhardt, L. Jackson, S. Clark, personal communication, March 8, 2018).

Part II: Legal Problems Among Veterans

Upon returning from service, many veterans encounter legal problems that negatively affect their health. In this section, we discuss the range of legal issues veterans face that can be remedied through the legal aid available through MLPs. We also discuss research by the VA that evidences the serious, negative impact unmet legal needs have on veterans' wellbeing.

Housing Stability

Veterans are more likely to experience homelessness than the non-veteran population (National Alliance to End Homelessness, 2015). By one estimate, 40,056 veterans were homeless in 2017 (United States Department of Housing and Urban Development, 2017), and the majority of these homeless veterans suffer from a mental health or substance abuse disorder (National Coalition for Homeless Veterans, n.d.). One factor in this crisis is unmet housing law needs, which MLP lawyers can help veterans resolve. For instance, lawyers can help veterans obtain housing subsidies to pay rent, can prevent illegal evictions, and can secure modifications of pre-foreclosure mortgage agreements. By way of specific example, a lawyer could help a veteran enforce proper notice before his landlord evicts him, buying him time to find a new place to live as opposed to living in a shelter. Alternatively, if an eviction has already occurred, a lawyer could prevent the eviction from appearing on a veteran's record. A court record of eviction can result in the loss of needed housing subsidies (National Housing Law Project, 2008).

One of the biggest benefits of an MLP in this context is that it promotes identification of the legal needs underlying homelessness before a loss of housing occurs. MLP clinicians are trained to spot nascent housing problems and can seamlessly refer patients to lawyers onsite, as opposed to lawyers coming on the scene when the veteran has already suffered a deprivation.

VA Disability Benefits

A legal need that is by definition unique to veterans is assistance with obtaining VA compensation for service-connected disabilities. Many service-members return to civilian life with disabilities stemming from their service—one estimate finds that over 4 million veterans have a service-connected disability rating—and this only includes veterans whose disabilities have been recognized by the VA (United States Census Bureau, 2016). These disabilities may be physical or psychological. Post-Traumatic Stress Disorder (PTSD), for instance, is a common service-connected disability, often stemming from combat or MST (VA, "How Common Is PTSD?", 2016a).

The monthly benefit amount for VA compensation for service-connected conditions varies according to the type (VA, "Schedule for Rating Disabilities", n.d.-b) and severity of the condition according to a percentage rating scale (VA, "Veterans Compensation", 2017g). Veterans who are totally disabled due to service-connection conditions, for instance, are entitled to be rated at the 100% level and to receive $2,973.86 per month (in 2018). The process for obtaining VA benefits is byzantine, with multiple tiers and forms of appeal, and some cases require complex medical evidence. Accordingly, legal assistance can be key to veterans accessing the benefits they earned through their service.

VA Benefit Overpayments

Though VA disability benefits provide critical income stability to millions of veterans, it is not uncommon for veterans who receive these benefits to face legal problems due to VA "overpayments." An overpayment occurs when the VA determines that it has paid too much to a veteran, which in effect creates a debt to the VA (Veterans' Benefits (2018)). Overpayments are a widespread problem: from January 1993 to 2009, for instance, the Veterans Benefits Administration (VBA) overpaid 27,500 disabled veterans a total of $943 million, an amount it asked these veterans to pay back (VA Office of Inspector General [OIG], 2014).

There are a number of ways veterans might find themselves subject to an overpayment, often related to major life changes. For example, failure to report a divorce while the VA continues to pay the higher disability benefit amount to which veterans with spouses are entitled creates an overpayment. The VA sometimes does not detect overpayments when they start to accrue, and indeed, sometimes does not detect overpayments until years after they began accumulating (VA OIG, 2014). This can leave veterans with very large and unexpected overpayment bills.

Time is of the essence for a veteran once the VA has identified what it believes is an overpayment. Unless the veteran appeals the alleged overpayment within 30 days of first receiving notice of the debt, the VA can begin to withhold the veteran's monthly benefits in full, and can continue until the debt is repaid (Pensions, Bonuses and Veterans' Relief, 2018a). This sudden loss of income can cause veterans to miss rent payments and to default on other financial obligations, and can eventually lead to eviction, bad credit, and other serious problems. With the assistance of a lawyer, however, veterans subject to an overpayment can avail themselves of several powerful legal remedies. For instance, lawyers can help veterans dispute the validity or amount of the debt (Pensions, Bonuses and Veterans' Relief, 2018b), request a waiver of the debt (Pensions, Bonuses and Veterans' Relief, 2018c), and appeal VA waiver decisions (Pensions, Bonuses and Veterans' Relief, 2018d).

Discharge Upgrades and Character of Discharge Determinations

Some veterans face an additional, substantial hurdle in accessing critical VA benefits: hundreds of thousands of Americans who served in the military are not considered "veterans" by the VA due to their discharge statuses (Veterans Legal Clinic, 2016). This is because only service-members discharged with an Honorable or General characterization are considered "veterans" under VA law, to the exclusion of service-members who received an Other Than Honorable, Bad Conduct, or other "bad paper" discharge (Veterans' Benefits (2011)). To access VA benefits, former service-members with bad paper have two options: apply for a discharge upgrade from the Department of Defense (discussed in Chap. 8) or for a Character of Discharge (COD) determination from the VA. The laws and adjudicative processes underlying these two options differ. However, a favorable determination in either venue is highly consequential, as it restores veterans' eligibility for VA healthcare, benefits, and housing programs (VA, "Claims for VA Benefits", n.d.-a).

The main regulation governing CODs contains a number of nuanced provisions that often call for argumentation only lawyers are equipped to provide (Pensions, Bonuses and Veterans' Relief, 2018e). For instance, one provision bars former service-members who were found guilty of a crime of "moral turpitude" during service, a concept that is only loosely defined (VA OGC, 1988). In addition, some of these provisions require medical evidence that calls for the joint efforts of lawyers and clinicians. A common issue in COD cases is whether the misconduct that led to the service-member's discharge was actually a symptom of an undiagnosed mental health condition (Pensions, Bonuses and Veterans' Relief, 2018f). On one hand, only a clinician can opine as to whether there is a nexus between a former service-member's behaviors and a mental health condition. On the other hand, clinicians often need the guidance of a lawyer in order to provide an opinion that is responsive to the VA's specific legal standards. VA MLPs are uniquely positioned to accommodate this interdisciplinary advocacy.

Family Law

Family law ranks among the greatest legal needs of veterans (VA, "CHALENG", 2017b). There is a high rate of separation and divorce in the veteran population, and the rate is even higher for veterans with PTSD (Price & Stevens, 2017). Research also suggests that women veterans are at greater risk than their non-veteran counterparts for intimate partner violence (VA, "Intimate Partner", 2015c) and perpetration of intimate partner violence by male veterans ranges from 13.5% to 42% (Gierisch et al., 2013). In addition, many veterans have child support obligations and if they fail to satisfy these dues, a lien can be placed against their bank accounts, they can be barred from obtaining credit, and their driver's licenses can be suspended (United States Department of Health and Human Services [U.S. DHHS], Administration for Children and Families [ACF], n.d.). Frequently, child custody arrearage occurs when a veteran is struggling with homelessness, a mental health condition, or a substance use disorder (U.S. DHHS, ACF, n.d.).

More often than not, veterans need legal assistance to resolve or manage these family law issues. For instance, an order of protection can help address intimate partner violence. In addition, lawyers can help veterans modify child support agreements to reflect income changes that make the veteran unable to pay in full. This type of legal aid can be critical as failure to pay child support can cause a cascade of legal problems: individuals who do not satisfy their support obligations are subject to arrest and nearly every state restricts, suspends, or revokes driver's licenses for failure to pay child support (National Conference of State Legislature, 2015). (See Chap. 6 of this book for a more detailed discussion of the intersection between veterans and family law, including family law courts.)

Other Legal Needs

Veterans face a host of other legal problems in addition to those just described. For instance, some veterans need help with driving related issues, such as restoring their driver's licenses and clearing negative driving records (Manchanda et al., 2016). Veterans also have consumer law needs, ranging from debt collection management, predatory lending scheme remedies, and enforcement of student loan discharge rights based on disability (Consumer Financial Protection Bureau, n.d.).

Certain subsets of the veteran population have unique legal needs. For instance, veterans with a criminal history may need assistance with outstanding warrants and fines, and expungements (Manchanda et al., 2016). (See Chap. 2 of this book for a discussion of veterans' involvement in the criminal justice system.) Older veterans' needs, in contrast, may center more on guardianships, wills, and advanced health-care directives. Roughly 75% of Vietnam era veterans are still alive (Gelman, 2013) and according the U.S. Census in 2012, there are more than 12 million veterans older than 65 years old (VA, "Elderly Veterans", 2017c).

Immigration law is another area of need for veterans. In 2016, more than 500,000 foreign-born veterans lived in the United States, accounting for three percent of the veteran population (Phillips, 2017). These veterans may need assistance obtaining citizenship status. Since October of 2001, the U.S. Citizenship and Immigration Services (USCIS) has naturalized 125,452 members of the military (United States Department of Homeland Security (DHS), 2018). While special provisions authorize USCIS to expedite the application and naturalization process for veterans, legal assistance can be crucial for complex naturalization applications (DHS, 2017). Although currently no VA MLPs focus on assisting veterans with immigration law matters, there is great potential for incorporation of this legal service into VA MLPs.

VA Research Shows That Veterans' Top Challenges Require Legal Assistance

VA research finds that veterans' needs for legal assistance with problems such as those discussed above are not being met. Each year, the VA conducts surveys of VA staff, community-based partners, and homeless veterans to determine the causes contributing to veteran homelessness (VA, "Project CHALENG", 2017d). Through this survey, known as Project CHALENG (Community Homelessness Assessment, Local Education and Networking Groups), participants rate the needs of homeless veterans in their communities (VA, "Community Homelessness Assessment, Local Education and Networking Groups [CHALENG]", 2017b). Although CHALENG data from the past ten years indicate that VA services meet many of the mental and physical health needs of veterans, the data also show veterans' legal needs are not being met.

Results from the most recent survey, conducted in 2016, reveal that four of the top ten unmet needs for both male and female homeless veterans require legal assistance (VA, "CHALENG", 2017b). These top legal needs concern: child support obligations, prevention of eviction or foreclosure, driver's license restorations, outstanding warrants and fines, and discharge upgrades (VA, "CHALENG", 2017b).

2016 VA CHALENG Survey, Top Unmet Legal Needs, Male Veterans

Rank	Male veteran unmet legal needs
1	Legal assistance for child support issues
2	Legal assistance to prevent eviction and foreclosure
3	Legal assistance to help restore a driver's license
4	Legal assistance for outstanding warrants and fines

2016 VA CHALENG Survey, Top Unmet Legal Needs, Female Veterans

Rank	Female veteran unmet legal needs
1	Legal assistance for child support issues
2	Legal assistance to prevent eviction and foreclosure
3	Legal assistance to help restore a driver's license
4	Discharge upgrade

In highlighting the underlying legal causes that contribute to veteran homelessness, CHALENG data have spurred legal services organizations and the VA to partner on innovative projects, like MLPs, to comprehensively address veterans' multi-faceted needs.

Part III: VA MLP Profiles

The growing number of VA MLPs serve increasingly diverse segments of the veteran population, are located at various types of VA sites, and assist with a range of legal problems. In this section, we provide snapshots of four VA MLPs that exemplify this variety. These profiles provide windows into the inner workings of these MLPs, showing how their legal services and processes are tailored to their veteran populations, and how lawyers and clinicians collaborate.

Profile I: VA Medical Center MLP, VA Maine Healthcare System

In 2015 in central Maine, Pine Tree Legal Assistance (Pine Tree) and VA Maine Healthcare System joined forces to form the Pine Tree-Togus MLP based at Togus VAMC. Pine Tree is a statewide non-profit civil legal aid organization that provides legal assistance to low-income Mainers, focusing on access to stable housing and income, healthy food, personal safety, and education (Pine Tree Legal Assistance, 2017). The MLP grew organically from Pine Tree's prior work providing legal assistance to homeless veterans in Maine (Liscord & Elliott, 2013) it became clear that an MLP was the ideal service model for bringing services to this hard to reach population.

The Togus VAMC provides office space to Pine Tree lawyers who manage an MLP clinic. Twice a week, lawyers meet with veterans onsite and provide legal consults to clinicians. These consults help clinicians navigate potential legal issues that put veterans at-risk of homelessness, suicide or mental health crises. Clinical staff from primary care, mental health, and social work attend MLP legal trainings once a month to learn how to issue spot potential legal issues and listen for magic words that indicate a veteran may need legal help. They screen for health-harming legal needs and refer veterans to Pine Tree lawyers using an integrated referral system hosted on

VA Maine Healthcare System's intranet. The MLP's legal staff provide assistance to veterans on housing and income issues, such as evictions and VA benefits overpayments, as well as represent veterans with PTSD or a history of MST in discharge upgrade and VA character of discharge determination proceedings.

The Pine Tree-Togus MLP developed its screening and referral system and clinical staff trainings based on the results of a community partner needs assessment at VA Maine Healthcare System, which included the Togus VAMC and the CBOCs. The needs assessment collected information about what legal issues clinicians observed in their patients and gauged clinicians' level of legal knowledge and understanding of the social determinants of health. The needs assessment, coupled with VA CHALENG survey data and Pine Tree's own study on veterans' legal needs in Maine (Liscord & Elliott, 2013), also served as the basis for the MLP's prioritization of legal assistance for housing, income, consumer matters, and discharge upgrades.

The Pine Tree-Togus MLP is one of the first VA MLPs to utilize VA Telehealth to reach veterans in rural locations (L. Eilhardt, personal communication, March 12, 2018; "What is Telehealth?", 2017). Generally, by way of a warm hand-off, a VA clinician onsite at Togus initiates a Telehealth meeting between a veteran located at a CBOC in a rural area and an MLP lawyer. Many CBOCs in Maine are several hours away from Togus, in rural communities. For example, the Caribou, Maine CBOC is a four-hour drive from Togus and serves 3500 rural Maine veterans (VA, "Caribou CBOC", 2017a). These veterans may need legal assistance but have limited access to lawyers in their remote location. Without the MLP's use of VA Telehealth, many rural veterans would not receive the help they need.

The Pine Tree-Togus MLP created the first VA MLP advisory council, which consists of leadership and staff from both the health and legal side of the partnership (L. Eilhardt, personal communication, March 12, 2018). The council developed a joint mission statement and works to develop mutual best practices. It also convenes regularly to ensure the MLP is running smoothly and to make adjustments to the processes underlying the collaboration, as needed.

To increase its ability to close the justice gap for Maine veterans, and to provide legal assistance outside of its areas of expertise, Pine Tree incorporates pro bono lawyers into its MLP. In 2017, Pine Tree partnered with the Maine State Bar Association to create the Veterans Legal Services Initiative (VLSI) (Weston, 2018). VLSI educates private Maine lawyers on the health-harming legal issues Maine veterans face and encourages pro bono representation of veterans referred to the MLP. VLSI also facilitates discrete and time-limited pro bono opportunities, like a wills legal clinic and a partnership with Starbucks called Military Mondays (Selnau & Jackson, 2018).

Profile II: Vet Center MLP, Oakland Vet Center

The Oakland Vet Center (OVC) in California is home to the first MLP at a VA Vet Center. The MLP at OVC was formed in 2016 between the OVC and Swords to Plowshares (Swords). Swords is a community-based organization that provides legal, employment, and housing assistance to over 3000 veterans in the California Bay Area every year (Swords to Plowshares, 2018). The OVC and Swords' Legal Unit had long had many veteran clients in common. However, they did not have a means of coordinating their respective behavioral health and legal services. An MLP provided the ideal framework for addressing these shared veteran clients' intertwined mental health and legal needs. By design, the Swords-OVC MLP's legal services focus on areas of law vital to veterans with mental health conditions: CODs, discharge upgrades, and VA disability compensation.

Chief among the benefits of the Swords-OVC MLP is the direct link between legal aid and veterans with Other Than Honorable discharges. (See Chap. 8 for more information about discharge statuses.) To be eligible for care at a Vet Center, such as the OVC, a veteran must have served in combat theater or an area of hostility, or have experienced MST (VA, "Vet Center Program", 2016b). Discharge status is not taken into account. Elsewhere in the VHA system, in contrast, an Other Than Honorable discharge is almost always an insurmountable obstacle to care (VA, "Applying for Benefits", 2015b). Eligibility for comprehensive treatment at VAMCs and CBOCs is contingent on either not having "bad paper" or on the VA making a legal determination that the veteran is "Honorable for VA purposes," despite his/her discharge status. Put simply, most veterans with Other Than Honorable discharges are not welcome at VAMCs or CBOCs. Thus, Vet Center MLPs like the Swords-OVC MLP fill a critical gap that other VA MLPs by definition cannot: they bring legal aid to veterans who are so marginalized, they cannot even access basic VA healthcare.

Filling this gap is important. Veterans with Other Than Honorable discharges have particularly acute legal and mental health needs—and compared to other veterans, they are more likely to be homeless and involved in the justice system, and are at greater risk of suicide (Veterans Legal Clinic, 2016). By helping these veterans obtain discharge upgrades and CODs, in effect restoring their veteran status, the Swords-OVC MLP pries open the door to life-saving VA benefits, such as subsidized housing and comprehensive healthcare.

In keeping with the motivating spirit of Vet Centers, which were formed to provide a more intimate space for therapy than large VAMCs, accessing legal services at the Swords-OVC MLP does not require veterans to navigate a sea of red tape. Counselors can refer veterans directly to the MLP lawyer simply by walking down the hall after a therapy session. OVC counselors also play a key role in the legal process itself. Importantly, they write medical opinions that are often integral to veterans' disability benefit, COD, and discharge upgrade cases, which frequently turn on evidence of mental health conditions. Moreover, Vet Center counselors regularly attend VA hearings to provide live testimony and answer adjudicators' questions, a level of clinical advocacy not common at other VA MLPs. Anecdotal evidence from the OVC-Swords MLP suggests that this testimony greatly increases veterans' chances of success: VA decisions often rely heavily on OVC counselors' opinions.

The Swords-OVC MLP's COD success rate is another testament to the power of the partnership, and by extension, the need for more Vet Center MLPs. CODs are notoriously difficult to win; the overall success rate varies between roughly 10–13%, depending on whether the COD is at the initial or appellate level of review (Veterans Legal Clinic, 2016). In stark contrast, to date the Swords-OVC MLP has won approximately 80% of its substantial caseload of COD cases. The remaining 300 or so Vet Centers across the country that have yet to form MLPs are ripe for this level of success.

Profile III: VA MLP for Women Veterans, Manhattan and Bronx VAMCs

The first VA MLP to exclusively serve women veterans launched in 2017. (See Chap. 10 for further information about the characteristics and special needs of women veterans.) This MLP is a partnership between the New York Legal Assistance Group's LegalHealth division and the Manhattan (VA, "New York Harbor", 2018c) and Bronx VAMCs (VA, "James J. Peters VA Medical Center [Bronx VAMC]", 2018b). LegalHealth currently runs three distinct legal clinics for veterans—the women's clinic, an older veterans clinic, and a general veteran clinic (New York Legal Assistance Group, 2017).

To meet the diverse needs of women veterans at the Manhattan and Bronx VAMCs, the Women Veterans MLP provides a range of legal services, including assistance with government benefits, discharge upgrades, family law matters (primarily orders of protection, custody, and child support), and housing. There is particularly high demand for assistance with VA benefits and family law issues. Almost all VA benefits matters relate to MST (Kubek, 2016).

Social workers within these two VAMCs make most of the referrals for legal assistance, though other VA providers, such as psychologists and primary care doctors, also make referrals. A great deal of referrals also come from word of mouth between women veterans: these VAMCs effectively operate as half hospital, half community center, with veterans and staff exchanging information about health and social services informally (S. Kubek, personal communication, November 14, 2017).

VA staff's role in the Women Veterans MLP extends beyond referrals. They also sometimes provide critical assistance in veterans' cases, for instance, by writing clinical statements regarding service-related mental health conditions in support of VA benefit claims or discharge upgrade applications. Moreover, social workers often play an invaluable role in ensuring women veterans take the steps necessary to advance their cases, such as writing affidavits about service traumas (S. Kubek, personal communication, November 14, 2017).

To support these forms of collaboration, as well as inform women veterans of their rights, the Women Veterans MLP lawyer conducts targeted trainings. For VA staff, trainings focus on how to spot legal issues early, so they can make referrals in time for the MLP lawyer to stop problems from snowballing or to maximize benefits. For veterans, the lawyer provides Know Your Rights trainings, a.k.a. "Legal Standowns," covering issues common to women veterans (Kubek, 2016).

Cultural competency is an essential component of the Women Veterans MLP. Women veterans often have experienced a multitude of traumas throughout their lifetime, not just MST, and legal services must be sensitive to these experiences. For instance, the MLP operates on the understanding that there is no one right way to write an affidavit. Veterans can write it at home, or with the lawyer, whatever minimizes the risk of re-traumatization (S. Kubek, personal communication, November 14, 2017).

The importance of providing culturally competent legal aid begs the question of why the Women Veterans MLP is one of only two VA MLPs that exclusively serve women veterans. This gap is likely due in part to a lack of awareness of the fact that women veterans' needs are best addressed through a gender-specific MLP. Granted, the legal issues most pressing for women veterans, such as access to stable housing and income, are similar to those faced by male veterans. Many women veterans, however, do not feel comfortable in settings populated by male veterans. This proximity may bring up memories of MST, which can prevent women from getting needed care (Murphy, Hans, & Reina, 2014). A separate MLP creates a safe space for women veterans to confront their pasts and to receive the legal aid they need to build better futures.

Profile IV: VA MLP for Senior Veterans, San Francisco VAMC

Senior veterans face many pressing health and legal challenges that younger veterans do not, and they constitute a significant portion of the veteran population. On average, veteran median age in the United States is 64 years old, compared with 44 for non-veterans (United States Department of Veterans Affairs, National Center of for Veterans Analysis and Statistics, 2018). However, few VA MLPs specifically serve senior veterans. One such MLP, the Medical-Legal Partnership for Seniors—Veterans Project, (MLPS Veterans Project) (University of California San Francisco/University of California Hastings College of the Law San Francisco [UCSF/UC Hastings XE], n.d.) is a partnership between UC Hastings College of the Law and the San Francisco VAMC. The idea to start the partnership started to take shape when staff at the San Francisco VAMC who were familiar with U.C. Hastings College of the Law's existing partnership with the nearby UCSF Center for Geriatric Care began to clamor for onsite legal services to address the legal problems with which they saw their elderly veteran patients struggling. The MLPS Veterans Project was created as an expansion of the existing MLP at UCSF in response to this demand in 2015 (S. Huffman, personal communication, November 14, 2017). It is based at the VAMC's Geriatric and Palliative Care Clinics, but referrals also come from hospital in-patient units and the Community Living Center nursing home.

Two legal issues predominate the MLPS Veterans Project: VA benefits and housing. With respect to VA benefits, the MLP most often helps veterans obtain non-service-connected benefits, such as pension (VA, "VA Pension", 2017e) and Aid & Attendance (VA, "Aid, & Attendance", 2015a). Most of the veterans who present to the MLP already receive service-connected benefits if they have a service injury or illness, perhaps because they have been in the VA system for a long time. Regarding housing, habitability and eviction notices are the most common issues that arise. The MLP engages in pre-litigation eviction advocacy and has been successful at settling housing disputes before eviction cases reach the courts (S. Huffman, personal communication, November 14, 2017).

Capacity and related estate planning issues are another core area of practice for the MLPS Veterans Project. For instance, if a veteran is newly diagnosed with dementia or another progressive debilitating or terminal disease, their VA clinician can make a legal referral for assistance with establishing an advance directive, power of attorney for finance, and simple will. These tools provide veterans an opportunity to express and protect their wishes before they lose the capacity to do so (Mendonca, 2016). Elder abuse, neglect, and financial abuse are other issues that occasionally arise. If the MLP cannot help with a given legal issue that presents, the MLP makes a targeted referral to a local legal services organization (S. Huffman, personal communication, November 14, 2017).

Collaboration between the VA staff and the lawyer partnered through this MLP takes several forms. In addition to making referrals, VA clinicians fill out VA Disability Benefit Questionnaires (VA, Disability Benefits Questionnaires [DBQ], 2018a) or other forms to help veterans access benefits, write medical necessity letters for American With Disabilities Act cases, and write letters to help with housing accommodation issues. VA clinicians also consult with the MLP lawyer about various legal issues that come up in the course of treatment, such as legal capacity. If the lawyer determines that the veteran may soon lose legal capacity or already has, they then advise about next steps in arranging the senior veteran's affairs (S. Huffman, personal communication, November 14, 2017).

The MLPS Veterans Project is different from most other VA MLPs in one important respect: the MLP lawyer makes home visits. Because accessibility can be a big issue for senior veterans, some of whom are housebound (Mendonca, 2016), many in this population simply would not get help without home visits.

The dearth of MLPs for senior veterans is likely due to several factors. First, there is an undersupply of elder law attorneys and geriatric doctors (Cottrell Houle, 2015), which creates a double gap for this vulnerable population. There is also a general lack of awareness of the depth of the needs of seniors. Many have not saved enough for retirement (Olen, 2016) or for long-term care (The Associated Press and the nonpartisan and objective research organization NORC at the University of Chicago Center for Public Affairs Research [AP-NORC], 2015) and dementia and other cognitive illnesses are on the rise (United States Department of Health and Human Services [U.S. DHHS], 2011). With medical advances in cancer, stroke, and chronic disease treatment, people are living longer (National Center for Health Statistics, 2017), but because of this they are living with things like dementia and Parkinson's disease for many more years than they would have before. Basically, they are living longer and sicker. VA MLPs are a powerful way to help senior veterans face these end-of-life challenges.

Part IV: VA MLP Participant Characteristics and Outcomes

Studies have shown that MLPs can benefit asthma patients (O'Sullivan et al., 2012), decrease barriers to healthcare for children (Weintraub et al., 2010), help underserved populations in rural areas (Teufel et al., 2012), improve the lives of cancer patients (Retkin, Brandfield, & Bacich, 2007), and reduce stress among low-income patients (Ryan, Kutob, Suther, Hansen, & Sandel, 2012). However, to date, only one study has examined the effects of MLPs on veterans' mental health (Tsai et al., 2017). In this section, we discuss this ground-breaking study's findings.

Benefits of MLPs for Veterans

In 2016, researchers conducted a study of VA MLPs in Connecticut and New York to assess the extent to which onsite legal services improve veterans' health and decrease VA healthcare spending. The study focused on four partnerships: (1) Connecticut Veterans Legal Center (CVLC) and the VA Connecticut Healthcare System in West Haven; (2) CVLC and the VA Connecticut Healthcare System in Newington; (3) LegalHealth, a division of the New York Legal Assistance Group, and the Manhattan Campus of the VA New York Harbor Healthcare System; and (4) LegalHealth and the James J. Peters VA Medical Center in the Bronx. Researchers analyzed MLP participant characteristics and legal services provided to 950 veterans who received MLP services from one of the VA MLP study sites during the period of June 2014 to January 2016. A subsample of 148 veterans were followed for up to one year to assess the impact legal services had on their mental health. This subsample group was selected based on their need for full legal representation for one of four legal problems: housing, consumer debt, child support payments, and disability benefits (Tsai et al., 2017).

Participant Characteristics

During the January 2014 to January 2016 study period, 950 veterans sought assistance from one of the VA MLP study sites in Connecticut and New York. Veterans presented with a total of 1384 legal issues or 1.5 legal issues per veteran. Most veterans seeking MLP services were male and unmarried, with an average age of 53. Mean annual income was below $25,000. Veterans' most commonly cited legal matters concerned VA benefits, housing, family law matters, and consumer issues (Tsai et al., 2017).

Participant Outcomes

Overall, veterans' legal goals were achieved in 51.4% of the legal issues presented to the VA MLPs during the two-year period. Goals were not achieved for 8.5% of issues presented and the remaining 40.1% had yet to reach an outcome during the study period. Legal goals were defined at the outset of representation between MLP legal staff and veterans. Notably, only 8.7% of the issues in which veterans' goals were achieved required lengthy court appearances or hearings, suggesting that most legal issues could be resolved with brief services, negotiation, or advice (Tsai et al., 2017).

Of the 148 veterans included in the yearlong assessment of mental health outcomes, 112 (75.7%) met their legal goals within the one-year study period. This subsample received "full" legal representation on housing issues, consumer debt, child support, and disability benefits. Full legal representation was defined as "an attorney's undertaking to provide the full range of legal services that are relevant to the existing factual situation and representing the client for as long as it takes to resolve the particular matter" (Tsai et al., 2017, p. 2197).

Researchers conducted outcome assessments using validated measures every three months for a one-year period. They observed that after only the first 3 months of the study period, these veterans showed "significant reductions in symptoms of hostility, paranoia, psychosis, generalized anxiety disorder (GAD-7), and posttraumatic stress disorder (PCL-5)" (Tsai et al., 2017, p. 2200). Furthermore, the study found significant improvements in physical health (Tsai et al., 2017, p. 2200). After 12 months, veterans continued to show significant reductions in mental health symptoms and also experienced improved housing status and income (Tsai et al., 2017, 2200). The increase in income was primarily from VA disability benefits, as opposed to other government benefits or employment. While these results are promising, the researchers also acknowledged that there is need for a more rigorous study employing a randomized controlled design.

Cost-Effectiveness

The study did not directly assess the cost-effectiveness of VA MLPs, in terms of VA healthcare spending or otherwise. However, it did raise some cost-effectiveness implications. The participating MLPs estimated the average total cost for each resolved legal issue as $270–$405 (Tsai et al., 2017). Compared to the average annual cost of $10,000–$60,000 to care for a person who is chronically homeless or who has a severe mental illness, study results suggest that focusing funding on legal programs that can prevent homelessness and improve mental health, like MLPs, can decrease costs (Jones et al., 2003; Rosenheck, Kasprow, Frisman, & Liu-Mares, 2003).

Part V: Veteran MLP Participant Profile

In this section, we profile a veteran who benefited from the assistance of a VA MLP. This concrete example showcases how collaboration between lawyers and clinicians can bring about positive change in veterans' lives that each profession is generally unable to effectuate on its own.

J.G., a Vietnam era Marine veteran, approached the Swords-OVC MLP in California for help accessing VA disability benefits, housing support, and healthcare in early 2017. He was homeless, moving between transitional housing sites, and his Other Than Honorable discharge stood in the way of the VA help he desperately needed. In step with the therapy provided by J.G.'s Vet Center counselor, the MLP lawyer began to build J.G.'s case for VA eligibility.

Prior to setting foot in the OVC, J.G. had not spoken about his service traumas in the decades that had passed since his discharge. It took some time, and the skill of J.G.'s Vet Center counselor, for J.G. to revisit the painful memories of his service in Vietnam. As a truck driver in Vietnam, J.G. had been charged with "deadruns," which required him to collect the bodies of dead service-members. Moreover, while driving in convoys J.G.'s own life was frequently in danger, as roadside attacks were common. Surrounded by so much loss of life and in fear for his own, J.G. began to manifest symptoms of PTSD. He went Absent Without Leave, got into fights, self-medicated with marijuana, and started abusing alcohol to escape his distress. However, PTSD was not yet recognized as a mental health diagnosis at this time, and J.G's symptoms were misinterpreted as misconduct. He was discharged from the Marines with an Other Than Honorable discharge. Upon returning to civilian life, J.G. was locked out of main VHA facilities because of his discharge status, and his PTSD symptoms and drinking worsened.

In the course of therapy and also by reviewing J.G.'s service records, provided by J.G.'s MLP lawyer, J.G.'s Vet Center counselor recognized what the Marines had failed to see decades ago: J.G. had incurred PTSD in service, and this condition had been the cause of his misconduct. With the guidance of J.G.'s lawyer, the counselor wrote a medical opinion explaining the nexus between J.G.'s traumas and the in-service behaviors that led to his discharge. When J.G. obtained a VA COD hearing, his counselor attended to testify, and his MLP lawyer explained how under VA laws, this medical evidence weighed in favor of granting J.G. a favorable COD. Importantly, J.G. overcame his decades of silence and testified, emboldened by the support of his OVC counselor and guided by moot preparation sessions with his MLP lawyer. J.G. gave a human voice to the hardships and distress he had experienced in Vietnam.

Based on these collective efforts, J.G. prevailed. He is now recognized by the VA as "Honorable," and is able to access the VA healthcare, disability benefits, and housing support he has been waiting for since the 1970s, when he first petitioned for VA eligibility. Today, J.G. is service-connected with a 100% rating for the PTSD he incurred in Vietnam. With this income, he is now able to afford housing and lives in a rental apartment. Without the Vet Center MLP, J.G. would likely still be without housing, income, and the peace of mind of having the honorableness of his service to his country finally recognized.

Part VI: Funding for VA MLPS

In this penultimate section, we discuss the current landscape of funding for VA MLPs, and point to some promising movement in Congress to increase funding.

Currently, VA does not have statutory authority to fund MLPs at its healthcare sites (VA MLP Task Force, n.d.). The legal services provided through VA MLPs tend to be funded by post-graduate legal fellowships (Skadden Foundation, 2018), the Legal Services Corporation (2018), Bar Associations (New Orleans Bar Association, 2018), law firms, (Equal Justice Works, 2017), private foundations (Elmina B. Sewall Foundation, 2018), and law school veterans clinics (Solomon Center for Health Law and Policy at Yale Law School, n.d.). That is, historically, funding for MLPs has fallen largely on the legal partner. Because much of the funding available to legal partners, such as post-law school fellowships, is short-term, VA MLPs are prone to suffer from funding instability and to struggle with sustainability.

Recognizing VA MLPs' need for enhanced financial support, several Members of Congress have proposed legislation that would authorize VA funding of legal services at its sites. For instance, on the Senate side, the *Homeless Veterans Prevention Act of 2017* (S. 1072) would have the VA enter into partnerships with public or private legal service entities, and would give VA the authority to fund a portion of the legal services these partners provide to veterans who are homeless or at risk of homelessness (United States Congress, "Homeless Veterans Prevention", 2017–2018). These legal services would cover housing, family law, income support, and criminal defense matters. Another Senate bill would have VA fund MLPs for women veterans. The *Deborah Sampson Act* (S. 681) directs the VA to enter into a partnership with at least one non-profit organization to provide legal services to women veterans that target their ten top unmet needs (United States Congress, "Deborah Sampson", 2017–2018).

Similar legislation has also been introduced on the House side. The *Legal Services for Homeless Veterans Act of 2017* (H.R. 2703) (United States Congress, "Legal Services", 2017–2018) and *Homeless Veterans Legal Services Act* (H.R. 1993) (United States Congress, "Homeless Veterans Legal", 2017–2018), for example, would each authorize VA to award grants or contracts to outside entities to fund a portion of pro bono legal services provided to veterans who are homeless or at risk of homelessness. In introducing these bills, Members of Congress have recognized the importance of legal aid in helping veterans readjust to civilian life and avoid or escape homelessness. For instance, in introducing H.R. 2703 Congressman Ted W. Lieu (2017) of Los Angeles, California explained that "[t]he research clearly shows that legal services are as necessary to addressing the Veteran homelessness epidemic as physical housing, but the VA does not have the flexibility it needs to fund those services."

Conclusion

In this chapter, we have discussed the unique powers of VA MLPs to address veterans' health-harming legal needs. VA MLPs increase veterans' access to needed legal aid by bringing lawyers to sites veterans frequent to receive healthcare. Critically, VA MLPs also foster the close collaboration between lawyers and clinicians that can be outcome determinative in cases affecting core aspects of veterans' lives, from housing to access to life-saving medical treatments. Despite the successes of the VA MLPs currently in operation and the research confirming that VA MLP services improve veterans' wellbeing, this model is underutilized: the demand for VA MLPs' unique integrated services far outstrips supply.

We predict that as research and awareness of VA MLPs grows, so will the availability of funding to expand the model. Research examining whether VA MLPs result in healthcare cost-savings is a particularly important area of research, as findings could provide financial incentive for VA to invest in MLPs at its sites. Additionally, research investigating differences between MLPs according to type of VA healthcare site and comparing the impact of legal aid provided at VA sites as opposed to at legal aid offices could aid in program design. This data could help service providers best reach the most vulnerable veterans and provide services targeted to their needs. Even without this data, Congress' growing interest in VA MLPs and push for federal funding bodes well for the future of this novel service model.

Acknowledgments The authors would like to acknowledge the contributions of Lara Eilhardt at the U.S. Department of Veterans Affairs (VA) Office of the General Counsel, Samantha Kubek at the New York Legal Assistance Group, Sara Huffman at U.C. Hastings College of Law, Ryan Lilly at the VA Maine Healthcare System, Dr. Linda Baggett at the Long Beach VA Healthcare System, Leila Jackson at the VA Office of Community Engagement, Sean Clark at the VA Veterans Justice Outreach program, and the VA Medical-Legal Partnership (MLP) Task Force.

References

Consumer Financial Protection Bureau (n.d.). Serving service members, veterans, and military families. Retrieved March 11, 2018, from https://www.consumerfinance.gov/practitioner-resources/servicemembers/

Cottrell Houle, M. (2015). An aging population, without the doctors to match. *The New York Times*. Retrieved March 11, 2018, from https://www.nytimes.com/2015/09/23/opinion/an-aging-population-without-the-doctors-to-match.html?_r=0

Curran, M. (2016). Medical-legal partnership legalserver configuration guide. Retrieved March 11, 2018, from http://medical-legalpartnership.org/legalserver-guide/

Elmina B. Sewall Foundation (2018). 2014–2015 Grantees. Retrieved June 8, 2018, from https://static1.squarespace.com/static/5a283583a803bb17b69fec72/t/5b22c5a61ae6cfc35594d9e3/1529005484764/2014-2015.pdf

Equal Justice Works (2017). 2014, Equal justice works fellowships, Devin Bissman. Retrieved March 11, 2018, from http://www.equaljusticeworks.org/node/80935

Gelman, A. (2013). How many Vietnam veterans are still alive? *The New York Times*. Retrieved March 11, 2018, from http://www.nytimes.com/2013/03/26/science/how-many-vietnam-veterans-are-still-alive.html
Gierisch, J., Shapiro, A., Grant, N., King, H., McDuffie, J., & Williams J. (2013). Intimate partner violence: Prevalence among U.S. Military Veterans and Active Duty Servicemembers and a review of intervention approaches. Department of Veterans Affairs, Evidence-based Synthesis Program Center, Project #09-010. Retrieved March 14, 2018, from https://www.hsrd.research.va.gov/publications/esp/partner_violence-REPORT.pdf
Gottlieb, L., Tirozzi, K., Manchanda, R., Burns, A., & Sandel, M. (2015). Moving electronic medical records upstream. *American Journal of Preventive Medicine, 48*(2), 215–218.
Jones, K., Colson, P., Holter, M., Lin, S., Valencia, E., Susser, E., & Wyatt, R. J. (2003). Cost-effectiveness of critical time intervention to reduce homelessness among persons with mental illness. *Psychiatric Services, 54*(6), 884–890.
Kremer, T., Lowell, M., & Zolezzi-Wyndham, V. (2015). Public/private partnership to address housing and health care for children with asthma. *Health Affairs Blog*. Retrieved March 11, 2018, from http://healthaffairs.org/blog/2015/07/22/publicprivate-partnership-to-address-housing-and-health-care-for-children-with-asthma/
Kubek, S. (2016). The invisible veterans. *The Huffington Post*. Retrieved March 14, 2018, from www.huffingtonpost.com/entry/the-invisible-veterans_us_585967c7e4b06ae7ec2a41c9
Lawton, E. (2014). A history of the medical legal partnership movement. *Community Health Forum (National Association of Community Health Forum Magazine)*, pp. 12–13.
Legal Services Corporation (2018). Veterans pro bono grant program. Retrieved March 11, 2018, from https://www.lsc.gov/media-center/blog/2015/07/28/veterans-pro-bono-grant-program
Liscord, R. & Elliott, C. (2013). Serving those who served: Understanding the legal needs of Maine's Veteran Community. Retrieved March 11, 2018, from https://statesidelegal.org/sites/default/files/Veteran%20Legal%20Needs%20Study.pdf
Manchanda, R., Murphy, S., Lawton, E., & Middleton, M. (2016). The invisible battlefield: Veterans facing health-harming legal needs in civilian life. Retrieved June 8, 2018, from http://medical-legalpartnership.org/wp-content/uploads/2016/06/The-Invisible-Battlefield.pdf
Marple, K. (2015). Messaging guide: Framing legal care as health care. Retrieved March 11, 2018, from http://medical-legalpartnership.org/mlp-resources/messaging-guide/
Mendonca, K. (2016). Medical legal partnership helps senior veterans. Retrieved March 11, 2018, from https://www.sanfrancisco.va.gov/features/Medical_Legal_Partnership.asp
Murphy, F., Hans, S., & Reina, B. (2014). Women veterans: The long journey home. Retrieved March 14, 2018, from DAV Website: https://www.dav.org/wp-content/uploads/women-veterans-study.pdf
National Alliance to End Homelessness (2015). Veteran homelessness. Retrieved March 11, 2018, from https://endhomelessness.org/resource/veteran-homelessness/
National Center for Health Statistics (2017). *Health, United States, 2016: With chartbook on long-term trends in health*. Hyattsville, MD.
National Center for Medical-Legal Partnership (2014). The medical-legal partnership toolkit, phase II: Building infrastructure. Retrieved March 11, 2018, from https://kresge.org/sites/default/files/Uploaded%20Docs/Medical-Legal-Partnership-toolkit-phase-2.pdf
National Center for Medical-Legal Partnership (2015). The medical-legal partnership toolkit, phase I: Laying the groundwork. Retrieved March 11, 2018, from http://medical-legalpartnership.org/wp-content/uploads/2017/11/MLP-Toolkit-Phases-I-and-II.pdf
National Center for Medical-Legal Partnership (n.d.-a). Retrieved March 11, 2018, from http://medical-legalpartnership.org/
National Center for Medical-Legal Partnership (n.d.-b). FAQ. Retrieved March 11, 2018 from http://medical-legalpartnership.org/faq/
National Coalition for Homeless Veterans (n.d.). Background and statistics. Retrieved March 11, 2018, from http://nchv.org/index.php/news/media/background_and_statistics/

National Conference of State Legislature (2015). Criminal nonsupport and child support. Retrieved March 11, 2018, from http://www.ncsl.org/research/human-services/license-restrictions-for-failure-to-pay-child-support.aspx#1
National Housing Law Project (2008). HUD-VASH: Long neglected program brought back to life. Retrieved March 11, 2018, from http://nhlp.org/files/06%20NHLP%20Bull%20Jul08%20072408_2%20(final)-2VASH.pdf
New Orleans Bar Association (2018). Veteran justice fellowship: Leave no veteran behind. Retrieved March 11, 2018, from http://www.neworleansbar.org/foundation.html
New York Legal Assistance Group (2017). NYLAG annual report. Retrieved March 14, 2017, from https://nylag.org/about-us/annual-report
O'Sullivan, M., Brandfield, J., Hoskote, S., Segal, S., Chug, L., Modrykamien, A., & Eden, E. (2012). Environmental improvements brought by the legal interventions in the homes of poorly controlled inner-city adult asthmatic patients: A proof-of-concept study. *Journal of Asthma, 49*(9), 911–917.
Olen, H. (2016). You call this retirement? Boomers still have work to do. *AARP The Magazine*. Retrieved March 11, 2018, from https://www.aarp.org/work/retirement-planning/info-2014/boomer-retirement-little-savings-means-working.html
Pensions, Bonuses and Veterans' Relief (2018a). 38 C.F.R. § 1.911(c)(1).
Pensions, Bonuses and Veterans' Relief (2018b). 38 C.F.R. § 1.911(c)(2).
Pensions, Bonuses and Veterans' Relief (2018c). 38 C.F.R. § 1.911(c)(3).
Pensions, Bonuses and Veterans' Relief (2018d). 38 C.F.R. § 1.912a.
Pensions, Bonuses and Veterans' Relief (2018e). 3.301(c)(3).
Pensions, Bonuses and Veterans' Relief (2018f). 38 C.F.R. § 3.12.
Phillips, K. (2017). The story behind this powerful photo of deported military veterans saluting the U.S. flag. *The Washington Post*. Retrieved March 11, 2018, from https://www.washingtonpost.com/news/checkpoint/wp/2017/11/16/the-story-behind-this-powerful-photo-of-deported-military-veterans-saluting-the-american-flag/?utm_term=.def18299b813
Pine Tree Legal Assistance (2017). Retrieved March 11, 2018, from www.ptla.org
Price, J. & Stevens, S. (2017). Partners of veterans with PTSD: Research findings. Retrieved June 6, 2018, from https://www.ptsd.va.gov/professional/treatment/family/partners_of_vets_research_findings.asp
Retkin, R., Brandfield, J., & Bacich, C. (2007). Impact of legal interventions on cancer survivors. Retrieved March 14, 2018, from http://www.bc.edu/content/dam/files/schools/law_sites/library/pdf/content/tremblay_schulman/2007-01-00.Retkin%20et%20al.pdf
Rosenheck, R., Kasprow, W., Frisman, L., & Liu-Mares, W. (2003). Cost-effectiveness of supported housing for homeless persons with mental illness. *Archives of General Psychiatry, 60*(9), 940–951.
Ryan, A., Kutob, R., Suther, E., Hansen, M., & Sandel, M. (2012). Pilot study of impact of medical-legal partnership services on patients' perceived stress and wellbeing. *Journal of Health Care for the Poor and Underserved, 23*(4), 1536–1546.
Selnau, K., & Jackson, F. (2018). A unique approach to pro bono: Legal help for Maine veterans at Starbucks. *Maine Bar Journal, 32*(4), 25–27. Retrieved March 11, 2018 from http://c.ymcdn.com/sites/www.mainebar.org/resource/resmgr/BarJournals/MBJonline_Fall-17_WINTER-18.pdf
Skadden Foundation (2018). Retrieved March 11, 2018, from https://www.skaddenfellowships.org/
Solomon Center for Health Law and Policy at Yale Law School (n.d.). Medical-legal partnerships. Retrieved March 11, 2018, from https://law.yale.edu/solomon-center/projects-publications/medical-legal-partnerships
Swords to Plowshares (2018). Retrieved March 11, 2018, from https://www.swords-to-plowshares.org/

Teufel, J., Werner, D., Goffinet, D., Thorne, W., Brown, S., & Gettinger, L. (2012). Rural medical-legal partnership and advocacy: A three-year follow-up study. *Journal of Health Care for the Poor and Underserved, 23*(2), 705–714.

The Associated Press and the Non-Partisan and Objective Research Organization NORC at the University of Chicago Center for Public Affairs Research (2015). Long-term care poll. Long-term care in America: Americans' outlook and planning for future care. Retrieved July 9, 2017, from http://longtermcarepoll.org/Pages/Polls/long-term-care-in-america-americans-outlook-and-planning-for-future.aspx

Tobin Tyler, E., Lawton, E., Conroy, K., Sandel, M., & Zuckerman, B. (2011). *Poverty, health and law: Readings and cases for medical-legal partnership* (1st ed.). Durham, NC: Carolina Academic Press.

Tsai, J., Middleton, M., Villegas, J., Johnson, C., Retkin, R., Seidman, A., ... Rosenheck, R. (2017). Medical-legal partnerships at veterans affairs medical centers improved housing and psychosocial outcomes for vets. *Health Affairs, 36*(12), 2195–2203.

United States Census Bureau (2016). Service-connected disability-rating status and ratings for civilian veterans 18 years and over, United States census bureau, 2016 American Community Survey 1-year estimates. Retrieved March 12, 2018, from https://factfinder.census.gov/faces/tableservices/jsf/pages/productview.xhtml?pid=ACS_16_1YR_C21100&prodType=table

United States Congress, 115th Congress (2017–2018). Deborah Sampson Act. Retrieved March 11, 2018 from https://www.congress.gov/bill/115th-congress/senate-bill/681

United States Congress, 115th Congress (2017–2018). Homeless Veterans Legal Services Act. Retrieved March 11, 2018 from https://www.congress.gov/bill/115th-congress/house-bill/1993

United States Congress, 115th Congress (2017–2018). Homeless Veterans Prevention Act of 2017. Retrieved March 11, 2018 from https://www.congress.gov/bill/115th-congress/senate-bill/1072

United States Congress, 115th Congress (2017–2018). Legal Services for Homeless Veterans Act of 2017. Retrieved March 11, 2018 from https://www.congress.gov/bill/115th-congress/house-bill/2703

United States Department of Health and Human Services, Centers for Disease Control and Prevention (2011). Cognitive impairment: A call for action now! Retrieved March 11, 2018, from https://www.cdc.gov/aging/pdf/cognitive_impairment/cogimp_poilicy_final.pdf

United States Department of Health and Human Services, Health Resources and Services Administration (HRSA) (n.d.). Service descriptors for form 5A: Services provided. Retrieved March 14, 2018, from https://bphc.hrsa.gov/about/requirements/scope/form5aservicedescriptors.pdf

United States Department of Homeland Security (2017). Naturalization through military service. Retrieved March 11, 2018, from https://www.uscis.gov/news/fact-sheets/naturalization-through-military-service-fact-sheet

United States Department of Homeland Security (2018). Military naturalization statistics. Retrieved March 11, 2018, from https://www.uscis.gov/military/military-naturalization-statistics

United States Department of Housing and Urban Development (HUD) (2017). 2017 Annual homeless assessment report, part I: Point-in-time estimates of homelessness. Retrieved May 6, 2018, from https://www.hudexchange.info/resources/documents/2017-AHAR-Part-1.pdf

United States Department of Veterans Affairs (2011). Directive 2011-034, homeless veterans legal referral process. Retrieved March 13, 2018 from, https://www.va.gov/vhapublications/publications.cfm?Pub=1

United States Department of Veterans Affairs (2012). Memorandum: Advising clients on working with non-VA legal service providers. Retrieved March 11, 2018, from http://statesidelegal.org/sites/default/files/VA%20Memo%20re%20Non-VA%20legal%20service%20providers.pdf

United States Department of Veterans Affairs (2015a). Aid & attendance and housebound. Retrieved March 11, 2018, from https://www.benefits.va.gov/pension/aid_attendance_housebound.asp

United States Department of Veterans Affairs (2015b). Applying for benefits and your character of discharge. Retrieved March 11, 2018, from http://www.benefits.va.gov/benefits/character_of_discharge.asp
United States Department of Veterans Affairs (2015c). Intimate partner violence. Retrieved March 14, 2018 from, https://www.ptsd.va.gov/public/types/violence/domestic-violence.asp
United States Department of Veterans Affairs (2015d). 300 Vet centers here for vets who served in combat zones. Retrieved March 11, 2018, from https://www.va.gov/health/NewsFeatures/20120227a.asp
United States Department of Veterans Affairs (2015e). Vet center program. Retrieved March 11, 2018, from https://www.vetcenter.va.gov/About_US.asp
United States Department of Veterans Affairs (2016a). How common is PTSD? Retrieved March 11, 2018, from https://www.ptsd.va.gov/public/PTSD-overview/basics/how-common-is-ptsd.asp
United States Department of Veterans Affairs (2016b). Vet center program eligibility. Retrieved March 11, 2018, from https://www.vetcenter.va.gov/eligibility.asp
United States Department of Veterans Affairs (2017a). Caribou CBOC. Retrieved March 11, 2018, from https://www.maine.va.gov/locations/caribou.asp
United States Department of Veterans Affairs (2017b). Community Homelessness Assessment, Local Education and Networking Groups (CHALENG). Retrieved March 11, 2018, from https://www.va.gov/HOMELESS/docs/CHALENG-2016-factsheet-508-2017-07-29.pdf
United States Department of Veterans Affairs (2017c). Elderly veterans. Retrieved March 11, 2018, from https://www.benefits.va.gov/persona/veteran-elderly.asp
United States Department of Veterans Affairs (2017d). Project CHALENG. Retrieved March 11, 2018 from https://www.va.gov/homeless/chaleng.asp
United States Department of Veterans Affairs (2017e). VA Pension. Retrieved March 11, 2018, from https://www.benefits.va.gov/pension/
United States Department of Veterans Affairs (2017f). VA telehealth services. Retrieved March 11, 2018, from https://www.telehealth.va.gov/
United States Department of Veterans Affairs (2017g). Veterans compensation benefits rate tables. Retrieved March 11, 2018, from https://www.benefits.va.gov/COMPENSATION/resources_comp01.asp
United States Department of Veterans Affairs (2018a). Disability Benefits Questionnaires (DBQs). Retrieved March 11, 2018, from https://www.benefits.va.gov/compensation/dbq_disabilityexams.asp
United States Department of Veterans Affairs (2018b). James J. Peters VA medical center. Retrieved March 11, 2018, from https://www.bronx.va.gov/
United States Department of Veterans Affairs (2018c). VA New York harbor health care system. Retrieved March 11, 2018, from https://www.nyharbor.va.gov
United States Department of Veterans Affairs (n.d.-a). Claims for VA benefits and character of discharge. Retrieved March 11, 2018, from https://www.benefits.va.gov/BENEFITS/docs/COD_Factsheet.pdf
United States Department of Veterans Affairs (n.d.-b). Schedule for rating disabilities. Retrieved March 11, 2018, from https://www.gpo.gov/fdsys/pkg/CFR-1998-title38-vol1/pdf/CFR-1998-title38-vol1-part4.pdf
United States Department of Veterans Affairs (n.d.-c). Vet center facility and service locator. Retrieved March 11, 2018, from https://www.va.gov/directory/guide/vetcenter.asp
United States Department of Veterans Affairs, MLP Task Force (n.d.). Medical-legal partnerships and community engagement. Retrieved March 11, 2018, from https://www.va.gov/ve/docs/medicalLegalPartnershipsAndCommunityEngagement.pdf
United States Department of Veterans Affairs, National Center of for Veterans Analysis and Statistics (2018). Profile of veterans: 2016 data from the American Community Survey. Retrieved June 8, 2018, from https://www.va.gov/vetdata/docs/SpecialReports/Profile_of_Veterans_2016.pdf
United States Department of Veterans Affairs, Office of General Counsel (1988). Precedential opinion 6–87.

United States Department of Veterans Affairs, Office of General Counsel (2018). Free legal clinics in VA facilities. Retrieved June 5, 2018, from https://www.va.gov/ogc/docs/LegalServices.pdf

United States Department of Veterans Affairs, Office of Inspector General (2014). Statement of Linda A. Halliday, Assistant Inspector General for Audits and Evaluations, Office of Inspector General, Department of Veterans Affairs Before the Committee on Veterans' Affairs, United States House of Representatives, Hearing on evaluation of the process to achieve VBA goals. Retrieved March 11, 2018, from https://www.va.gov/oig/pubs/statements/vaoig-statement-20140714-halliday.pdf

United States Department of Veterans Affairs, VAntage Point, Official Blog of the United States Department of Veterans Affairs (2017). Medical Legal Partnerships: Veterans health beyond the stethoscope. Retrieved on March 11, 2018, from https://www.blogs.va.gov/VAntage/38055/medical-legal-partnerships-veterans-health-beyond-stethoscope/

United States Department of Veterans Affairs, Veterans Health Administration (2018a). Retrieved March 11, 2018, from https://www.va.gov/health/aboutVHA.asp

United States Department of Veterans Affairs, Veterans Health Administration (2018b). Where do I get the care I need? Retrieved March 11, 2018, from https://www.va.gov/health/findcare.asp

United States Representative Ted Lieu (2017). Press release: Rep. Lieu introduces legislation to give homeless veterans access to legal services. Retrieved March 11, 2018 from https://lieu.house.gov/media-center/press-releases/rep-lieu-introduces-legislation-give-homeless-veterans-access-legal-0

University of California San Francisco/University of California Hastings College of the Law San Francisco Consortium on Law, Science, and Health Policy (n.d.). Medical-legal partnership for seniors clinic. Retrieved March 11, 2018, from http://www.ucconsortium.org/our-work/training-and-services/medical-legal-partnership-seniors-clinic/

Veterans Legal Clinic Legal Services Center Harvard Law School (2016). Underserved: How the VA wrongfully excludes veterans with bad paper. Retrieved March 11, 2018, from https://www.swords-to-plowshares.org/wp-content/uploads/Underserved.pdf

Veterans' Benefits (2011). 38 U.S.C. § 101(2).

Veterans' Benefits (2018). 38 U.S.C. § 3685.

Weintraub, D., Rodgers, M., Botcheva, L., Loeb, A., Knight, R., Ortega, K., … Huffman, L. (2010). Pilot study of medical-legal partnership to address social and legal needs of patients. *Journal of Health Care for the Poor and Underserved, 21*(2 suppl), 157–168.

Weston, A. (2018). From the executive director: A review of 2017, and a peek ahead to 2018. *Maine Bar Journal, 33*(1), 6–7.

What is Telehealth? (2017). Retrieved March 11, 2018, from https://www.healthit.gov/telehealth

Chapter 5
Veterans Treatment Courts

Janice D. McCall and Benjamin Pomerance

> *"The court reflects the structure of a military unit: The judge becomes the commanding officer; the volunteer Veteran mentors act as fire team leaders; the court team becomes the company staff; and the Veteran defendants become the troops"*
>
> —Bryan Lett, Reporter for Disabled American Veterans (DAV), April 11, 2017

Abbreviations

ACLU	American Civil Liberties Union
AUDIT	Alcohol Use Disorders Identification Test
DAST	Drug Abuse Screening Test
DAV	Disabled American Veterans
DoD	Department of Defense
DWI	Driving while intoxicated
IOM	Institute of Medicine
MOAS	Modified Overt Aggression Scale
NADCP	National Association of Drug Court Professionals
NIJ	National Institute of Justice
OEF	Operation Enduring Freedom
OIF	Operation Iraqi Freedom
PCL	PTSD Checklist
PHQ	Patient Health Questionnaire
PTSD	Posttraumatic stress disorder
SDVTRC	San Diego, California, Veterans Treatment Review Calendar

J. D. McCall, PhD, MSW, LSW (✉)
Department of Social Work, California University of Pennsylvania, California, PA, USA
e-mail: mccall@calu.edu

B. Pomerance, Esq.
New York State Division of Veterans' Services, Albany, NY, USA

J. Tsai, E. R. Seamone (eds.), *Intersections between Mental Health and Law among Veterans*, https://doi.org/10.1007/978-3-030-31664-8_5

U.S.	United States
VA	Department of Veterans Affairs
VJO	Veterans Justice Outreach
VTC	Veterans Treatment Court

Introduction

Treatment courts, also known as problem-solving courts, offer an alternative to incarceration in the form of mandated individualized treatment. Born from the need to address the root cause of criminal conduct among many justice-involved Veterans—untreated behavioral health needs that are often related to trauma incurred during the Veteran's military service—Veterans Treatment Courts (VTCs) operate as a collaborative effort among the presiding judge and the prosecuting and defense attorneys in the courtroom, the Veterans Justice Outreach (VJO) Program of the United States Department of Veterans Affairs (VA), and partners from multiple medical, legal, criminal justice, social services, and community-based entities. For a substantial number of Veterans, reintegration into civilian life is rife with the complexities of navigating various interlocking challenges such as battling alcoholism or substance abuse, treating trauma, and addressing service-related mental health needs. By offering eligible justice-involved Veterans treatment focusing on these issues and tailored to their individual needs, VTCs demonstrate that the law, through its procedures and rulings, can be a therapeutic agent, serving as an active force to effect change in a defendant's life and guiding court interventions for the purpose of improving defendants' lives.

VTC Participant Characteristics

According to the 2016 demographics report on the Profile of the Military Community (United States Department of Defense (U.S. DoD), 2016), the average age of the Active Duty force is 28.5 years, which is younger than the median adult age in the United States (37.8 years) (U.S. Census Bureau, n.d.-a). Eighty-five percent of officers in the Armed Forces compared to 31% of the national population have a Bachelor's degree or higher (U.S. Census Bureau, n.d.-b; U.S. DoD, 2016). In terms of racial diversity in the Armed Forces, while nationally 24% of the population is non-white, among Active Duty members nearly one-third (31%) identify themselves as a racial minority (i.e., Black or African American, Asian, American Indian or Alaska Native, Native Hawaiian or Other Pacific Islander, Multi-racial, or Other/Unknown) (U.S. Census Bureau, n.d.-b; U.S. DoD, 2016). Overall, 41% of military personnel have children (U.S. DoD, 2016). Additionally, individuals who are recruited into military services are often "selected against factors that are correlated with community crime, such as a history of mental illness, a prior criminal record, or a history of drug abuse" (Guy Gambill, Soros Senior Justice Fellow, Justice Policy Institute, as cited in Cartwright, 2011). However, sometimes what we find is that when service members return to civilian life, the process of their civilian reintegration may include the presence of trauma—both physical and psychological—that are tied to their deployment and combat exposures.

Veterans experience a range of comorbid physical health needs and yet, given the increase in popularity of the VTC model across the country, little is known about the medical care profiles among Veterans who become VTC participants. Studies on Veterans, who are not justice-involved, have reported complications stemming from comorbid posttraumatic stress disorder (PTSD) and chronic pain (Outcalt, Hoen, Yu, Franks, & Krebs, 2016); greater comorbid health problems, including liver disease, among dually diagnosed Veterans with major depressive disorders and alcohol use disorder (Yoon, Petrakis, & Rosenheck, 2015); and key treatment priorities among female Veterans to include depression, pain management, and coping with chronic general medical conditions (Kimerling et al., 2014). The physical and psychological traumas experienced by Veterans are also linked to increased risk of the development of behavioral health disorders (Miller, Pederson, & Marshall, 2017; Seal et al., 2011). Unfortunately, for some Veterans, these traumas remain unaddressed and complications from untreated behavioral health needs may result in justice involvement. For example, a 2019 scoping study reviewing literature on the health and healthcare of Veterans involved in the criminal justice system reported substance use disorders (e.g. alcohol use disorder, opioid use disorder, co-occurring substance use and other mental health diagnoses) as the most common condition examined in their sample of 191 studies (Finlay et al., 2019). Several articles in Finlay et al. (2019) also examined experiences related to PTSD and trauma. For justice-involved populations, this is particularly salient as studies have provided supporting evidence for the link between PTSD and crime (Collins & Bailey, 2007; Kulka et al., 1990; Wilson & Zigelbaum, 1983).

Moreover, recent research suggests that for those serving in the U.S. Armed Forces the unique circumstances of the wars in Afghanistan and Iraq (Operation Enduring Freedom (OEF) and Operation Iraqi Freedom (OIF)) pose significant challenges. For example, those serving in these current conflicts are faced with an increased number of multiple and lengthier deployment. According to the Institute of Medicine (IOM) (2013), the average length of deployments is 7.7 months—from an average of 4.5 months in the Air Force to an average of 9.4 months in the Army. As suggested by the IOM, "if deployment itself is considered an exposure, the 'dose' may impact health, so more deployment time would theoretically be worse for subsequent health outcomes." Furthermore, for military members, the importance of a period of time between deployments, also known as "dwell cycle," helped urge a 24-month dwell cycle in the Army, however, due to demand for personnel, average dwell time was 21 months (ranging from 16 months in the Marine Corps to about 22 months in the Army and Navy) for military personnel with two or more deployments (IOM, 2013). In addition, advancements in technology have enabled military personnel to survive traumatic combat experiences that would have likely been deadlier in previous conflicts (Tanielian & Jaycox, 2008). Thus, Veterans of OEF/

OIF conflicts are exposed to combat that is more frequent and of longer duration placing these Veterans at a higher risk of PTSD (Cavanaugh, 2011). Approximately 10–20% of troops returning from OEF/OIF conflicts exhibit psychological problems that warrant treatment (Tanielian & Jaycox, 2008).

For Veterans, justice-involvement presents further obstacles and more service complexity when engaging services to meet their health care needs. If the Veteran has been incarcerated, the Veteran will likely face new barriers upon release related to poverty and lower socioeconomic status, including access to ongoing health care—especially if the Veteran's character of discharge from the military excludes them from enrolling in the VA's healthcare system. Securing health care benefits, accessing care, and ensuring continuity of care for former prison inmates upon release remains a nationwide public health concern. Thus, it is not surprising that most justice-involved Veterans remain at risk for poor health outcomes. According to the general population of OEF/OIF Veterans surveyed in a 2008 RAND study, only 53% of Veterans had sought professional help in the previous year, and only half of those who did seek care received adequate treatment. The potential association between stigma and accessing mental health treatment could be particularly salient for female Veterans who also experience high rates of military sexual trauma that have been associated with PTSD (Kimerling et al., 2010; Kimerling et al., 2014; Yaeger, Himmelfarb, Cammack, & Mintz, 2006). The opportunity for team-based access to health and mental health services presented by a VTC program could also potentially connect the minority of justice-involved female Veterans to needed assessments and services.

As we continue in this chapter, it has been important to acknowledge the context and characteristics of individuals who serve in the U.S. Armed Forces, the conditions of their service that are associated with their civilian reintegration, and the risks posed to Veterans who may become involved in the justice system. For Veterans who are identified and referred into a VTC program, the assessing VJO Specialist will likely focus on areas such as mental health, substance use, trauma exposure, physical health, family relationships, social support, housing, employment, and education needs (Please see Chap. 3 for further descriptions on VJOs).

We would like to now provide you with a description of known characteristics of VTC participants as recently reported in a large national study of VTCs. Among 7, 931 Veterans in the VJO program across 115 associated VA sites, the majority of VTC participants were white, male, with at least a high school education, aged in their 40s, and less than half were employed in the past three years (Tsai, Finlay, Flatley, Kasprow, & Clark, 2018; Tsai, Flatley, Kasprow, Clark, & Finlay, 2017). Compared to non-VTC participants who were also criminal justice-involved, VTC participants were more likely to have served in Iraq and Afghanistan, to have reported combat exposure, and to have a drug offense (Tsai et al., 2017). Notably, over one-third of VTC participants were judged to have probable PTSD (Tsai et al., 2018). A separate 2018 scoping study that examined 15 VTC-related articles similarly reported that most VTC participants were white, male, middle-aged (30–50 years of age), and had mental health and substance use disorders (McCall, Tsai, & Gordon, 2018). In one of the national studies, some Veterans entering a

VTC program were characterized as not being stably housed, less than half were employed in the past three years, and over half reported symptoms consistent with substance use disorders (Tsai et al., 2018). Another national study compared Veterans who were justice-involved to VTC participants and found that VTC participants were less likely to be in jail at program admission, to be chronically homeless, to have a probation offense, to have any prior psychiatric hospitalizations, and to report having spent fewer days in a corrections institution in the past month (Tsai et al., 2017). Among this discussion of VTC participant characteristics, we do not want to neglect the demographic of female Veterans who, in most studies, are consistently reported in the minority, accounting for a range of only 4–12% of VTC study populations (Ahlin & Douds, 2016; Baldwin & Rukus, 2015; Hartley & Baldwin, 2019; Knudsen & Wingenfeld, 2016; Tsai et al., 2017). Finally, we want to also mention that VTCs may differ in their choice about whether to admit violent offenders and in their decisions about whether to limit their services to Veterans who served in a combat zone. In a 2016 national study on VTCs, Baldwin reported that more than half of the VTCs in her study (57%) excluded some type of violent felony charge, and approximately half reported military discharge and conduct exclusions (46%) or violent felony charge exclusions (43%) (Baldwin, 2016).

Despite this knowledge of extensive health and behavioral health needs among Veterans who are justice-involved, VTCs are confronted by critics who may argue that medical care does not fall under the jurisdiction of the courts; however, it is widely acknowledged that VTCs use an interdisciplinary team approach to address Veterans' health care needs while under the close supervision of the court system, which becomes a major component in the efforts to coordinate the Veterans' subsequent civilian reintegration efforts.

Origins of Problem-Solving Courts

As we have just presented the characteristics that are common among VTC participants, this segment of the chapter presents the history of the problem-solving court, and its trajectory as becoming a space to practice therapeutic jurisprudence. While present-day practices in problem-solving courts recognize the needs of the defendant and employ the help of behavioral health interventions and a close interaction with a treatment team, recognizing the root causes of criminal justice involvement and addressing treatment remedies in the court system are only concepts adopted in the last 30 years.

In the late twentieth century, the United States experienced a surge in corrections spending and a growing prison population. In 1975, 27% of the total sentenced federal prison population (20,692) was serving time due to a drug offense. Over the next ten years, this number had grown to reflect 34% (27,623) by 1985 (Maguire, 2003). During the mid-1990s' peak of the "tough on drugs" policy approach, 61% of the total sentenced population (80,872) was serving time in federal prison due to drug offenses (Maguire, 2003). During this tough-on-crime era, the number of people in federal prisons for drug offenses increased 1,950% between 1980 and 2010 growing from 4,749 people to 97,472 people. At the time, the War on Drugs was in full-force, demonstrated by the increases in numbers of offenders, many of whom who were dealing with active substance use and addiction. For example, among nonviolent state prisoners, drug offenders (44%) reported the highest incidence of drug use at the time of the offense (Mumola & Karberg, 2006). As reported in the Bureau of Justice Statistics' 2006 report on drug use and drug dependence, 32% of state prisoners and 26% of federal prisoners committed their offense under the influence of drugs (Mumola & Karberg, 2006).

Around the country, jurisdictions had become increasingly aware of the opportunity to shift classes of offenders away from costly incarceration while maintaining offender accountability to the offense and addressing rehabilitation and criminogenic needs via the provision of alternative sentencing. The emergence of the drug court, as a specialized court or a specialized court docket for drug offenders, offered an alternative to incarceration while also applying therapeutic jurisprudence to this special class of offenders. In drug courts, addiction was believed as a root cause which, left untreated, may promote criminal behavior. Drug courts are judicially supervised and handle the cases of nonviolent, substance-addicted offenders under the adult, juvenile, and family justice systems. Drug courts operate under a model that combines intensive judicial supervision, mandatory drug testing, escalating incentives and sanctions, and treatment. Often, it is the relationship between the offender and judge that drives adherence of a drug treatment program and its related court appearances. For example, in a 2011 multi-site drug court evaluation funded by the National Institute of Justice (NIJ), drug court participants who received higher levels of judicial praise, judicial supervision, and case management reported fewer crimes and fewer days of drug use (Rossman et al., 2011). The level of supervision in drug court permits the program to support the recovery process, but also allows program supervisors to react swiftly to impose appropriate therapeutic sanctions or to reinstate criminal proceedings when participants do not comply with the program.

The designation of specialized court dockets and courts for specialized populations in the United States have been documented for at least the last 30 years. The first drug court prototype was established in Miami-Dade, Florida in 1989, presided over by Judge Stanley Goldstein, grounded in procedures combining teamwork, cooperation, and collaboration, and drawing from the framework of therapeutic jurisprudence. Family treatment court (which is addressed in Chap. 6), is a model that seeks to improve parent(s)' treatment retention and family reunification rates in the child welfare system. The family treatment court has been described as the firm foundation of success upon which a rational and humane approach to protect children is built (Marlowe & Carey, 2012). It was in 1995 that the first family treatment courts began concurrently in Reno, Nevada and Pensacola, Florida (National Association of Drug Court Professionals (NADCP), 2018). By the year 2000, as many as 472 drug treatment courts were in operation across the United States. By 2006, at least 1,621 treatment courts were in operations, and by 2009 there were 2,459 treatment courts in the United States (NADCP, 2018). As of

June 2015, there were 1,558 adult drug courts in the United States. However, the estimated total number of drug courts operating in the U.S. is over 3,000 of which the majority target adults including DWI (driving while intoxicated) offenders, Veterans, and other drug courts which address juvenile, child welfare, and others (National Institute of Justice, 2018). Among VTCs, the first can be traced to 2004 in Anchorage, Alaska (Hawkins, 2010; Holbrook & Anderson, 2011; Johnson et al., 2016) and the 2008 VTC from Buffalo, New York (Cavanaugh, 2011; Johnson et al., 2016). The Buffalo VTC was the first instance of manualizing and operationalizing a VTC into its component parts. Today, there are at least 461 operational VTCs and Veterans dockets within drug, mental health, or criminal courts (Flatley, Clark, Rosenthal, & Blue-Howells, 2017).

Components of Veterans Treatment Courts

VTCs defy a "one size fits all" approach. Studies demonstrate that each VTC maintains its own standards and employs its own methods concerning justice-involved Veterans, sometimes leading to tremendous procedural variety among these courts (Arno, 2015; Baldwin, 2016). However, there are certain broad elements that typically appear in most, if not all, of these tribunals.

Eleven years ago, the ground-breaking Buffalo VTC established a set of ten key components for the successful operation of VTCs which is outlined in Table 5.1 (Huskey, 2017). Today, several widely used training programs for VTCs use this document as the basis for their guidance to court personnel. A few states even enacted laws requiring all of their VTCs to abide by these ten principles (Pomerance, 2018).

Similar to the United States Department of Justice's January 1997 document titled "Defining Drug Courts: The Key Components"—the document on which the Buffalo VTC based their creation—the key components for VTCs include early identification and placement of eligible VTC participants; interdisciplinary education of all VTC staff concerning topics such as military cultural competence and criminal justice system goals; monitoring and enforcement of abstinence from drug and alcohol abuse among program participants; and close collaboration among actors within the legal, mental health, drug and alcohol rehabilitation, and Veterans' services systems (Arno, 2015; Rogers, 2018). Taken together, this document provides a starting point for the types of processes, policies, ideals, and objectives that many VTCs share. It is neither, however, a mandate for all VTCs nationwide, nor does every VTC follow each of these ten key components in the same manner (Baldwin, 2016; Baldwin & Brooke, 2019). A closer look, therefore, is necessary to determine the measures that VTCs commonly take to perform their work.

VTC participant eligibility requirements differ by jurisdiction and one of the challenges in establishing eligibility for VTCs is the availability of identification protocols for Veterans who are entering the criminal justice system. There is a general lack of uniformity in intake questionnaires (Baldwin, 2013; Christy, Clark,

Table 5.1 The ten key components of Veterans Treatment Court

Key Component #1
Veterans Treatment Court integrate alcohol, drug treatment, and mental health services with justice system case processing
Key Component #2
Using a non-adversarial approach, prosecution and defense counsel promote public safety while protecting participants' due process rights
Key Component #3
Eligible participants are identified early and promptly placed in the Veterans Treatment Court program
Key Component #4
Veterans Treatment Court provide access to a continuum of alcohol, drug, mental health and other related treatment and rehabilitation services
Key Component #5
Abstinence is monitored by frequent alcohol and other drug testing
Key Component #6
A coordinated strategy governs Veterans Treatment Court responses to participants' compliance
Key Component #7
Ongoing judicial interaction with each Veteran is essential
Key Component #8
Monitoring and evaluation measure the achievement of program goals and gauge effectiveness
Key Component #9
Continuing interdisciplinary education promotes effective Veterans Treatment Court planning, implementation, and operations
Key Component #10
Forging partnerships among Veterans Treatment Court, Department of Veterans Affairs, public agencies, and community-based organizations generates local support and enhances Veteran Treatment Court effectiveness

Frei, & Rynearson-Moody, 2012). In addition, Veterans' identification occurs across various stages of their involvement with the criminal justice system (refer to Chap. 3 for Sequential Intercept Model). While prior military service is reported among 8% of incarcerated individuals in the United States (Bronson, Carson, Noonan, & Berzofsky, 2015), the majority of participants of VTCs are not identified in incarcerated settings. In Baldwin's 2016 study, she reported that among her national survey of 79 VTCs, the majority of Veterans who were potential participants in VTCs were not incarcerated and were identified elsewhere in the justice system: 70% of VTCs reported that potential participants were identified at booking, 62% of VTCs reported that Veterans were identified at pretrial services, 46% of VTCs identified potential participants at the time of arrest, and nearly 71% of Veterans were identified at arraignment (Baldwin, 2016). Furthermore, in a 2017 study, Tsai and colleagues compared VTC participants with non-treatment court participants and reported that VTC participants were less likely to have been in jail at VTC admission. Baldwin and colleagues' study found that only 2.5% of VTC participants were Veterans who had been convicted and were identified during incarceration (Baldwin, 2016).

Once accepted into a VTC, a justice-involved Veteran may likely be linked by the court with a Veteran peer mentor (Arno, 2015; Perlin, 2013). To increase the likelihood of mentor and mentee developing a bond based on shared experiences, VTCs typically try to match mentors and mentees from the same branch of service and the same era of service. Most courts also try to link mentors and mentees of the same gender. This last objective has proved challenging, however, as many VTCs face an overall scarcity of female Veteran mentors. In most VTCs, these peer mentors are all volunteers, at times creating difficulties when the ever-rising out-of-pocket costs of travel to and from court appearances and mentor-mentee meetings, courthouse parking, and other recurring expenses of mentorship understandably provoke some mentors to leave the program (Jaafari, 2019).

Like drug courts, the vast majority of VTCs establish a treatment team of subject-matter experts who collectively link a justice-involved Veteran with key resources, guide the Veteran through the assigned VTC steps, and monitor and evaluate the Veteran's progress (Baldwin, 2016). Where possible, each member of the treatment team in a VTC should have particular experience and expertise in working with Veterans, ensuring that the people providing both the assistive tasks and the oversight functions of the court possess the cultural competence necessary to give the justice-involved Veteran the best possible chance of success (Jones, 2014). One crucial member of the VTC team is a VJO Specialist from the VA, linking Veterans with localized healthcare services and other fundamental forms of assistance. Veterans Service Officers often play an important role on treatment teams, too, connecting justice-involved Veterans with the federal, state, and local benefits for which they are eligible by virtue of their military service—benefits about which a substantial number of Veterans are often completely unaware (Pomerance, 2019). Other key treatment team members commonly include alcohol and substance abuse specialists, social workers, and employment counselors. Again, while the members of the treatment team do not necessarily need to be Veterans, successful VTCs emphasize a high level of military cultural competence among the members of these teams (Shah, 2014).

VTCs often go to significant lengths to distinguish themselves from a traditional courtroom setting. The implicit environment of a VTC may resemble military culture as a reimagining and interpretation for use within the courtroom. The military experience is one that Veterans have self-reported as a distinguishing feature and likened to membership of a subculture (Ahlin & Douds, 2016; Baldwin & Rukus, 2015). Additionally, prosecutors and defense attorneys interact in a non-adversarial manner, with the judge working with both lawyers and with the justice-involved Veteran in a less-formal manner than one typically witnesses in a criminal court proceeding (Russell, 2009; Seamone, 2019). Some judges even abandon their customary place on the bench to create a more collegial atmosphere in the courtroom (Shevory, 2011). Placing military flags or patriotic insignia in the courtroom in recognition of the service rendered by the justice-involved Veterans coming before the court is another common practice.

Individualization of treatment plans is another central component of VTCs (Cartwright, 2011; Seamone, 2019). Every justice-involved Veteran entering a court may receive a set of assignments, goals, and strategies that are uniquely tailored by the treatment team and the presiding judge to that particular Veteran's pre-military, military, and post-military experiences (Shah, 2014). While every treatment team takes their own unique approach regarding which factors to apply and how much emphasis to place upon each element, the most common criteria that treatment teams consider include the presence of any diagnosed medical conditions, the existence of any substance use histories on illegal drugs and/or alcohol, the nature and resolution of any prior criminal convictions on the Veteran's record, the degree to which family members play an active role in the Veteran's life, the stability or instability of the Veteran's housing situation, the Veteran's current and future educational and employment prospects, and other bedrock elements of rehabilitating the Veteran from present status to a more constant and sustainable life (Baldwin, 2016).

All VTCs must establish a process for deciding whether a justice-involved Veteran is eligible for admission into a VTC. Typically, this process involves some variety of dialogue among the judges presiding over the traditional criminal court and the VTC, as well as the District Attorney's Office and the justice-involved Veteran's defense counsel, focusing on the balancing of interests between public safety concerns and the desire to avoid unnecessary incarceration when rehabilitative options are reasonably available. Courts differ regarding the level of involvement and influence for each of these parties in making this decision. In some locations, for instance, the District Attorney's Office plays the key "gatekeeping" role in deciding whether a justice-involved Veteran should be eligible for admission to a VTC, while other jurisdictions permit the VTC's presiding judge to make this final call (Pomerance, 2018). From court to court, the assessment instruments used to decide whether an individual presents a low risk of recidivism and a substantial likelihood for rehabilitation differ as well (Baldwin, 2016). This allows local legal systems the flexibility necessary to make case-by-case decisions without the rigidity that has led to criticism in other areas of criminal law, but also creates understandable questions about whether greater standardization in this process is necessary (Arno, 2015).

Similarly, VTCs maintain a set of standards concerning when a justice-involved Veteran is eligible to graduate from the treatment court program, as well as a set of policies regarding the rewards for successfully reaching all of the assigned milestones (McMichael, 2011). Sometimes, graduation from a VTC can result in full dismissal of the criminal charges against the justice-involved Veteran. Other times, graduation leads to withdrawal of the criminal charges in exchange for the justice-involved Veteran accepting a non-criminal disposition or a lower-level criminal offense (Baldwin, 2016). In a minority of jurisdictions, these standards are codified in state statutes (Pomerance, 2018). Most VTCs, however, are free to set whatever policies they deem most appropriate, with the approval of their state's judicial oversight agency (McMichael, 2011). On the negative side, all VTCs must determine what penalties will be imposed if a justice-involved Veteran fails to timely complete the milestones on the assigned treatment court plan (McMichael, 2011). This assessment includes the decision of when a VTC will expel a justice-involved

Veteran from the program, as well as the consequences—a list that customarily involves incarceration—that result from an individual's dismissal (Hawkins, 2010; Jones, 2014). Again, while a minority of states maintains laws that address this issue, most VTCs possess the authority to set these standards without any statutory authority (Pomerance, 2018).

A final commonality among most VTCs is the positive political and mainstream media attention that most of these courts have received. Starting with the creation of the Buffalo VTC in 2008, the opening of new VTCs has been hailed with largely glowing news reports, as well as acclamation by politicians from all sides of the political aisle (Renz, 2014). One can logically presume that this bipartisan positive attention encouraged a continually growing number of jurisdictions to establish and sustain VTCs (Pomerance, 2018). While critics of these courts undoubtedly exist, the fact that VTCs have received lofty acclamation and substantial funding from both Barack Obama and Donald Trump, and praise-filled reports from media outlets of seemingly every political affiliation, VTCs will likely be kept in the spotlight of criminal justice reform conversations for the foreseeable future (Arno, 2015; Jaafari, 2019; Renz, 2014).

Outcomes for VTC Participants

The question as to whether VTCs are effective remains an important one that drives VTC scholarship and practices today. Varied measures have been used when reporting on outcomes for VTC programs. Among existing studies, VTC outcomes have been measured as a reduction in participants' criminal recidivism, a reduction in adverse health conditions, successful community reintegration, and reductions in recidivism, among others. For example, one jurisdiction's VTC program reported on its six program goals which included: reduced criminal recidivism, promotion of participant sobriety, increased compliance with treatment and court-ordered conditions, improved access to VA benefits and services, improved family relationships and social support connections, and improved life stability (Caron, 2012). In a national study on VTCs, outcomes included domains such as housing stability, employment, receipt of VA benefits, and criminal justice (Tsai et al., 2018). Another study reported on 24 infractions (such as failure to complete treatment, missed hearings, failure to comply with judge's order) and 18 types of sanctions (such as verbal reprimand, behavioral contract, and community service) as outcome metrics used in their analyses (Johnson, Stolar, Wu, Coonan, & Graham, 2015). A variety of outcome studies are essential as they can demonstrate effectiveness, efficiency, and key behavioral changes necessary for a Veteran to complete a VTC program and be released into the community.

Given the centrality of the behavioral health needs as root problems among VTC participants, an important outcome for VTCs is the reduction of behavioral health challenges which have triggered criminal involvement among Veterans. For example, Derrick et al. (2018) reported on 82 participants of the San Diego,

California, Veterans Treatment Review Calendar (SDVTRC) Pilot Program and examined 12 clinical measures from baseline to 12-months using the following scales: PTSD Checklist (PCL) a 17-item Likert-type checklist that measures PTSD symptoms (Weathers, Litz, Herman, Huska, & Keane, 1993); Modified Overt Aggression Scale (MOAS) a 16-item Likert-type scale (Cicerone & Kalmar, 1995); Drug Abuse Screening Test (DAST-10) a 10-item yes/no inventory to measure illegal drug use over the prior four weeks; Alcohol Use Disorders Identification Test (AUDIT-C) a three-question tool that measures frequency and volume of alcohol consumption over the prior four weeks; Patient Health Questionnaire-9 (PHQ-9) a 9-item Likert-type scale to measure symptoms of depressed mood over the prior two weeks. For 52 participants with both a baseline and 12-month scores, Derrick et al. (2018) reported reductions in drug use; depressed mood; trauma and four subscales measuring re-experiencing, avoidance, hyperarousal, and total trauma and stress; and anger and aggression subscales including verbal aggression, physical aggression toward objects, physical aggression toward others, physical aggression toward self, and total anger and aggression. Improvements in behavioral health measures such as emotional well-being, social functioning, reductions in self-harm, reductions in substance use were also reported in Knudsen & Wingenfeld's, 2016 study on 86 Veterans.

Another important outcome for a problem-solving court is reducing recidivism, which is the reduction of an offender's tendency to reoffend. Reoffense can be measured as new arrests, new incarcerations, or new offenses. In some outcome studies, recidivism reduction is measured as the percentage difference of number of arrests at VTC program entry compared to number of arrests at VTC program exit. For example, in Hennepin County, Minnesota's 2012 VTC program review, 83% of Veterans had fewer number of charges at six months after entering their VTC program compared to six months prior to their start of their VTC program, and 72% of Veterans had fewer number of charges at 24 months after entering their VTC program compared to 24 months prior to their start of their VTC program. For VTC participants in Hennepin County, Minnesota, 66% of active VTC participants and 76% of VTC graduates did not have any misdemeanor or felony reoffenses within 12 months of VTC program entry; at 24 months of program entry, 40% of active VTC participants and 56% of VTC graduates did not have any misdemeanor or felony reoffenses (Caron, 2012). In Smith's, 2012 study on the Anchorage, Alaska VTC, recidivism was defined as a return to custody or a violation of probation. In the Smith (2012) study, a recidivism rate of 45% was reported, which was presented in comparison to the 50% recidivism rate experienced by offenders of the state system who were not participants in the VTC. In Tsai et al.'s 2018 national study, they reported that 20% of VTC participants received jail sanctions and 14% reported a new incarceration within an average of nearly one-year in a VTC program, which is lower than the 23–46% one-year recidivism rate found among U.S. prisoners. Finally, in Hartley and Baldwin's (2019) study of 144 Veterans in a VTC and a control group of 157 VTC-eligible Veterans, they reported that the VTC group had lower total number of arrests (34 compared to 44) and a lower recidivism rate (14% compared to 17%). In addition, Hartley and Baldwin (2019) also compared their

VTC graduates to VTC terminations and found that the Veterans who graduated has the lowest recidivism rate overall (8%) and the Veterans who were terminated from the VTC program had the highest recidivism rate (56%).

Outcome measures have also included community reintegration domains such as housing and employment indicators. In Caron's 2012 report which included 41 VTC graduates, 35% maintained their level of employment or student status throughout their VTC participation, and 19% increased their level of employment throughout their VTC participation. In terms of living situation, it was reported that among VTC graduates, 73% did not experience changes to their private residence status, and 15% increased their housing stability during the course of their VTC participation (Caron, 2012). In Johnson et al.'s 2017 study of 1,224 Veterans, lower rates of incarceration during VTC participation was more likely associated with having stable housing (compared to being homeless), and with program referrals to substance use treatment (which authors had noted that nearly all VTCs utilized this treatment approach). In the national study by Tsai et al. (2018), 58% of VTC participants were in private residence at program exit, which was an increase from 48% measured at VTC program admission. They also reported that 28% of VTC participants were employed at program exit compared to 27% at admission, and 50% were receiving VA benefits compared to 38% at admission (Tsai et al., 2018).

Given the delivery of a VTC and its use of sanctions and rewards, some outcomes for VTC participants can also take the form of increased jail sanctions, increased new arrests, and increased new incarcerations for VTC participants. Outcomes for an intensive program like the VTC where the VTC participant is subjected to more program requirements, more drug testing, and more careful surveillance by program officials also affords the VTC participant more opportunities to accumulate sanctions while remaining a program participant. In a 2016 study, researchers described predictors of program termination across 302 VTCs and Veterans' dockets in a treatment court and reported higher rates of termination were associated with phase progression based on measurable goals, programs that permitted post-plea Veterans, programs that accepted outside of jurisdiction Veterans, programs that conducted more frequent drug and alcohol testing, programs with more severe sanctions for meeting immediate goals versus long-term goals, and programs classified Veterans' courts as opposed to other treatment courts with Veterans dockets (Johnson et al., 2016). Johnson et al. (2016) also reported that lower rates of termination from these Veterans court programs included those programs that allowed National Guard/Reserve participants, programs that permit later phases to have less stringent testing, programs utilizing behavioral contracts, programs utilizing brief incarcerations, and programs that work closely with a VA Health Care Network. Increases in sanctions, arrests, and incarcerations were experienced by VTC participants when compared to non-treatment court participants in a national study (Tsai et al., 2017). While relapse and failure are components of the recovery and rehabilitation process for individuals in substance use treatment, some VTC programs may penalize relapse as a violation of program compliance and thus result in a participant's discharge from the VTC program. A retrospective study of 100 participants in the Harris County, Texas VTC reported that arrests after discharge from a VTC were predicted by a prior diagnosis of opiate misuse as well as arrests during VTC enrollment (Johnson et al., 2015). Thus, some scholars have urged that VTC administrators examine ways of continuing enrollment for Veterans at highest risk of recidivism.

Criticisms of Veterans Treatment Courts

Despite the abundant positive attention lavished upon VTCs since their inception, plenty of observers criticize these courts for a variety of reasons. Some critics condemn VTCs for offering too many second chances to criminal court defendants. Others insist that VTCs are traps for the unwary, leading defendants to unwittingly forfeit basic legal rights. Still others allege that these courts, while well-intentioned, perpetuate stereotypes and stigmas that harm Veterans overall. Finally, some critics state that VTCs can establish a system of fundamental unfairness in statewide criminal justice structures, conferring some privileges upon certain defendants in particular jurisdictions that may not be available in neighboring jurisdictions. In this section, we summarize each of these common critiques.

Critique 1: Veterans Treatment Courts Offer Unnecessary Favoritism to Certain Criminals

Individuals and groups advancing this argument state that VTCs provide a particular group of lawbreakers with a baseless pathway to escape incarceration. To the surprise of many observers, the American Civil Liberties Union (ACLU) has strenuously objected to the creation of many VTCs (Shevory, 2011). According to the ACLU, these courts needlessly favor Veterans over other criminal court defendants whose traumatic life experiences are equally deserving of the treatment, mentorship, sustained assistance, and second chances that justice-involved Veterans receive in a VTC (Perlin, 2013). Barry Schaller opined that this model runs afoul of the Equal Protection Clause of the Fourteenth Amendment, stating that VTCs improperly offer privileges to Veterans because of "who they are rather than what they are accused of doing or what problems they have" (Schaller, 2012). Allison Jones raised similar concerns in a law review article that examined whether VTCs unjustly establish a special class of criminal court defendants, offering options to Veterans that are not available to civilians without a legitimate basis for doing so (Jones, 2014). A justice-involved Veteran with PTSD can receive a multitude of services in a VTC, Jones pointed out, while a civilian with equally severe PTSD does not receive these benefits and services, even if the civilian's PTSD directly contributed to that civilian committing the charged criminal offense.

Some commentators voice concerns that VTCs proliferated throughout the United States substantially because of emotionally patriotic responses, not because empirical research solidly demonstrated that these courts truly possess the capacity to advance the public good (Baldwin & Brooke, 2019; Huskey, 2017; Jaafari, 2019). Julie Baldwin, the associate director for research for justice programs at American University in Washington, D.C., pointed out in 2019 that VTCs "evolved like many of the other specialty courts, just out of [judges who] believed there was a need from what they saw in their courtrooms … and it spread without scientific evaluation" (Jaafari, 2019). As we have previously discussed in this chapter, despite the fact that VTCs have existed for more than a decade, more empirical data about the efficacy of these courts remains scarce, leading to questions about why separate court dockets and special privileges for justice-involved Veterans should exist in the absence of clear signs that these courts are functioning in a manner that benefits society overall (Baldwin & Brooke, 2019; Jaafari, 2019; Rogers, 2018; Schaller, 2012).

Lastly, some critics consider VTCs acceptable conceptually, but object to these courts admitting certain categories of offenders (Jones, 2014; Kravetz, 2012). Pamela Kravetz, for instance, is one of many commentators arguing that VTCs should not accept Veterans charged with crimes of intimate partner violence (Kravetz, 2012). To Kravetz, and to other observers who echo her comments, "Veterans courts are a dangerous forum for intimate partner violence cases until reliable research has uncovered the complicated interplay between symptoms of combat trauma and domestic violence and evidence-based interventions have proved effective." Similar arguments exist from individuals who believe that VTCs should reject all cases involving the possession of a weapon, all cases involving any form of violent act by the defendant, and—in the views of some critics—all cases involving any felony offense (Arno, 2015; Cartwright, 2011; Cavanaugh, 2011; Merriam, 2015; Shah, 2014).

Critique 2: Veterans Treatment Courts Trap Veterans into Forfeiting Fundamental Rights

In a rare instance of uniformity, jurisdictions offering one or more VTCs legally view admission to such courts as a privilege, not a right (Merriam, 2015). Consequently, a justice-involved Veteran seeking to participate in a VTC must acquiesce to the conditions established by the leadership of that particular court. Commonly, these conditions may include entering a guilty plea for the crimes with which the Veteran has been charged (Baldwin, 2016; McMichael, 2011).

The National Association of Criminal Defense Lawyers objects to this practice, calling the requirement of pleading guilty "a forced waiver of rights" (Brown, 2012). These attorneys fear that a Veteran facing criminal charges will view a VTC as an "easy way out," far simpler than defending their case in a traditional criminal court, and will plead guilty to all of the offenses even if they are innocent of some or all of the charges. As a result, some members of the criminal defense bar object that VTCs are a tool that prosecutors can use to rid themselves of complex criminal cases by enticing a Veteran into the VTC rather than engaging in a trial (Brown, 2012; Shah, 2014). This prevents such Veterans and their attorneys from presenting evidence and calling witnesses in their own defense, cross-examining hostile witnesses, confronting their accusers, demonstrating any existing violations in law enforcement practices, and other due process rights that a criminal court defendant would otherwise possess.

Other critics claim that VTCs are false friends to justice-involved Veterans, promising far more benefits than they could ever possibly deliver. Barry Schaller argues that "[c]ourts are not agencies created or equipped to solve the social problems of society through policymaking and delivery of social services" (Schaller, 2012). Again, due to the lack of empirical data nationwide regarding VTCs, it is difficult to definitively refute this claim that these courts are not fully equipped to provide the services and supports that encourages justice-involved Veterans to waive their due process rights in the first place. Notably, though, this critique does fail to acknowledge that the most effective VTCs do not attempt to manage all of these issues internally. On the contrary, a VTC's success typically depends on the ability of the court to cultivate and utilize public sector and private sector partnerships with providers of these essential services (Renz, 2014; Russell, 2009; Shevory, 2011).

Critique 3: Veterans Treatment Courts Create Inequity Within the States Where They Exist

Only a handful of states have statutes governing the conduct of VTCs within their borders (Pomerance, 2019; Shah, 2014). Of these states, an even smaller number maintain laws that truly standardize and regulate the activities of VTCs. Thus, the vast majority of states lack statutory uniformity for their VTCs. While some commentators have discussed the desirability of enacting state laws containing standards by which all VTCs in the state must abide, such laws appear in only a minority of jurisdictions (Arno, 2015; Pomerance, 2019; Shah, 2014). So, when states lack statutory uniformity for VTCs, fundamental differences can—and do—exist between any two VTCs within the same state (Arno, 2015; Pomerance, 2019; Shah, 2014). For instance, one VTC may accept only justice-involved Veterans with an honorable discharge from the military, while a VTC in a neighboring county may welcome all Veterans regardless of their character of discharge. One VTC may be willing to admit Veterans charged with a violent felony offense, depending on the facts and circumstances of the case, while another VTC located only a few miles away may maintain an automatic ban on all cases involving an act of violence. The list of significant distinctions exists leading to extreme inconsistencies in the standards for admission, participation, and graduation among the VTCs in virtually any given state (Arno, 2015; Baldwin, 2016; Pomerance, 2019; Shah, 2014).

Even more complicated are situations where a Veteran's ability to access a VTC depends entirely on the county in which the Veteran is charged with the crime. In New York State, for example, a Veteran arrested in the Bronx may be eligible for entry into the Bronx County VTC. However, as of this writing, a Veteran arrested for the same crime only a few miles away across the border of Westchester County would not have this opportunity, as Westchester County has not created a VTC. States that do not establish a VTC in every county, and that fail to enact legislation allowing the transfer of a case from a traditional criminal court in a county with no VTC into a VTC in a nearby county, create a damaging inequity for justice-involved Veterans within their state (Pomerance, 2019). Access to the services, resources, and advantages of a VTC should not depend on the county within the state in which the Veteran happened to wind up in the criminal justice system.

Critique 4: Veterans Treatment Courts Encourage Unwanted Stigmatization of Veterans

Paradoxically, the courts that were created to focus on unique needs and take into account the unique experiences of Veterans run the risk of arousing undesirable social stereotypes about individuals who serve in the military. Yale Law School's Jerome N. Frank Legal Services Organization, for example, has criticized VTCs for perpetuating the wide military-civilian divide in the United States. "Veterans' courts prevent civilians from learning from Veterans and vice versa," stated members of this legal clinic in public testimony. "It is important for the general population to see Veterans so they can understand and sympathize with them. In addition, it is important for Veterans to witness civilians being held accountable for their actions." According to the members of this clinic, VTCs ran contrary to these goals by segregating Veterans from the other members of society. "When Veterans are secluded in Veterans' courts none of these observations and interactions can occur," the clinic's testimony concluded. "Moreover, Veterans' courts prevent reintegration by ghettoizing Veterans and secluding them from the general population" (Levy, 2015).

Other critics raise an equally concerning issue: the possibility that the widespread publicity surrounding VTCs perpetuate an all-too-common myth that the vast majority of Veterans struggle with mental health conditions, alcoholism or substance abuse, suicidal ideation, heightened risk of homelessness, criminal behavior, or are otherwise "broken" in some form. For instance, Anne Douds and Eileen Ahlin point out that "labeling a court a 'Veterans court' may lead some to speculate that the number of Veteran offenders is so disproportionally high that they need a new court just to process them" (Douds & Ahlin, 2019). Such assumptions can unjustly stigmatize not only justice-involved Veterans, but all Veterans, placing the people who served our country at risk of anti-Veteran discrimination by employers, landlords, creditors, and other individuals who believe that they are taking a heightened risk whenever they engage in an interaction with a Veteran. Such prejudices toward Veterans already exist in multiple forms and forums throughout this nation (Perlin, 2013). Without question, every effort must be made to ensure that any initiative, no matter how well-intentioned, does not inflame the biases and assumptions that already exist throughout the United States concerning Veterans.

Conclusions

VTCs typically are able to tailor many of their methods to the needs presented in individual cases, this flexible system can be—for better and for worse—devoid of foundational standards. While certain attributes are common to the majority of VTCs, and the "Ten Key Components" drafted in Buffalo, NY, more than a decade ago remains a keystone document to which most of these courts look for guidance, the lack of standardization and consistency raises concerns among some commentators who fear that VTCs are too loosely constructed to meet their purported societal objectives. An overall lack of a strong empirical foundation from evaluations of these courts creates concerns that the growth and development of VTCs is based largely on popular sentiment rather than evidence-based practices. Although a handful of states have enacted statutes standardizing eligibility requirements, standards for participation, and graduation requirements, the majority of jurisdictions do not have such laws. Again, this leads to substantial variances among the VTCs in the states without a governing statute, meaning that two VTCs in neighboring counties are permitted to implement and maintain entirely different procedures and standards. As we have presented in this chapter, the implementation of these well-intentioned problem-solving courts does not come without legitimate concerns.

Despite these critiques, this still-young judicial movement offers plenty of life-changing benefits for their participants and graduates, and thus provides substantial hope for their future. Given the extremes to which many members of the military are subjected during their service, a program insisting that these individuals are not abandoned by their government's justice system when they struggle during their reintegration to civilian life is not only reasonable, but ethically and morally imperative. VTCs appear to offer plenty of praiseworthy benefits for justice-involved Veterans throughout this country, including suggestions for cost-savings by way of carefully tailored rehabilitation rather than widespread incarceration and social benefits on the class of Veterans who have served the United States. Graduates of VTCs have perceived the program to be life-changing and have expressed gratitude toward the VTC treatment team, the path toward treatment readiness, and the success of their civilian reintegration (McCall, Rodriguez, Barnisin-Lange, & Gordon, 2019; Montgomery & Olson, 2018). A treatment-based approach focusing on the unique aspects and impacts of military service fulfills two basic premises of justice: to ensure that the full story of an individual charged with a crime is heard by the court and to provide a framework in which eligible individuals receive the best possible opportunity for genuine rehabilitation. Thus, the VTC as a widely popular, innovative, multi-faceted, and individualized treatment program further encourages the pursuit of increased understanding and evaluation of its components, and the enhanced pursuit of a fair balance between individualization and standardization, particularly as VTCs continue to rapidly proliferate across the country.

References

Ahlin, E. M., & Douds, A. S. (2016). Military socialization: A motivating factor for seeking treatment in a Veterans Treatment Court. *American Journal of Criminal Justice, 41*, 83–96. https://doi.org/10.1007/s12103-015-9332-4

Arno, C. (2015). Proportional response: The need for more--and more standardized--Veterans Treatment Courts. *University of Michigan Journal of Law Reform, 48*, 1039–1072.

Baldwin, J. M. (2016). Investigating the programmatic attack: A national survey of Veterans Treatment Courts. *Criminal Law & Criminology, 105*(3), 705–752.

Baldwin, J. M., & Brooke, E. J. (2019). Pausing in the wake of rapid expansion: A call to critically examine the veterans treatment court concept. *Journal of Offender Rehabilitation, 58*, 1–29.

Baldwin, J. M., & Rukus, J. (2015). Healing the wounds: An examination of Veterans Treatment Courts in the context of restorative justice. *Criminal Justice Policy Review, 26*, 183–207. https://doi.org/10.1177/0887403413520002

Bronson, J., Carson, E. A., Noonan, M., & Berzofsky, M. (2015). Veterans in prison and jail, 2011–12. Retrieved from http://www.bjs.gov/index.cfm?ty=pbdetail&iid=547.

Brown, K. (2012). Are Veterans Treatment Courts preferential? *Sobering Up*. Retrieved from https://www.scramsystems.com/blog/2012/11/are-veterans-treatment-courts-preferential/

Baldwin, J. (2013). Executive Summary: National Survey of Veterans Treatment Courts. Retrieved from https://doi.org/10.2139/ssrn.2274138

Caron, A. (2012). Fourth judicial district Veterans court—Two year review: July 2010–June 2012. Retrieved from http://www.mncourts.gov/Documents/4/Public/Research/Veterans_Court_Two_Year_Review.pdf

Cartwright, T. (2011). "To care for him who shall have borne the battle": The recent development of Veteran Treatment Courts in America. *Stanford Law and Policy Review, 22*, 295–316.

Cavanaugh, J. M. (2011). Helping those who serve: Veterans treatment courts foster rehabilitation and reduce recidivism for offending combat Veterans. *New England Law Review, 45*, 463–487.

Christy, A., Clark, D., Frei, A., & Rynearson-Moody, S. (2012). Challenges of diverting Veterans to trauma informed care: The heterogeneity of intercept 2. *Criminal Justice and Behavior, 39*(4), 461–474.

Cicerone, K. D., & Kalmar, K. (1995). Persistent post-concussive syndrome: Structure of subjective complaints after mild traumatic brain injury. *The Journal of Head Trauma Rehabilitation, 10*(3), 1–17.

Collins, J. J., & Bailey, S. L. (2007). Traumatic stress disorder and violent behavior. *Journal of Traumatic Stress, 20*, 203–220. https://doi.org/10.1002/jts.2490030204

Derrick, R. M., Callahan, L., Vesselinov, R., Krauel, R. W., Litzenberger, J. A., & Camp, L. R. (2018). Serving those who served: Outcomes from the San Diego Veterans Treatment Review Calendar (SDVTRC) Pilot Program. *Psychological Injury and the Law, 11*, 171–183. https://doi.org/10.1007/s12207-017-9308-4

Douds, A.S., & Ahlin, E.M. (2019). The Veterans Treatment Court movement: Striving to serve those who served. Retrieved from https://play.google.com/books/reader?id=Z2N8DwAAQBAJ&hl=en

Finlay, A. K., Owens, M. D., Taylor, E., Nash, A., Capdarest-Arest, N., Rosenthal, J., … Timko, C. (2019). A scoping review of military Veterans involved in the criminal justice system and their health and healthcare. *Health & Justice, 7*(1), 6. https://doi.org/10.1186/s40352-019-0086-9

Flatley, B., Clark, S., Rosenthal, J., & Blue-Howells, J. (2017). Veterans court inventory 2016 update: Characteristics of and VA involvement in Veterans Treatment Courts and other Veteran-focused court programs from the Veterans Justice Outreach Specialist Perspective. 2017 Retrieved from Washington, D.C.: U.S. Department of Veterans Affairs.

Hartley, R. D., & Baldwin, J. M. (2019). Waging war on recidivism among justice-involved Veterans: An impact evaluation of a large urban Veterans Treatment Court. *Criminal Justice Policy Review, 30*, 52–78. https://doi.org/10.1177/0887403416650490

Hawkins, M. D. (2010). Coming home: Accommodating the special needs of military Veterans to the criminal justice system. *Ohio State Journal of Criminal Law, 7*, 563–573.

Holbrook, J. H., & Anderson, S. (2011). Veterans courts: Early outcomes and key indicators for success. Retrieved from https://papers.ssrn.com/sol3/papers.cfm?abstract_id=1912655

Huskey, K. A. (2017). Justice for Veterans: Does theory matter? *Arizona Law Review, 59*, 698–735.

Institute of Medicine (IOM). (2013). *Returning home from Iraq and Afghanistan: Assessment of readjustment needs of veterans, service members, and their families*. Washington, DC: The National Academies Press. Retrieved from https://www.ncbi.nlm.nih.gov/books/NBK206864/pdf/Bookshelf_NBK206864.pdf

Jaafari, J. D. (2019). Special courts for Veterans languish. *The Marshall Project*. Retrieved from https://www.themarshallproject.org/2019/02/19/special-courts-for-veterans-languish

Johnson, R. S., Stolar, A. G., McGuire, J. F., Clark, S., Cooman, L. A., Hausknecht, P., & Graham, D. P. (2016). U.S. Veterans court programs: An inventory and analysis of national survey data. *Journal of Community Mental Health, 52*, 180–186. https://doi.org/10.1007/s10597-015-9972-3

Johnson, R. S., Stolar, A. G., McGuire, J. F., Mittakanti, K., Clark, S., Coonan, L. A., & Graham, D. P. (2017). Predictors of incarceration of Veterans participating in U.S. Veterans Courts. *Psychiatric Services, 68*, 144–150. https://doi.org/10.1176/appi.ps.201500266

Johnson, R. S., Stolar, A. G., Wu, E., Coonan, L. A., & Graham, D. P. (2015). An analysis of successful outcomes and associated contributing factors in Veterans' court. *Bulletin of the Menninger Clinic, 79*, 166–173.

Jones, A. E. (2014). Veterans Treatment Courts: Do status-based problem-solving courts create an improper privileged class of criminal defendants? *Washington University Journal of Law and Policy, 43*, 307–331.

Kimerling, R., Bastian, L. A., Bean-Mayberry, B. A., Bucossi, M. M., Carney, D. V., Goldstein, K. M., … Frayne, S. M. (2014). Patient-centered mental health care for female Veterans. *Psychiatric Services, 66*(2), 155–162. https://doi.org/10.1176/appi.ps.201300551

Kimerling, R., Street, A. E., Pavao, J., Smith, M. W., Cronkite, R. C., Holmes, T. H., & Frayne, S. M. (2010). Military-related sexual trauma among Veterans Health Administration patients returning from Afghanistan and Iraq. *American Journal of Public Health, 100*(8), 1409–1412. https://doi.org/10.2105/AJPH.2009.171793

Knudsen, K. J., & Wingenfeld, S. (2016). A specialized treatment court for Veterans with trauma exposure: Implications for the field. *Community Mental Health Journal, 52*, 127–135. https://doi.org/10.1007/s10597-015-9845-9

Kravetz, P. (2012). Way off base: An argument against intimate partner violence cases in Veterans Treatment Courts. *Veterans Law Review, 4*, 162–205.

Kulka, R. A., Schlenger, W. E., Fairbank, J. A., Hough, R. L., Jordan, B. K., Marmar, C. R., & Weiss, D. S. (1990). *Brunner/Mazel psychosocial stress series, No. 18. Trauma and the Vietnam war generation: Report of findings from the National Vietnam Veterans Readjustment Study*. Philadelphia, PA, US: Brunner/Mazel.

Levy, S. (2015). Testimony concerning S.B. 1015: An act expanding programs for Veterans in the Judicial Department. Retrieved from https://www.cga.ct.gov/2015/vadata/tmy/2015SB-01015-R000303-Steven%20Levy,%20Veterans%27%20Legal%20Services%20Clinic,%20Yale%20Law%20School-TMY.PDF

Maguire, K. (Ed.) (2003). Sourcebook of criminal justice statistics, Bureau of Justice Statistics, Table 6.57. Retrieved from http://www.albany.edu/sourcebook/pdf/t657.pdf

Marlowe, D. B., & Carey, S. M. (2012). *Need to know: Research update on family drug courts* (p. 10). Alexandria, VA: National Association of Drug Court Professionals. Retrieved from https://www.nadcp.org/wp-content/uploads/Reseach%20Update%20on%20Family%20Drug%20Courts%20-%20NADCP.pdf

McCall, J. D., Rodriguez, K., Barnisin-Lange, D., & Gordon, A. J. (2019). A qualitative examination of the experiences of Veterans Treatment Court graduates in Allegheny County, Pennsylvania. *International Journal of Offender Therapy and Comparative Criminology, 63*, 339–356. https://doi.org/10.1177/0306624X18801462

McCall, J. D., Tsai, J., & Gordon, A. J. (2018). Veterans Treatment Court research: Participant characteristics, outcomes, and gaps in the literature. *Journal of Offender Rehabilitation, 57*, 1–18. https://doi.org/10.1080/10509674.2018.1510864

McMichael, W. (2011). The battle on the homefront: Special courts turn to Vets to help other Vets. *American Bar Association Journal, 97*, 44–49. Retrieved from http://www.abajournal.com/magazine/article/the_battle_on_the_home_front_special_courts_turn_to_vets_to_help_other_vets

Merriam, E. (2015). Non-uniform justice: An equal protection analysis of Veterans Treatment Courts' exclusionary qualification requirements. *Mississippi Law Journal, 84*, 686–743.

Miller, S. M., Pederson, E. R., & Marshall, G. N. (2017). Combat experience and problem drinking in Veterans: Exploring the roles of PTSD, coping motives, and perceived stigma. *Addictive Behaviors, 66*, 90–95. https://doi.org/10.1016/j.addbeh.2016.11.011

Montgomery, L. M., & Olson, J. N. (2018). Veterans Treatment Court impact on Veteran mental health and life satisfaction. *Journal of Psychology and Behavioral Science, 6*, 1–4. https://doi.org/10.15640/jpbs.v6n1a1

Mumola, C. J. & Karberg, J. C. (2006). Drug use and dependence, state and federal prisoners, 2004. Retrieved March 28, 2019 from https://www.bjs.gov/content/pub/pdf/dudsfp04.pdf

National Association of Drug Court Professionals (NADCP). (2018). Drug court history. Retrieved from https://www.nadcp.org/test-timeline/

National Institute of Justice. (2018). Drug courts. Retrieved from https://www.nij.gov/topics/courts/drug-courts/pages/welcome.aspx

Outcalt, S. D., Hoen, H. M., Yu, Z., Franks, T. M., & Krebs, E. E. (2016). Does comorbid chronic pain affect posttraumatic stress disorder diagnosis and treatment? Outcomes of posttraumatic stress disorder screening in Department of Veterans Affairs primary care. *Journal of Rehabilitation Research and Development, 53*, 37–44.

Perlin, M. L. (2013). "John Brown Went Off To War": Considering Veterans Treatment Courts as problem-solving courts. *Nova Law Review, 37*, 445–475.

Pomerance, B. (2018). The best-fitting uniform: Balancing legislative standards and judicial processes in Veterans Treatment Courts. *Wyoming Law Review, 18*, 179–236.

Pomerance, B. (2019). Rational justice: Equal protection problems amid Veterans Treatment Court eligibility categorizations. *Oregon Law Review, 97*, 425–475.

Renz, T. (2014). Veterans Treatment Court: A hand up rather than lock up. *Richmond Public Interest Law Review, 17*, 697–705.

Rogers, K. N. (2018). The importance of cultural competence: The defining characteristic separating Veterans Treatment Courts from other specialized dockets. *UNLV Theses, Dissertations, Professional Papers, and Capstones, 3321*. Retrieved from https://digitalscholarship.unlv.edu/cgi/viewcontent.cgi?article=4324&context=thesesdissertations

Russell, R. T. (2009). Veterans Treatment Court: A proactive approach. *New England Journal on Civil and Criminal Confinement, 35*, 357–372.

Rossman, S. B., Rempel, M., Roman, J. K., Zweig, J. M., Linquist, C. H., Green, M., ... Farole, Jr., D. J. (2011). The multi-site adult drug court evaluation:The impact of drug courts, volume 4. Washington, DC: The Urban Institute.

Schaller, B. R. (2012). *Veterans on trial: The coming court battles Over PTSD*. Dulles, VA: Potomac Books.

Seal, K. H., Cohen, G., Waldrop, A., Cohen, B. E., Maguen, S., & Ren, L. (2011). Substance use disorders in Iraq and Afghanistan Veterans in VA healthcare, 2001–2010: Implications for screening, diagnosis and treatment. *Drug and Alcohol Dependence, 116*, 93–101. https://doi.org/10.1016/j.drugalcdep.2010.11.027

Seamone, E. R. (2019). Rescuing soldiers of misfortune: A full-spectrum approach to Veterans in the criminal justice system from arrest to reentry. Retrieved from https://books.google.com/books/about/Rescuing_Soldiers_of_Misfortune.html?id=h7V9DwAAQBAJ&printsec=frontcover&source=kp_read_button#v=onepage&q&f=false

Shah, S. (2014). Authorization required: Veterans Treatment Courts, the need for democratic legitimacy, and the separation of powers doctrine. *Southern California Interdisciplinary Law Journal, 23*, 67–106.

Shevory, K. (2011). Why Veterans should get their own courts. *The Atlantic*. Retrieved from https://www.theatlantic.com/magazine/archive/2011/12/why-veterans-should-get-their-own-courts/308716/

Smith, J. W. (2012). The Anchorage, Alaska Veterans Court and recidivism: July 6, 2004–December 31, 2010. *Alaska Law Review, 29*, 93–111.

Tanielian, T., & Jaycox, L. H. (Eds.). (2008). *Invisible wounds of war: Psychological and cognitive injuries, their consequences, and services to assist recovery*. Santa Monica, CA: RAND Corporation. Retrieved from https://www.rand.org/pubs/monographs/MG720.html

Tsai, J., Finlay, A., Flatley, B., Kasprow, W. J., & Clark, S. (2018). A national study of Veterans Treatment Court participants: Who benefits and who recidivates. *Administration and Policy in Mental Health and Mental Health Services Research, 45*, 236–244.

Tsai, J., Flatley, B., Kasprow, W. J., Clark, S., & Finlay, A. (2017). Diversion of Veterans with criminal justice involvement to treatment courts: Participant characteristics and outcomes. *Psychiatric Services, 68*, 375–383. https://doi.org/10.1176/appi.ps.201600233

United States Census Bureau. (n.d.-a). American Fact Finder: Median age. Retrieved from https://factfinder.census.gov/bkmk/cf/1.0/en/nation/UnitedStates/AGE

United States Census Bureau. (n.d.-b). Quick facts United States. Retrieved from https://www.census.gov/quickfacts/fact/table/US/PST045218

United States Department of Defense (DoD), Office of the Deputy Assistant Secretary of Defense for Military Community and Family Policy. (2016). Demographics: Profile of the military community. Retrieved from https://download.militaryonesource.mil/12038/MOS/Reports/2016-Demographics-Report.pdf

Wilson, J. P., & Zigelbaum, S. D. (1983). The Vietnam veteran on trial: The relation of Post-Traumatic Stress Disorder to criminal behavior. *Behavioral Sciences & the Law, 1*(3), 69–83. https://doi.org/10.1002/bsl.2370010308

Weathers, F. W., Litz, B. T., Herman, D. S., Huska, J. A., & Keane, T. M. (1993). The PTSD checklist (PCL): Reliability, validity, and diagnostic utility. Paperpresented at the 9th Annual Convention of the International Society for Traumatic Stress Studies, San Antonio, TX.

Yaeger, D., Himmelfarb, N., Cammack, A., & Mintz, J. (2006). DSM-IV Diagnosed posttraumatic stress disorder in women Veterans with and without military sexual trauma. *Journal of General Internal Medicine, 21*(S3), S65–S69.

Yoon, G., Petrakis, I. L., & Rosenheck, R. A. (2015). Correlates of major depressive disorder with and without comorbid alcohol use disorder nationally in the Veterans health administration. *The American Journal on Addictions, 24*(5), 419–426.

Chapter 6
Family Courts: The Next Frontier for Veteran-Informed Services

Janice M. Rosa

> *"Happy families are all alike; every unhappy family is unhappy in its own way."*
>
> Leo Tolstoy (1828–1910), Anna Karenina (Chapter 1, first line)

Abbreviations

ABA	American Bar Association
ACE	Adverse childhood experiences
CCR	Coordinated Community Response
CPS	Child protective services
DoD	Department of Defense
DV	Domestic violence
FAP	Family Assistance Program
GWOT	Global war of terror
ICEOMC	Interstate Compact on Educational Opportunity for Military Children
IPV	Intimate partner violence
NCJFCJ	National Council of Juvenile and Family Court Judges
NCTSN	National Child Traumatic Stress Network
PTSD	Post-traumatic stress disorder
SAMSHA	Substance Abuse and Mental Health Services Administration
SCRA	Servicemembers Civil Relief Act
SUD	Substance abuse disorder
TBI	Traumatic brain injury
UDPCVA	Uniform Deployed Parents Custody and Visitation Act
VA	Veterans Administration
VHA	Veterans Health Administration
VTC	Veterans Treatment Court

J. M. Rosa (✉)
New York Supreme Court (Ret.), 8th Judicial District, Buffalo, NY, USA

Adverse Childhood Experiences, Denver, CO, USA

J. Tsai, E. R. Seamone (eds.), *Intersections between Mental Health and Law among Veterans*, https://doi.org/10.1007/978-3-030-31664-8_6

The continued popularity of Tolstoy's epic tale more than a hundred years later testifies to the enduring truth of the mix of love, drama, and dysfunction in family life. It is the country's family courts that serve this population of "unhappy families" as they arrive at the courthouse doors with all the varied needs that modern families have. They ask the judicial system for dispute resolution and determination of rights, often with unrealistic hopes of what a court can do to remedy the problem. When referenced in this chapter, unless otherwise specified, the term "family court" is broad and it extends beyond divorce and custody proceedings to any proceeding involving a parent, a spouse, a partner, a relative, and a child. This chapter highlights the need to consider family courts as a fundamental component in systemic responses to justice-involved veterans (including active duty, reserve component, and separated service members), including successful community re-entry following release from confinement.

Turning to Tolstoy's quote about families, based on additional risks that are likely to impact their interpersonal relationships, veterans, spouses, and children of military families are some of the most unhappy families in the courts (Seamone, 2012). In 2014, a special edition of the *Family Court Review* addressed several key issues facing military and veteran families impacted by the courts. One of the volume's articles, a first of its kind, addressed family law considerations for veterans in the criminal justice system. The article concluded that a substantial number of justice-involved veterans had families and, in fact, most would return to live with a family member following release from incarceration (Clark, McGuire, & Blue-Howells, 2014). These observations make it necessary for criminally-involved veterans and those professionals who assist this population to understand how family courts operate and the constraints they operate under in serving veteran family legal needs. To the extent that veteran-specific mental health treatments, family services, domestic violence accountability measures, and benefit eligibility can be incorporated into or leveraged by the family and juvenile courts' approach, these interventions may translate directly to a reduction of recidivism, and more importantly to a true healing of the trauma suffered by a veteran and the veteran's family.

This chapter lies at the intersection of family and criminal law, two systems that have tremendous influence on one another but lack the slightest degree of interaction. The chapter urges a more responsible approach for those in the criminal justice system who are dealing with veteran inmates who have families. First, this chapter identifies the benefits of a trauma-informed approach in the family law system, which should naturally extend to veterans with traumatic experiences when they are identified. Second, this chapter discusses the different points at which veterans might interact with the family law system in order to create realistic expectations of what the family courts can, and cannot, do. Finally, the chapter discusses the all-too-common issue of domestic and interpersonal violence perpetrated by veterans. The chapter shares a newly developed battery of tests that can assist in evaluating the influence of veterans' mental health symptoms on assaultive situations. It is hoped that this chapter will better equip criminal justice system members to engage in an ongoing and long-overdue dialogue with the family courts regarding their shared clientele.

Where Justice-Involved Veterans and Family Courts Intersect

In a typical county courthouse, on any given day, you will see the depth and breadth of family distress. For veterans and their families, some examples of issues might be:

- The magistrate in the *child support* enforcement courtroom has a busy calendar of a newly created Stand Down child support docket for homeless, at-risk, and other veterans.
- Down the hall, the family courtroom hearing *juvenile delinquency* matters has a full docket, including the disposition for an adolescent male of a military veteran found to have committed petit larceny, illegal drug use, and trespass.
- The *divorce and child custody* courtroom is full of divorcing couples, some with attorneys, most without. In that group, a veteran and spouse are seeking to uncouple and move on. Another litigant, a divorced veteran wife of an active duty servicemember, seeks to relocate with the children to her hometown. And yet a third unhappy couple is dealing with the ravages of his severe Posttraumatic Stress Disorder (PTSD) and self-medication with alcohol. It has broken the marriage and now the mother wants the veteran father, a decorated war hero, to have only supervised visits with his young daughter, fearing for the child's safety.
- In the next courtroom, in the midst of several other families whose children are in foster care, sits a recently-discharged veteran and his wife, newly arrived back in their hometown, accused of *child maltreatment*.
- In the last courtroom, the judge hearing the emergency *civil protective order* requests has more than a dozen hearings scheduled, including one of a respondent veteran under partial disability from PTSD and Traumatic Brain Injury (TBI) whose female partner alleges ongoing and escalating events which cause her to fear for her and the children's safety.

Veterans and Family Courts: At-Risk Populations Hidden in Plain Sight

A dilemma facing virtually every court system is the inability to identify when a case involves a servicemember or veteran. In family courts, no designated computer field records this data, as it is not required for state civil case management purposes (Rosa, 2014). If veteran status is identified at all, this normally occurs in default cases against defendants where the moving party must prove that the defendant is not in active military service (and thus under the protection of the Servicemembers Civil Relief Act (SCRA)) (Odom, 2011; Sullivan, 2011). It appears that the exception to the prevailing lack of inquiry into veteran status occurs mainly in the context of criminal courts with special dockets for veterans (Veterans Treatment Courts (VTCs)) or criminal courts that must apply sentencing guidelines that are only applicable to veterans. In contrast to family courts, most VTCs use questionnaires or pre-trial release interviews to determine military service. Referring once again to the array of case scenarios at the outset of the chapter, the veteran status or the prior military service and history of the litigants are seldom known, and often only by happenstance. In cases where the family courts forego obtaining this vital knowledge of veteran status, the opportunity for the court or other civilian professionals to access possible VA or military service-related resources is a lost one.

Even in jurisdictions with sizeable armed forces and veteran populations, the struggles of military and veteran families have fallen largely under the courts' radar. With increased pressures from state budget cutbacks affecting all branches of government, courtrooms are struggling simply to maintain their core responsibility to dispense justice. New courthouse initiatives that could result in saving considerable time and money in other non-judicial systems (such as schools, housing, law enforcement, public assistance, mental health care) unfortunately find little purchase in a country where every state judiciary consumes only a shockingly tiny percent of any state's total budget (the remainder of course used by the executive and legislative branches) (Rosa, 2014). For instance, in Montana and Hawaii, the percent allotted for the entire state judicial branch hovers at about 2%; in Louisiana and Florida, it is less than 1% (National Center for State Courts, n.d.).

One compounding factor for family law matters is the lack of federal or congressional attention to, and limited mandates about, family law issues (with the exceptions of child welfare measurements, child support enforcement, and domestic violence). Long the sole domain of state courts by constitutional division of federal versus state rights, Congress does not fund, and the Executive Branch has no departmental home for, matters affecting families such as divorce, separation, custody, paternity, spousal support, or property rights (Rosa, 2014).

By 2016, about 3.9 million of the nation's veterans had served since 9/11 and nearly half of them were between the child-rearing ages of 25–34, precisely the demographic served by family court (Department of Labor, n.d.; Department of Defense, 2016). Quite literally, virtually every family courtroom in the country now has contact with active, retired, or veteran populations of these latest conflicts encompassed by the Global War on Terror (GWOT).

In the previously mentioned 2014 special issue of the *Family Court Review*, this author commented on the unrelenting pace of forever wars and nonstop military fronts since 9/11, noting that these cases in family courts "have increased like a rising tide, silently but inexorably. Much like slowly heating water in the lobster pot, … the court system did not at first consider them any more than anomalies until their numbers and the presenting problems were epidemic" (Rosa, 2014, p. 512).

In nearby courtrooms, these issues are spilling into mortgage foreclosures and consumer credit transaction litigation as well (Rosa, 2014). Family court judges across the country have voiced a consistent desire for more training and education on the military family, not only the laws applicable, but more importantly the unique challenges, stressors, strengths, and resources available to both active servicemembers, guard, reserve, and veterans (Seamone, 2014). Based on the lack of communication between family courts and prisons or the criminal justice system, it is vital to consider ways to integrate responses for better informed approaches and outcomes in community reentry and decreased criminal recidivism. This remainder of this chapter examines common dynamics within family courts with the hopes of improving coordination on behalf of justice-involved and incarcerated veterans.

Family Court, in the Context of the Judicial System

The federal Constitution divides national government into three co-equal branches: the Executive, the Legislative with law-making powers and the "power of the purse," and the Judiciary, created to resolve disputes in a consistent orderly process, relying on the rule of law, due process, and equal access to the courts. Our state governments are virtual mirrors of this schematic.

Each state judicial branch is constituted differently, but all share a consistent hierarchy of trial (lower) courts along with one and more levels of appellate courts, to which trial court decisions may be appealed. Depending on the state, trial courts will have jurisdiction (power) over different types of cases, or cover different geographical boundaries. Family Courts are trial courts, and might bear that name or another name (e.g., "juvenile court" or "domestic relations court"). In still other states, family law cases are not provided a court "home," but instead are mingled with all other types of cases. There is a national trend for the creation of specialized family courts to handle these increasingly complex and convoluted cases, particularly as states realize the large percentage of the total civil docket that family law cases occupy. For instance, in Maryland, family law cases are nearly 46% of the state trial court docket; in New Jersey they comprise 41%; in Nevada, they are 49%; and in Nebraska family cases are 58% of the total civil case docket. Considering the lack of attention and resources that most family law cases receive in the courts' systems, the numbers of these cases are astonishing (Babb, 2008, 2014). Although specialization extends to juvenile drug courts and family drug courts, there is no similar interest in or development of veteran-focused family court dockets (Rosa, 2014).

Historically, legal disputes in the judicial system were handled by attorneys, and it was unheard of to have a lay person handle his or her own case. That time is long past, and in most states the typical family law case has one or both litigants "self-represented," some by choice, but most by dint of economics (National Center for State Courts, 2017). This directly impacts the veteran population. *The Justice Gap* noted that 71% of households with veterans or other military personnel reported experiencing a civil legal problem in the year preceding the survey, including 13% as veteran-specific issues (Legal Services Corporation, 2017).

Neither the Armed Forces nor the judicial branches of state government are monolithic, cohesive, or able to act with one voice across the country. While there are five branches of the active Armed Forces under the Department of Defense (DoD), multiple components of the National Guard and Reserves, and an entirely separate Department of Veterans Affairs (VA), there are 50 different state judicial systems, the District of Columbia, and the territories. No two of these jurisdictions are the same, and each has dozens of districts and hundreds of judges with juvenile and family law dockets. Some state judiciaries are more hierarchical than others; some are composed of appointed judges, and some have an elected judiciary. While some family court systems are static and may have a judge assigned to one courthouse and one case type for many years (thus gaining an expertise and familiarity), others have frequent judicial rotations and pride themselves on that (Rosa, 2014).

In our system of jurisprudence there is a stark division in every state and federal level between criminal cases and civil cases. The divide is real, even so deep as to have different courthouses, different judges who might never handle the other type of case, and case management computer systems that are not integrated between the two case types. Entire bodies of case law for criminal cases and civil cases have evolved, and there are declared constitutional rights afforded to criminal defendants which do not accrue to the same person in a civil case. For instance, in criminal cases, veteran defendants have a right to an attorney, and a "speedy trial," etc. So, a veteran facing a domestic abuse charge in criminal court could have an attorney appointed if indigent, whereas that same person (now, as a "respondent") facing the same allegations brought by his or her partner in a civil protective order case, would not have that right. In criminal cases, the charging party is always the state, acting in its capacity to enforce law and order. In civil cases, the moving party is nearly always a private individual or a corporation (two exceptions relevant to family law cases are child maltreatment and juvenile justice cases, where once again the charging party is the state).

Trauma, Veterans, and Family Court

The overwhelming percentage of family court cases involve trauma—current, past, and unfortunately future. Few and far between are the happy cases of adoption, family reunification, or amicable settlement, and even those are formed out of traumatic events. One might conclude, then, that the professionals populating courthouses around the country are trained to intervene with the psychological and emotional needs of the litigants and schooled in veteran's issues. But that would largely be a mistake, despite recent inroads. Perhaps because of their genesis in the measured, cool, and collected structures of the civil court system, family courts are populated more by attorneys (some with litigious bents) than by psychologists and social workers.

Veterans entering through the family courthouse doors carry in trauma baggage that is the same as their fellow civilians, and at the same time, unique due to what they have experienced with the demands and expectations of military life. In the veteran population, trauma can run through servicemember and family members, and be the result of long-term negative experiences and disruptive childhoods, but also can arise from the stressors arising from deployments, reintegration, injuries, and return to civilian life (Seamone, 2012). This is crucial to understand because military-specific trauma often requires military-specific treatments. When military trauma remains untreated, the veteran's symptoms can continue, worsen, and spill-over to influence other family members. Ironically, while the family courts have begun to recognize the impact of prior traumatic experiences on parents, children, and family members, they have not juxtaposed this same approach on traumatic experiences related to combat, specifically.

Fortunately, there is a growing movement to approach the families and veterans entering the family courthouse with a "trauma-informed" lens, Leading the national conversation of what is a "trauma-informed response" is the Substance Abuse and Mental Health Services Administration (SAMHSA) (Substance Abuse and Mental Health Services Administration, 2014, p. 7).

In courtrooms, forensic trauma from rigid protocols, intimidating, adversarial approaches, and a foreign environment is a real and present daily occurrence (Marsh & Bickett, 2015). Changing that courthouse experience to take into account the public health concerns of the litigants takes awareness, and connections with other community partners. The first courtrooms to experience this approach were the criminal drug treatment courts, followed soon by courts in the juvenile justice and child welfare systems (Marsh & Bickett, 2015). The National Council of Juvenile and Family Court Judges (NCJFCJ) under its "Trauma Informed System of Care" practice, provides practical training for courthouses (National Council of Juvenile and Family Court Judges, n.d.-a, n.d.-b). Because research has confirmed an "elevated prevalence of ACEs among men and women who have served in the military" (Blosnich, Dichter, Cerulli, Batten, & Bossarte, 2014, p. 1044; Cabrera, Hoge, Bliese, Castro, & Messer, 2007), these new ACEs-based standards directly implicate the unique challenges facing veterans and underscore the need for veteran-informed family court interventions.

Veteran-Specific Considerations for Family Courts

Considering the need for greater responsiveness to veterans, demonstrated through the additional lens of ACES, the following subsections address five family court proceedings with clear military intersections: (1) Child support enforcement proceedings; (2) juvenile justice; (3) divorce and custody; (4) child maltreatment; and (5) intimate partner violence (Centers for Disease Control and Prevention, n.d.; Felitti et al., 1998; Katon et al., 2015; Montgomery, Cutuli, Evans-Chase, Treglia, and Culhane, 2013; Oshiri et al., 2015). Each subsection highlights opportunities to develop more effective veteran-focused interventions.

Child Support Enforcement Proceedings

The support magistrate handling the support proceeding is part of her community's recent initiative targeting veterans who have unpaid child support obligations. Data analysis in 2010 indicated that veterans were a small but significant portion of the noncustodial parent child support caseload (just over 5%) (U.S. Department of Health and Human Services, 2017a). This translated to more than half a million veterans among the nearly 11 million noncustodial parents in the group, and was likely an underestimate. The arrears owed by this veteran group was more than $7 billion, with an average support arrears owed of almost $25,000 per veteran. Interestingly, this cohort is substantially older than the average child support debtor, and more than three times as likely to be older than the average. The results revealed that many of the homeless and at-risk veterans are Vietnam-era veterans, with children long-ago emancipated (U.S. Department of Health and Human Services, 2017a).

With no federal funding, a national collaboration began in 2010 with the Department of Health and Human Services through the Office of Child Support Enforcement, together with the VA, and the American Bar Association (ABA) aiming to address homeless veterans' child support matters, in an effort to remove existing barriers to housing and employment. Nine pilot sites and other jurisdictions partnered with local state child support agencies, the VA, a legal provider, and other community resources focused on veteran support. They pooled their experiences and distilled the lessons learned into a toolkit identifying components of effective outreach programs for veterans (U.S. Department of Health and Human Services, 2017b). Their efforts have yielded fruit: while actual outcome measures at the pilot sites were incomplete, critical connections among community stakeholders were formed, legislative reforms were proposed, and anecdotally veterans were better served. The toolkit created from their efforts leads other jurisdictions in similar reform (U.S. Department of Health and Human Services, 2017a).

Juvenile Justice

With a juvenile delinquency charge, Johnny sits in the juvenile division courtroom of the family courthouse with his parents, awaiting his case to be called. Last month, after a hearing, the judge found Johnny to be a juvenile delinquent, determining the proof showed Johnny had trespassed on a neighbor's property, stolen a bicycle leaning against the house, and was increasingly found intoxicated by his parents and teachers. After multiple transfers around the country, and two deployments that left the servicemember father suffering from TBI and depression, Johnny's father had recently transitioned from the Marine Corps, and the family had returned to their home state last summer. Johnny was now in his seventh school setting, and had been held back.

By good fortune, the juvenile court judge and juvenile probation in this jurisdiction are trauma-informed and trauma-responsive, and in the past month Johnny has undergone a battery of tests and interviews. Judge and officer know that up to 90% of juvenile system-involved youth will reveal being exposed to some type of traumatic event, and about one-third of these will meet the diagnostic criteria for PTSD (Dierkhising & Marsh, 2015).

The investigating probation officer was, by luck, also well versed in the unique characteristics, strengths, and stressors of the family of a military veteran injured and recently released from service. So, the judge had been made aware of a recent study linking increased risk of alcohol and drug use among children from deployed military families (Acion, Ramirez, Jorge, & Arndt, 2013). These children are at a higher risk, so Johnny's dispositional order would have a substance abuse evaluation and outpatient treatment component. His parents will be provided with community resources, including referral to the local Vet Center, as a voluntary option.

A large body of research spanning 30 years has examined the culture of military youth and adolescents (Lemmon & Stafford, 2014). Johnny's father's multiple deployments, and Johnny's increasingly lackluster academic performance were in line with other military adolescents who show higher rates of anxiety symptoms and behavioral issues while a parent is deployed, in general more symptoms than his younger siblings. Thirty-two percent of children of deployed parents were classified as "high risk," a number two-and-a-half times the national average (Mischel et al., 2017).

As of 2009, the average military child could expect to have changed schools between six and nine times before twelfth grade (Howell & Wool, 2016). For this reason, the Interstate Compact on Educational Opportunity for Military Children (ICEOMC), creating a uniform policy for all military children, was adopted (Farmer, Jackson, & Franklin, 2014). Begun in 2006, the Compact was rapidly adopted in all states and the District of Columbia. All school districts agree to coordinate public school enrollment, attendance, grade placement, records transfers, and on-time graduation requirements, with a view to standardizing practices, and the ultimate goal of easing stresses and problems for military children (Military Interstate Children's Compact Commission, n.d.).

ICEOMC covers children of all active-duty military personnel of all branches as well as uniformed services, and it applies to veterans' families of those services for up to 1 year following retirement, disability, or death (Esqueda, Astor, & Tunac De Pedro, 2012). While it applies now to Johnny and his current placement, the prior school disruptions have taken their toll; remedial work set up by the probation officer with the school district will be needed to ensure that the youth engages and completes school.

Johnny's parents are going to ask the judge to send their son to a program they've heard about, similar to the military boot camp training that his father had undergone as a young recruit; they think it would do a world of good for Johnny. After hearing from the parents about their desire that he be placed in a "scared straight" program, the judge declines, and gives his reasoning. Conclusive empirical studies and meta-analyses over the past decade and more have unequivocally found that such programs not only do not help, in fact they are more harmful to juveniles than doing nothing, clearly a poor crime prevention strategy (Lilienfeld & Arkowitz, 2014; Petrosino, Turpin-Petersino, & Buehler, 2003; Petrosino, Turpin-Petrosino, Hollis-Peel, Lavenberg, & Stern, 2014).

By applying a trauma-informed lens to this youth, and seeing the military history and trauma of both parents and child as relevant to the disposition, the judge and probation officer have set the stage for a comprehensive strengths-based healing for the youngster and his family.

Divorce and Custody

The post 9/11 era of never-ending military engagement around the world has highlighted to the public in ways not seen in decades the stressors experienced by military families compared to their civilian counterparts (Seamone, 2014). Less information about the lot of National Guard and Reserve families exists; they tend to disappear into the civilian landscape. Likewise, there is a similar lack of visibility—and therefore, study and responses—for veteran families. The buffering effects of structural and functional supports for children and families of active duty servicemembers help mitigate some of the costs of combat, deployment, and change of duty stations (Sheppard, Malatras, & Isreal, 2010). Housing, education, health care, child care, community support from a cohesive group, and family advocacy groups provide the wrap around services for the families (Clever & Segal, 2013). While available, the supports for guard and reserve are more tenuous and the immersion in a military culture is absent (Lapp et al., 2010). For families of veterans, they experience even fewer supports (Zogas, 2017). The most obvious are the loss of the "military family" and the formal Family Assistance Programs (FAPs) operating in each branch of the armed services once a servicemember transitions to veteran status. Add to that the increased uncertainty in obtaining employment, housing, and health services and, "all told, the transition from military to civilian status may be one of the most precarious stages in the life of the family" (National Child Traumatic Stress Network, n.d.-a, para. 2).

While there are many programs under FAPs to assist with mental, physical, and social issues of active duty servicemembers, they are not a resource for veterans. Children and families of veterans, like their veteran family member, can become adrift or stranded in the civilian community (Zogas, 2017). No studies exist to document the plight of children and spouses of veterans, but these stress factors—loss of military housing, education, income, and community—would seem to increase the likelihood of worse outcomes.

Forty-four percent of active servicemembers are less than 25 years, the largest segment of that population; more than half of all servicemembers are married, and of those, about 40% have children. Of those with children, nearly two thirds of the children are less than 11 years of age, with the largest group aged birth to 5 years (Clark et al., 2014; Department of Defense, 2016). When divorce occurs in this group, the parents are dealing with the care of very young children. If intimate partner violence or coercive controlling behavior is being exhibited, or the servicemember is stressed or injured, this complicates exponentially the judge's task to determine parenting rights and responsibilities (Jaffe, Crooks, & Bala, 2009).

Although active duty military families experience lower rates of divorce than their civilian neighbors, divorce has been on the rise in the post 9/11 era, and veteran families have a divorce rate three times higher than their non-military service neighbors (National Child Traumatic Stress Network, n.d.-a). Those divorces come at a time when finances, the future, and hope are stretched to the breaking point. These individuals appear in the family court of the state they reside in, often bewildered to learn that their current state may have very different laws and expectations than where they resided during their term of service. They learn that divorce is a civil matter with no constitutional right to the services of an attorney. Like the other couples in the courtroom, they are trying to represent themselves, in a legal world whose language and customs are foreign (National Center for State Courts, n.d., 2017). If they reside in a state that is in step with the growing numbers of unrepresented family court litigants, there will be online resources, questionnaires, and information. If their state is well-resourced, there might even be self-help centers in the courthouse with staff to assist in navigating the system (Kourlis & Samnani, 2017). But none of these resources is mandated by statute, and all are subject to abandonment in the face of judicial budget constraints that are never far away.

While only about one-fifth of civilian families will uproot themselves and relocate in any year, nearly one-third of military families will be relocated (Farmer et al., 2014). For the veteran spouse seeking to relocate out of state with the children, leaving her military spouse behind, she will learn that the SCRA has a limited role to play unless her spouse is deployed or stationed away. This federal law is a protective shield for servicemembers unable to attend to legal matters, and does not provide substantive rights about custody, relocation, access, etc. (Odom, 2011). Those rights come from the state law and appellate decisions, except for the growing number of states adopting the Uniform Deployed Parents Custody and Visitation Act (UDPCVA) uniform code (Sullivan, 2014).

With increasing numbers of veteran parents returning with the invisible wounds of PTSD, depression, and TBI, and perhaps addiction to alcohol or prescription drugs, the concerns of child-rearing with safe parents has taken on new urgency. Veterans with impeccable records of service, the very epitome of good citizens, can return with serious impairments to their parenting abilities. The need for careful nuanced forensic custodial evaluations is slow to come to family courts (Seamone, 2012; Simon, 2014). As Professor Seamone noted, there is a sharp distinction between how PTSD is addressed in criminal court sentencing compared to family court civil custody decisions: "Curiously, this sense of urgency and recognition that combat veterans require a specially-tailored approach to their combat-related problem, is utterly absent in the family law system, which unavoidably inherits marital disputes as a result of the same psychiatric conditions" (Seamone, 2012, p. 312).

These cases require experts who have a working knowledge of the military culture that has shaped the veteran and family, to avoid stereotyping parents, and to choose a frame of reference of recovery. Many veteran parents will recover from the more temporary impairments in relatively short order, and only a small percentage will continue with symptoms. For those, delaying final custody decisions while a parent heals and is able to undertake full parenting responsibilities makes good long-term sense (Seamone, 2012). But for a severely impaired parent, family court judges are faced with the heartbreaking task of suspending or restricting contact between the veteran and his vulnerable children.

Child Maltreatment

Many military families have young children, and are expected to accept frequent moves, separations from extended family and their cities, deployments, and transitions back home of servicemembers, some with catastrophic wounds, external or internal. Adjustments to new schools, communities, duties, and responsibilities are a way of life for every active duty family member. Fortunately for them, coupled with these demands is the wide variety of family support services provided by the armed forces. These families have a strong sense of duty, hold a steady job, have access to health care, housing, education and higher training, all serving to provide preventive measures for the family's wellbeing. Those strengths may be largely absent, or difficult to secure, once the servicemember returns to civilian life as a veteran.

There is a wide variation of definitions and protocols used in the Armed Forces and in the various states for child maltreatment cases, so comparing trends between civilian and military families has always been a challenge. While rates of suspected child abuse and maltreatment for both civilian and military families have been increasing over the years, military rates are reported to be much lower than civilian rates, historically half the rates (Mischel et al., 2017; National Child Traumatic Stress Network, n.d.-c). However, military communities also saw an uptick in the past decade. Some experts believe even that increase may be a serious understatement of the level of child maltreatment within the armed services. Dr. David Rubin noted that between 2004 and 2007 (the period studied), only 20% of medically confirmed child abuse and neglect cases in Army children were found to have Family Advocacy Program (FAP) involvement. This is a rate less than one half of the substantiated cases in the civilian child protective services (CPS) group (Rubin, 2016; Wood et al., 2017).

Research has shown there is an increase in child neglect cases when a spouse is deployed, with stay-at-home parents three times more likely to be abusive or neglectful when the military spouse is away (Gibbs, Martin, Kupper, & Johnson, 2007; National Child Traumatic Stress Network, n.d.-a, n.d.-b, n.d.-c).

Findings during the post-deployment period are mixed and sometimes contradict each other (e.g., Rentz et al., 2007). However, child abuse most often occurs at the hands of the military parent, most often the father. Military families have higher rates of fatal child abuse and have higher rates of substance abuse disorder and intimate partner violence, both of which have strong links to child maltreatment. About 20% of troops returning from Iraq and Afghanistan meet the diagnostic criteria for PTSD or depression and TBI. Those adult stressors can increase the risk of child maltreatment. In the Army, child maltreatment occurs twice as often where domestic violence is present in a family. Those issues follow the family when they transition out of the military and into the civilian community (National Child

Traumatic Stress Network, n.d.-c). Likewise, drug and alcohol addiction follows the veteran home after discharge. One third of all soldiers were taking prescription medication and 14% were on potent painkillers (Howell & Wool, 2016).

FAPs under the Department of Defense are tasked with investigating suspected child maltreatment and domestic violence. Undoubtedly the stressors unique to the GWOT—improved survivability but with more life-altering disabilities, TBI and PTSD, multiple deployments with short returns—all have contributed to the stress on the family (Mischel et al., 2017; National Child Traumatic Stress Network, n.d.-a, n.d.-b, n.d.-c, n.d.-d). However, Dr. Rubin's work cited earlier is troubling, if it proves accurate across other regions and other branches of the military. The disconnect between state CPS and Armed Forces FAPs occurs because there is no statutory mandate and no process for civilian health professionals to report a servicemember and his family to the Armed Forces FAP (Fifield, 2017).

For the veteran family with child maltreatment concerns, departure from the Armed Forces means loss of the supportive factors and preventive measures (steady employment, child care, FAP preventive services) that military life can provide. There is no parallel support system for families at risk for child maltreatment in the VA, they are not included in the panoply of family services continuum offered (Sayers, Glynn, & McCutcheon, 2014). If they have come under FAP jurisdiction while on active duty because of concerns with the family, that oversight will end upon transition out of the service, and that information will very likely be lost to the new state when the veteran relocates. It is possible they may never have come to the attention of the FAP (Rubin, 2016). In any event, if the servicemember and family transition back into civilian life, into a new city or state, their home life is nearly a blank slate for the new state's CPS, unless there are indicated (substantiated) reports to be found in another state's database. As for the prior military status, and the effect it may have had on the family, both state CPS, and the state family court may mark it as a footnote, if at all. The state's attention will be focused on present neglect and risk and future remediation, and little on how prior military life exacerbated family dysfunction. Only in states whose child welfare agency is beginning to adopt "trauma-informed" and "strengths based" clinical approaches will military history inform the case plan.

Intimate Partner Violence

Intimate partner violence (IPV) is the term most descriptive of the dangerous dysfunctional dynamics that can occur between partners when one partner seeks power and control over the other (U.S. Department of Veterans Affairs, n.d.-a, n.d.-b). Other terms such as "battering," "assault," and "domestic violence" are often used interchangeably, but IPV includes a broad range of behaviors where physical violence and assault may be only one tactic, or may only be threatened. These tactics serve the purpose of reminding the victim (often female—more than four out five IPV victims are women) that violence is on the horizon, that she is at risk of harm

(Tinney & Gerlock, 2014). While the tactics are as broad as imagination and cruelty can concoct, they often include actions that do not, in and of themselves, fit the legal definition of criminal behavior. IPV includes use of power and control tactics such as: intimidation, coercion, threats, emotional abuse, economic control and coercion, sexual assault and rape, use of children, pets, and loved ones to control the victim, stalking, denial, and lying and blaming (in the vernacular of "gaslighting") (Tinney & Gerlock, 2014). Between 2 and 10 million children witness IPV every year in the United States (Summers, 2006).

Over the several decades that IPV and domestic violence has been named and studied, it has become clear that not all violence is equivalent. In fact, the context in which the violence and coercion occurs is critical to an understanding of the dangerousness, the dynamics, likely recidivism, and possible interventions (Tinney & Gerlock, 2014). IPV with its strong coercive controlling component (actions of the perpetrator are geared to exerting control over the victim) is at one end of the spectrum. "Resistive" violence, or action taken in self-defense or in direct response to a threat to safety, is not aimed at exerting control as much as it is used as a shield to stop the violence of the other person. "Situational" violence, which does not have the coercive component, may be used by either or both of the parties as a relationship behavior, and might only occur briefly at the time of separation. And then there is "pathological" violence, exhibited because of mental or psychological problems such as brain injuries, PTSD, mental illness, or substance abuse (Stamm, 2009; Tinney & Gerlock, 2014). History is key to understanding context, but risk and lethality are dynamic elements front and present in each case. Only be assessing *both* contextual history *and* present risk and lethality can effective interventions and responses to IPV be crafted (Battered Women's Justice Project, 2018).

Some studies have reported the prevalence of IPV in the Armed Forces as higher than the civilian population. Most victims are under 25 years of age; as with the occurrence of child abuse incidents, the perpetrator is predominantly a male servicemember (Stamm, 2009). IPV is prevalent among women veterans, with one third of them—as compared to one quarter of civilian women—reporting experiencing it (U.S. Department of Veterans Affairs, n.d.-b). Reluctance to report IPV is similar for both military and civilian families. But with the military there is the increased risk that ensues due to limited confidentiality of IPV cases, or the perception of same, even when command is not involved. In the past decade and-a-half the DoD has taken steps to better respond to IPV in its forces, to hold offenders accountable, and provide victims with safety, services, and protection (Battered Women's Justice Project, n.d.-b; Howell & Wool, 2016).

The overlay of the invisible wounds of TBI, PTSD, depression, and substance use disorder (SUD) vastly complicates the assessments and interventions for IPV victims and children. Veterans, as compared to active duty servicemembers, are more likely to have a diagnosed mental health issue, such as PTSD and depression, along with IPV. There is actually stronger evidence to link IPV with depression and substance abuse problems than with PTSD (Sparrow, Kwan, Howard, Fear, & MacManus, 2017).

PTSD adversely affects family relationship problems (Cesur & Sabia, 2016; Taft, Watkins, Stafford, Street, & Monson, 2011). Several studies have shown that veterans with PTSD are two to three times more likely to perpetrate IPV than those without the diagnosis (Finley, Baker, Pugh, & Peterson, 2010; Marshall, Panuzio, & Taft, 2005). The more severe the PTSD the more severe the IPV (Tinney & Gerlock, 2014). In a retrospective study of 117 respondents with military service, over half of Operation Iraqi Freedom War veterans with PTSD reported committing at least one act of physical aggression against their partner in the preceding 4 months before the survey (Jakupcak et al., 2007). Veterans with PTSD and their family members have noted three patterns associated with violence in the relationship—violence committed in anger; dissociative violence; and parasomatic/hypnopompic violence—suggesting that the people involved can at times differentiate between IPV and PTSD (Finley et al., 2010). It appears that anger is related but independent from PTSD, and that underlying anger and resulting IPV may predate the onset of PTSD (Tinney & Gerlock, 2014). But often—and quite erroneously, and with great risk—veterans and their partners see IPV as a result of the PTSD, rather than attributing the violence to a co-occurring and possibly pre-existing pattern of coercive control and violence tactics (Finley et al., 2010; Jakupcak et al., 2007).

TBI may be obvious or more subtle, may present as similar to PTSD, and may aggravate PTSD, and vice versa. Most military personnel and veterans who have sustained a TBI are not violent, but when IPV is present as well, TBI can be an aggravator (Battered Women's Justice Project, n.d.-a, n.d.-b, 2018). In illness-based violence, just as with behavior while intoxicated, the violence is usually directed at a handy target, perhaps even involuntarily, rather than a particular single individual.

To further complicate the analysis, PTSD is a treatable condition, capable of improvement and remediation. Only about 10% of the cases prove intractable, and one third to one half will go into complete remission, one third of them within the first year (Seamone, 2012). A family court system that can accurately assess and then direct treatment for PTSD can be vital element in reducing the risks of situational IPV resulting from the PTSD symptoms (Seamone, 2012). Sufficient reduction of the risks will require the court to access effective veteran-related interventions. For this, the civil family court system can learn a great deal from the tested veteran-focused treatment used in the nation's VTCs (Clark et al., 2014; Rosa, 2014).

The multiplier effect of PTSD, TBI, SUD, and depression to the risk posed to a veteran's family is well documented. But veterans who have no such conditions can still be violent and even lethal. It will always be a challenge to distinguish between IPV's coercive control aims and the violence of PTSD and other illness-based behavior, and even more so in a court setting without the benefit of differential diagnoses that are so important. There is no single factor that predicts violence, but well tested, evidence-based research provides law enforcement, other first responders, victim safety advocates, attorney, probation officers, and the courts with some guidance. For example, threats of suicide, access to firearms, loss of employment, substance abuse, jealousy, attempted strangulation, etc. are all proven risk factors, with a long history of research and validation (Campbell, 2007).

The VA did not have a robust program similar to DoD's FAP available to veterans to address IPV. In the past, routine screening for IPV was highly variable (Battered Women's Justice Project, n.d.-b), and only a handful of VA medical centers had offender programs (for example Tampa, Florida, Phoenix, Arizona, and Buffalo, New York) (Schaffer, 2016). However, in 2014, the VA began the rollout of the DV/IPV Assistance Program for a more integrated approach to IPV.

A major obstacle was the lack of any supportive evidence to show that existing IPV interventions such as the Duluth model (Pence & Lizdas, 1998) or other more recent modalities are effective in treating IPV (Sayers et al., 2014). The personality profiles of offenders indicate high levels of overall psychopathology, including narcissism and other counseling-resistant disorders (Tasso, Whitmarsh, & Ordway, 2016). However, the VA has noted the high rates of IPV among female veterans (nearly two out of five), and the deleterious effects of the veteran victim's healthcare needs (Boyle, 2018). Almost three-quarters of the women receiving care at women's healthcare clinics in VHA facilities report experiencing some form of IPV over their lifetime (Iverson, Wells, Wiltsey-Stirman, Vaughan, & Gerber, 2013). Training and services have recently rolled out to all centers, with IPV coordinators in all locations. Given the high incidence rates, emphasis has turned to routine screening of IPV for female veterans, and referrals for services and treatment (Iverson et al., 2013).

A recent breakthrough assessment and screening for IPV in veterans, which addresses the interplay of co-occurring PTSD and TBI, has been developed by Glenna Tinney, M.S.W., and April Gerlock, Ph.D., in a comprehensive model: *Screening, Assessment, and Intervention Model for Intimate Partner Violence Perpetration and Co-Occurring Combat-Related Conditions* (Battered Women's Justice Project, 2018). With the developers' permission, a list of the assessments used in this evaluative tool is attached as the Appendix at the end of this chapter. Its focus is on correctly identifying IPV veteran offenders by a community-wide response that incorporates sensitivity to military and veteran culture, and assesses and distinguishes between IPV, PTSD, SUD, depression, and lethality. Its comprehensive approach underscores the many moving components that must be weighed; it incorporates time-tested screening and assessment tools. It is the first undertaking to screen and assess for the co-occurring combat conditions, and it bodes well for the future of differential diagnoses of veteran IPV. It is no overstatement to say that this tool should be utilized in all cases involving the veteran suffering with PTSD or other combat-related conditions and facing civil allegations or criminal charges.

For a veteran's victim, whether married or divorced, there are no comparable resources or assistance to the DoD's FAP. There might be a Vet Clinic with an experienced IPV counselor, although not likely, and some family resources may be available for Guard and Reserve depending on location and branch of service. For the most part, all professionals serving veterans will refer IPV victims and offenders to civilian community resources (Tinney & Gerlock, 2014). In the civilian arena, the victim can access local domestic violence programs, and may seek court intervention in the civil (family court) or criminal court (assuming the prosecutor files charges).

Family Courts, the Interplay with Veterans Treatment Courts

The family court has long played several roles in administering justice to families. In some cases, it is a restorative "problem-solving" court, and in others it is more concerned with safety and accountability. For instance, in juvenile justice and divorce/custody matters, the judge will follow the law with an eye toward finding a resolution that will increase the future wellbeing of the family members, i.e., solving the problems now and for the future. In cases involving child maltreatment and IPV, however, the family court will have a mandate to first secure safety and then enforce accountability of the abusing/neglectful parent or the battering partner.

Over the years, criminal courts have developed the "problem-solving" methods used in the drug treatment courts and mental health treatment courts, which—as their names imply—have an overarching intervention component rather than a punitive one (National Institute of Justice, n.d.). VTCs, as described earlier in this volume, began in Buffalo, New York, and grew out of both the criminal drug and mental health treatment models (Rosa, 2014).

For nearly all other criminal matters, criminal courts are "accountability" courts. This enforcement and community safety model includes another type of problem-solving courts, such as dedicated criminal domestic violence courts. There are over 300 specialized domestic violence (DV) courts in the country and over 400 VTCs (Tsai, Finlay, Flatley, Kasprow, & Clark, 2018). In larger regions, these courts will often be siloed from each other despite some overlap in jurisdiction. In more rural areas, the same judge or group of judges will be handling all of these cases. While DV courts and VTCs are both problem-solving—meaning they are using intense approaches to a specific crime or specific offender—they have important differences.

In both courts, a single judge will hear all cases, thus increasing consistency. Offenders are sanctioned with a specific and known range of severity for infractions—the "graduated response." Very often, a court or community "resource coordinator" manages the referrals and reports of the defendants. The defendant's progress is monitored by regular appearances before the judge to ensure compliance and increase motivation. Other supports incorporated into VTCs include interdisciplinary treatment teams and peer mentors.

But only in VTCs is there systemic coordination with the local VA office, something sorely lacking in family law cases unless the family court develops a docket devoted to military families, as described by this author (Rosa, 2014). In VTCs, the VA will provide a Veterans Justice Outreach specialist who refers eligible veteran-defendants to VA services (Clark et al., 2014). These services are focused on treating the veteran-defendant's drug addiction or mental health concerns. In VTCs there is often a mentoring component providing peer support for the defendant, yet another source of motivation to foster compliance.

Absent from the VTC model is the coordinated community response (CCR) with the domestic violence provider community effectively used in specialized DV courts. The community group not only ensures mandated programs, they also connect victims of IPV with services for the adult survivor and children. This coordinated response has proven essential to ensuring victim and community safety and increasing batterer compliance, thus reducing recidivism and re-offense. The CCR is composed of law enforcement, first responders, health professionals, mental health services, probation services, advocacy services for both victim and offender, and sometimes the courts. Importantly, in DV courts, victim, family, and community safety is front and center of every discussion, with defendant mental health and drug addictions taking a back seat to that top priority. Support for defendant offenders is not built into most DV court models, but support for the victim always is.

The pressure to serve veterans facing criminal charges of any nature has changed the profile of litigants deemed appropriate for VTC services. Over time, a large majority of VTCs—over 80%—now enroll IPV perpetrators (Seamone, Holliday, & Sreenivasan, 2018; Tsai et al., 2018). Initially there was opposition in the DV-services groups to the inclusion of IPV cases in the VTC format (Kravetz, 2012), but once precautions were incorporated by the VTCs handling IPV cases the arguments against have subsided. That most VTCs accept DV perpetrators does not guarantee successful outcomes in such cases. The disturbing consequence of ignoring the safety needs of the victims and families and exalting military service can and has cost lives. In at least three known cases a current or former VTC defendant was involved in a domestic-related homicide (Seamone et al., 2018).

Those VTCs that are successfully accepting IPV cases are screening for a defendant's violence history, recognizing the need for staff training on the dynamics of IPV, and using sound protocols to provide victim and family safety (Center for Court Innovation, n.d.). Now victim advocates and law enforcement are involved in the VTC process, and weapons safety and confiscation protocols are in place.

Both VTCs and DV courts are part of the criminal justice system, and there is little to no connection with the plight of civil family law litigants in family courts, even if veterans might have cases in both courthouses. There is no VA staff person available to help veterans in family courts, although in communities with a VTC already in operation, the opportunity can be found to create coordination (Rosa, 2014). A veteran in need of special services from the VA should not have to commit a crime to merit attention. A knowledge of the issues facing court-involved veterans, particularly those with minor children, is informative, and underscores the value of formal or informal family court—VA connections (Clark et al., 2014).

The Honoring Military Families docket initiated by this author in Buffalo, New York, was able to benefit from the smooth trusted relationships between veterans agencies at the county, state, and federal levels working in the local VTC, as they stepped forward with assistance for the veterans involved in divorces (Rosa, 2014). It proved that there is much that can be gained from a concerted effort by the criminal VTCs and the civil family courts to conserve their limited resources by active coordination to assess and treat veterans with cases (often the same veteran), in both courthouses. A truly trauma-responsive justice system would have that as a core principle.

Conclusion

Family courts are probably, without exaggeration, the first "problem-solving" courts in the judicial system, dating back many decades before that concept came to criminal courts (Rosa, 2016a). Family court judges are expected to know a great deal of information from a range of sources that have nothing whatever to do with law. Some lawyers may even derisively refer to family courts as social work offices. Yet the job is demanding and complex, requiring proficiency in many family dynamics and issues. The qualities and skills that make an effective and successful family court judge were codified for the first time in a project this author was fortunate to be a part of (Knowlton, 2015). The list includes subject knowledge of the law, evidence, ethics, domestic violence and child maltreatment, and complex financial matters. But it also extends to include a working knowledge of forensic trauma ("trauma-informed care"), substance abuse and addiction, mental health, child development (both normal and abnormal and the causes and remedies), family dynamics, and cultural and implicit biases. Then, add into that mix the universally desired skills of timeliness, decisiveness, listening skills, dispute resolution techniques, stress management (for staff, public and self), respectfulness and courtesy, humility, and thoughtfulness. Top off that offering with a generous dollop of judicial leadership both on and off the bench, administrative capacity, and knowledge of community resources (Rosa, 2016a).

Regardless of the family courts' desires to serve their communities, veteran families still face near invisibility in and about the family court. As a system, none of the courts—criminal or civil—focus on identifying the servicemember or veteran family. Beyond that, judges may know little about the needs of the veterans and their families, and less about the resources available for veterans that might be tapped for them. A few glimmers of light dot the national landscape. There are some family courts situated near military installations that have limited memoranda of understanding about specific family court matters (for example, juvenile delinquency). There is a project underway with the National Council of Juvenile and Family Court Judges, funded by the State Justice Institute, that will yield promising practices in fostering coordinated military-court response in juvenile justice matters. It builds on the momentum generated by a unique gathering of military, court, and legal professionals at a 2015 National Courts and the Military Summit at Fort Benning (Rosa, 2015).

Family courts are the backbone of every community's response to family disputes for civilian and veteran families. They are the first responders, the emergency room if you will, to which families in need, or families in anger, will turn for direction, adjudication, and enforcement. While they are the workhorses of the court system, they labor under a lack of resources, including judicial time, to handle the heavy demands. The adversarial process that is the foundation for our dispute resolution method does not suit these family disputes well, and are in fact antithetical to trauma-responsive practices that are proven to be far more effective. Family court judges are asked to make binding decisions about the future. Unlike their counterparts in the malpractice, contract, or criminal divisions who are asked to adjudicate past events, family court judges must make predictions of future behavior and wellbeing. While those other cases are snapshots of past events, family law cases are a moving docu-drama occurring in real time (Rosa, 2016b). All too often, the unique circumstances of the veteran and family are overlooked, not for lack of desire, but for lack of information and coordination between the military, the civilian community, and the courts.

Family court is and will be the unwitting and not-altogether prepared witness to the casualties of the GWOT, to what one author refers to the "ugliest" costs of this war, the effects of the war on families and children, and the unknowable impact on future generations to come (Baker, 2014). Family courts and the judicial branch are committed to serving all families who come seeking resolution of issues—that is their mission, after all—and are eager for more information, more resources, and more coordination with the military, VA, and the community at large. They owe no less to veterans who have served the country, and their families who stood with them.

Appendix

Screening, Assessment, and Intervention Model for Intimate Partner Violence Perpetration and Co-Occurring Combat-Related Conditions

Tinney and Gerlock (2018)

- *Military Service Screening Tool*—1 page inquiry about branch of service, deployment into war zone or combat
- *Intimate Partner Violence Assessment Tool*—15 pages, demographics of both adults, court/law enforcement involvement, protective orders, past experiences and abusive relationships, medical and mental health history, effects of violence on children in household, types of abuse/violence experienced
- *IPV Perpetration Screening Tool*—1 page, offender questions
- *Abusive Behavior Inventory (ABI—Offender Form)*—2 pages, offender questions
- *Abusive Behavior Inventory (ABI—Partner Form)*—2 pages, adult victim form, listing of abusive/coercive behavior
- *Dangerousness/Risk Assessment Protocol (Perpetrator)*—4 pages, inquiries about physical harm to others, risk of suicide, homicidal ideation
- *Dangerousness/Risk Assessment Protocol (Adult Victim)*—4 pages, same inquiries as prior assessment above, for adult victim
- *PTSD Screening Tool*—1 page, 5 questions, developed for primary care medical care
- *TBI Screening Tool*—2 pages screening, answers indicate referral for further testing
- *Alcohol Abuse Screening Tool*—2 pages screening from AUDIT-C.
- *Drug Abuse Screening Tool*—1 pages, DAST-10, (shortened version)
- *Depression Screening Tool*—1 pages, shortened version of Patient Health Questionnaire-9 (PHQ-9)

References

Acion, L., Ramirez, M. R., Jorge, R. E., & Arndt, S. (2013). Increased risk of alcohol and drug use among children from deployed military families. *Addiction, 108*, 1418–1425. https://doi.org/10.1111/add.1216

Babb, B. A. (2008). Reevaluating where we stand: A comprehensive survey of America's family justice systems. *Family Court Review, 46*(2), 230–257.

Babb, B. A. (2014). Family courts are here to stay, so let's improve them. *Family Court Review, 52*(4), 642–647.

Baker, M. S. (2014). Casualties of the Global War on Terror and their future impact on health care and society: A looming public health crisis. *Military Medicine, 179*(4), 348–355.

Battered Women's Justice Project. (n.d.-a). Military and veterans. Retrieved March 3, 2018 from http://www.bwjp.org/our-work/projects/military-and-veterans-advocacy-program.html

Battered Women's Justice Project. (n.d.-b). Military and veteran IPV. Retrieved March 3, 2018 from http://www.bwjp.org/our-work/topics/military-ipv.html

Battered Women's Justice Project. (2018). Screening, assessment, and intervention model for intimate partner violence perpetration and co-occurring combat-related conditions. Retrieved March 8, 2018 from http://www.bwjp.org/resource-center/resourceresults/screening_assessment_and_intervention_model_for_intimate_partner_violence_perpetration_and_cooccurring_combat_related_conditions.html

Blosnich, J. R., Dichter, M. E., Cerulli, C., Batten, S. V., & Bossarte, R. M. (2014). Disparities in adverse childhood experiences among individuals with a history of military service. *JAMA Psychiatry, 71*(9), 1041–1048. https://doi.org/10.1001/jamapsychiatry.2014.724

Boyle, A. M. (2018). Domestic abuse tied to range of health issues, U.S. medicine. Retrieved from http://www.usmedicine.com/agencies/department-of-veterans-affairs/va-launches-new-initiative-to-recognize-respond-to-intimate-partner-violence-subhead-domestic-abuse-tied-to-range-of-health-issues/

Cabrera, O. A., Hoge, C. W., Bliese, P. D., Castro, C. A., & Messer, S. C. (2007). Childhood adversity and combat as predictors of depression and post-traumatic stress in deployed troops. *American Journal of Preventive Medicine, 33*(2), 77–82. https://doi.org/10.1016/j.amepre.2007.03.019

Campbell, J. C. (2007). *Assessing dangerousness: Violence by batterers and child abusers* (2nd ed.). New York, NY: Springer.

Center for Court Innovation. (n.d.). Breaking barriers: Enhancing responses in veterans treatment courts and domestic violence courts. CourtInnovation.org. Retrieved March 5, 2018 from http://www.courtinnovation.org/sites/default/files/documents/breaking_barriers.pdf

Centers for Disease Control and Prevention. (n.d.). ACE study. Retrieved March 5, 2018 from https://www.cdc.gov/violenceprevention/acestudy/index.html

Cesur, R., & Sabia, J. J. (2016). When war comes home: The effect of combat service on domestic violence. *Review of Economics and Statistics, 98*(2), 209–225. https://doi.org/10.1162/REST_a_00541

Clark, S., McGuire, J., & Blue-Howells, J. (2014). What can family courts learn from veterans treatment courts. *Family Court Review, 52*(3), 417–424.

Clever, M., & Segal, D. R. (2013). The demographics of military children and families. *The Future of Children, 23*(2), 13–39.

Department of Defense. (2016). 2016 demographics: Profile of the military community. Retrieved from http://download.militaryonesource.mil/12038/MOS/Reports/2016-Demographics-Report.pdf

Department of Labor, Bureau of Labor Statistics. (n.d.). Employment situation of veterans summary. Retrieved March 6, 2018 from https://www.bls.gov/news.release/vet.nr0.htm

Dierkhising, C. B., & Marsh, S. C. (2015). A trauma primer for juvenile probation and juvenile detention staff. Retrieved from http://www.ncjfcj.org/sites/default/files/NCJFCJ-Trauma-Primer-Final-10.08.15.pdf

Esqueda, M. C., Astor, R. A., & Tunac De Pedro, K. M. (2012). A call to duty: Educational policy and school reform addressing the needs of children from military families. *Educational Researcher, 41*(2), 65–70. https://doi.org/10.3102/0013189X11432139

Farmer, A. N., Jackson, A. M., & Franklin, S. L. (2014). Enduring hope and support: Helping family court professionals incorporate programs to build resilient families. *Family Court Review, 52*(3), 425–439.

Felitti, V. J., Anda, R. F., Nordenberg, D., Williamson, D. F., Spitz, A. M., Edwards, V., … Marks, J. S. (1998). Relationship of childhood abuse and household dysfunction to many of the leading causes of death in adults. *American Journal of Preventive Medicine, 14*(4), 245–258. https://doi.org/10.1016/S-0749-3797(98)00017-8

Fifield, J. (2017). Why child abuse in military families may go unreported. Retrieved March 3, 2018, from http://pewtrusts.org/en/research-and-analysis/blogs/stateline/2017/06/07/why-child-abuse-in-military-families-may-be-going-unreported

Finley, E. P., Baker, M., Pugh, M. J., & Peterson, A. (2010). Patterns and perceptions of intimate partner violence committed by returning veterans with post-traumatic stress disorder. *Journal of Family Violence, 25*, 737–743. https://doi.org/10.1007/s10896-010-9331-7

Gibbs, D. A., Martin, S. L., Kupper, L. L., & Johnson, R. E. (2007). Child maltreatment in enlisted soldiers' families during combat-related deployments. *JAMA, 298*(5), 528–535.

Howell, A., & Wool, Z. H. (2016). The war comes home: The toll of war and the shifting burden of care. In S. Sharoni, J. Welland, L. Steiner, & J. Pedersen (Eds.), *Handbook on gender and war* (pp. 249–269). Northampton, MA: Edward Elgar Publishing. https://doi.org/10.4337/9781849808927

Iverson, K. M., Wells, S. Y., Wiltsey-Stirman, S., Vaughan, R., & Gerber, R. M. (2013). VHA primary care providers' perspectives on screening female veterans for intimate partner violence: A preliminary assessment. *Journal of Family Violence, 28*, 823–831.

Jaffe, P. G., Crooks, C. V., & Bala, N. (2009). A framework for addressing allegations of domestic violence in child custody disputes. *Journal of Child Custody, 6*(3), 169–188. https://doi.org/10.1080/15379410903084517

Jakupcak, M., Conybeare, D., Phelps, L., Hunt, S., Holmes, H. A., Felker, B., … McFall, M. E. (2007). Anger, hostility and aggression among Iraq and Afghanistan war veterans reporting PTSD and subthreshold PTSD. *Journal of Traumatic Stress, 20*(6), 945–954. https://doi.org/10.1002/jts.20258

Katon, J. G., Lehavot, K., Simpson, T. L., Williams, E. C., Barnett, S. B., Grossbard, J. R., … Reiber, G. E. (2015). Adverse childhood experiences, military service, and adult health. *American Journal of Preventive Medicine, 49*(4), 573–582.

Knowlton, N. A. (2015). The modern family court judge: Knowledge, qualities, and skills for success. *Family Court Review, 53*, 203–216.

Kourlis, R. L., & Samnani, R. (2017). Court compass: Mapping the future of user access through technology. Retrieved March 3, 2018 from http://iaals.du.edu/honoring-families/publications/court-compass-mapping-future-user-access-through-technology

Kravetz, P. (2012). Note, way off base: An argument against intimate partner violence cases in veterans treatment courts. *Veterans Law Review, 4*, 162–205.

Lapp, C. A., Taft, L. B., Tollefson, T., Hoepner, A., Moore, K., & Divyak, K. (2010). Stress and coping on the home front: Guard and reserve spouses searching for a new normal. *Journal of Family Nursing, 16*(1), 45–67. https://doi.org/10.1177/1074840709357347

Legal Services Corporation. (2017). *The justice gap: Measuring the unmet civil legal needs of low-income Americans*. Washington, DC: NORC at University of Chicago for Legal Services Corporation. Retrieved March 6, 2018 from https://www.lsc.gov/sites/default/files/images/TheJusticeGap-FullReport.pdf

Lemmon, K., & Stafford, E. (2014). Advocating for America's military children: Considering the impact of parental combat deployment to Iraq and Afghanistan. *Family Court Review, 52*(3), 343–354.

Lilienfeld, S. O., & Arkowitz, H. (2014, November 1). How to turn around troubled teens. *Scientific American*. Retrieved March 3, 2018 from https://www.scientificamerican.com/article/how-to-turn-around-troubled-teens/?print=true

Marsh, S. C., & Bickett, M. K. (2015). Trauma-informed courts and the role of the judge. Retrieved April 30, 2018 from https://www.ncjfcj.org/trauma-informed-courts-and-role-judge

Marshall, A. D., Panuzio, J., & Taft, C. T. (2005). Intimate partner violence among military veterans and active duty servicemen. *Clinical Psychology Review, 25*, 862–876. https://doi.org/10.1016/j.cpr.2005.05.009

Military Interstate Children's Compact Commission. (n.d.). Background. Retrieved April 29, 2018 from http://www.mic3.net/background.html

Mischel, E., Smischney, T., Lu, Z., Otto, M., Schroeder, B., Root, H, … Borden, L. M. (2017). Child maltreatment in the military: Understanding the research. Retrieved March 3, 2018 from https://reachmilitaryfamilies.umn.edu/research/document/13588

Montgomery, A. E., Cutuli, J. J., Evans-Chase, M., Treglia, D., & Culhane, D. P. (2013). Relationship among adverse childhood experiences, history of active military service, and adult outcomes: Homelessness, mental health, and physical health. *American Journal of Public Health, 103*(52), 5262–5268.

National Center for State Courts. (n.d.). State of the judiciary quotes related to budgetary issues. Retrieved March 12, 2018 from http://www.ncsc.org/information-and-resources/budget-resource-center/budget_funding/state-of-the-judiciary-quotes-related-to-budgetary-issues.aspx

National Center for State Courts. (2017). Self-represented litigants. Retrieved March 6, 2018 from http://www.ncsc.org/topics/access-and-fairness/self-representation/resource-guide.aspx

National Child Traumatic Stress Network. (n.d.-a). After service: Veteran families in transition. Retrieved March 2, 2018, from http://www.nctsn.org/sites/default/files/assests/pdfs/veterans_families_final.pdf

National Child Traumatic Stress Network. (n.d.-b). NCCTS leadership: Military children and families. Retrieved March 2, 2018 from http://www.nctsnet.org/nctsn_assets/pdfs/MilitaryFamilies_InfoBrief_FINAL.pdf

National Child Traumatic Stress Network. (n.d.-c). Child maltreatment in military families. Retrieved March 2, 2018 from http://www.nctsn.org/sites/default/files/assets/pdfs/mfchildmaltreatment.pdf

National Child Traumatic Stress Network. (n.d.-d). Military children and families: Programs and projects. Retrieved March 5, 2018 from http://nctsn.org/resources/military-children-and-families-programs-and-projects

National Council of Juvenile and Family Court Judges. (n.d.-a). Trauma informed system of care. Retrieved April 30, 2018 from http://www.ncjfcj.org/our-work/trauma-informed-system-care

National Council of Juvenile and Family Court Judges. (n.d.-b). NCTSN bench card. Retrieved April 30, 2018 from http://www.ncjfcj.org/sites/default/files/NCTSN%20Bench%20Cards.pdf

National Institute of Justice. (n.d.). Drug courts. Retrieved March 10, 2018 from https://www.nij.gov/topics/courts/drug-courts/Pages/welcome.aspx

Odom, J. S. (2011). *A judge's benchbook for the servicemembers civil relief act*. Chicago, IL: ABA Publishing.

Oshiri, A., Lucien-Greer, M., O'Neal, C. W., Arnold, A., Mancini, J. A., & Ford, J. L. (2015). Adverse childhood experiences, family functioning, and resilience in military families: A pattern-based approach. *Family Relations, 64*(1), 44–63.

Pence, E., & Lizdas, K. (1998). *The Duluth safety and accountability audit: A guide to assessing institutional response to domestic violence*. Duluth, MN: Minnesota Program Development Inc.

Petrosino, A., Turpin-Petersino, C., & Buehler, J. (2003). Scared straight and other juvenile awareness programs for preventing juvenile delinquency: A systematic review of the randomized experimental evidence. *Annals of the American Academy of Political and Social Science, 589*(1), 41–62.

Petrosino, A., Turpin-Petrosino, C., Hollis-Peel, M. E., Lavenberg, J. G., & Stern, A. (2014). Scared straight and other juvenile awareness programs for preventing juvenile delinquency. *Crime Prevention Research Review* (No. 12). Washington, DC: Office of Community Policing Services. Retrieved March 5, 2018 from https://ric-zai-inc.com/Publications/cops-p288-pub.pdf

Rentz, E. D., Marshall, S. W., Loomis, D., Casteel, C., Martin, S. L., & Gibbs, D. A. (2007). Effect of deployment on the occurrence of child maltreatment in military and nonmilitary families. *American Journal of Epidemiology, 165*(10), 1199–1206.

Rosa, J. M. (2014). Mission critical: A call to action for juvenile and family court judges, the U.S. Armed Forces, and Veterans Affairs. *Family Court Review, 52*(3), 511–528.

Rosa, J. M. (2015). Report on the 2015 National Summit on Courts and the Military. Reno, NV: National Council of Juvenile and Family Court Judges. Retrieved March 6, 2018 from http://www.ncjfcj.org/resource-library/national-summit-courts-and-military-final-report

Rosa, J. M. (2016a). Family courts. In P. M. Koelling (Ed.), *The improvement of the administration of justice* (8th ed., pp. 799–822). Chicago, IL: ABA Publishing.

Rosa, J. M. (2016b, Spring). The judge as community first responder: Because ACEs high is a losing hand. *Synergy, 19*, 16–17.

Rubin, D. (2016, December 13). Study raises concern of significant under-reporting of child abuse within the U.S. Army. December 13, 2016 statement, PolicyLab Director Dr. David Rubin. Retrieved from http://policylab.chop.edu/press-releases/study-raises-concern-significant-under-reporting-child-abuse-within-us-army

Sayers, S. L., Glynn, S. M., & McCutcheon, S. (2014). Family court and a review of family services in the Department of Veterans Affairs. *Family Court Review, 52*(3), 371–380.

Schaffer, B. J. (2016). Male veteran intimate partner violence (IPV) program outcomes. *Journal of Evidence-Informed Social Work, 13*(2), 133–141. https://doi.org/10.1080/23761407.2015.1006943

Seamone, E. R. (2012). Improved assessment of child custody cases involving combat veterans with posttraumatic stress disorder. *Family Court Review, 50*(2), 310–343.

Seamone, E. R. (2014). Educating family court judges on the front lines of combat readjustment: Toward the formulation and delivery of a core curriculum on military family issues. *Family Court Review, 52*(3), 458–510.

Seamone, E. R., Holliday, S. B., & Sreenivasan, S. (2018). Veteran *non grata*: Veteran sex offenders with service-related mental health conditions and the need to mitigate risk. *Virginia Journal of Criminal Law, 6*(1), 182–237.

Sheppard, S. C., Malatras, J. W., & Isreal, A. C. (2010). The impact of deployment on U.S. military families. *American Psychology, 65*(6), 599–609. https://doi.org/10.1037/a0020332

Simon, R. A. (2014). Special considerations in conducting psychological custody evaluations with military families. *Family Court Review, 52*(3), 440–457.

Sparrow, K., Kwan, J., Howard, L., Fear, N., & MacManus, D. (2017). Systematic review of mental health disorders and intimate partner violence victimization among military populations. *Social Psychiatry & Psychiatric Epidemiology, 52*, 1059–1080. https://doi.org/10.1007/s00127-017-1423-8

Stamm, S. (2009). Intimate partner violence in the military: Securing our country, starting with the home. *Family Court Review, 47*(2), 321–339.

Substance Abuse and Mental Health Services Administration. (2014). SAMHSA's concept of trauma and guidance for a trauma-informed approach. Retrieved April 30, 2018 from https://store.samhsa.gov/shin/content/SMA14-4884/SMA14-4884.pdf

Sullivan, M. E. (2011). *The military divorce handbook* (2nd ed.). Chicago, IL: ABA Publishing.

Sullivan, M. E. (2014). Military custody and visitation: Problems and solutions in the twenty-first century. *Family Court Review, 52*(3), 355–370.

Summers, A. (2006). Children's exposure to domestic violence: A guide to research and resources. Retrieved March 8, 2018 from http://www.ncjfcj.org/sites/default/files/Childrens%20Exposure%20to%20Violence.pdf

Taft, C. T., Watkins, L. E., Stafford, J., Street, A. E., & Monson, C. M. (2011). Posttraumatic stress disorder and intimate relationship problems: A meta-analysis. *Journal of Consulting and Clinical Psychology, 79*, 22–33.

Tasso, A., Whitmarsh, L., & Ordway, A. (2016). Intimate partner violence within military families: Intervention guidelines for relational aggressors. *The Family Journal: Counseling and Therapy for Couples and Families, 24*(2), 114–121. https://doi.org/10.1177/1066480716628622tfj.sagepub.com

Tinney, G., & Gerlock, A. A. (2014). Intimate partner violence, military personnel, veterans, and their families. *Family Court Review, 52*(3), 400–416.

Tsai, J., Finlay, A., Flatley, B., Kasprow, W. J., & Clark, S. (2018). A national study of veterans treatment court participants: Who benefits and who recidivates. *Administration and Policy in Mental Health and Mental Health Services Research, 45*(2), 236–244.

U.S. Department of Health and Human Services, Administration of Children and Families. (2017a). Toolkit: Child support collaborations to engage and assist veterans (No. IM-17-03). Retrieved from https://www.acf.hhs.gov/css/resource/toolkit-collaborations-to-assist-veterans

U.S. Department of Health and Human Services, Administration of Children and Families. (2017b, November). Toolkit: Child support collaborations to engage and assist veterans. Retrieved from https://www.acf.hhs.gov/sites/default/files/programs/css/vt_cs_collaborations.pdf

U.S. Department of Veterans Affairs. (n.d.-a). Intimate partner violence (IPV) assistance program. Retrieved March 3, 2018 from https://www.socialwork.va.gov/IPV/Index.asp

U.S. Department of Veterans Affairs. (n.d.-b). Women veterans health care. Retrieved March 3, 2018 from https://www.womenshealth.va.gov/WOMENSHEALTH/outreachmaterials/abuse-andviolence/intimatepartnerviolence.asp

Wood, J. N., Griffis, H. M., Taylor, C. M., Strane, D., Harb, G. C., Lanyu, M., … Rubin, D. M. (2017). Under-ascertainment from healthcare settings of child abuse events among children of soldiers by the U.S. Army Family Advocacy Program. *Child Abuse and Neglect, 63*, 202–210. https://doi.org/10.1016/j.chiabu.2016.11.007

Zogas, A. (2017). US military veterans' difficult transitions back to civilian life and the VA's response. Retrieved from http://watson.brown.edu/costsofwar/files/cow/imce/papers/2017/Zogas_Veterans%27%20Transitions_CoW_2.1.17.pdf

Chapter 7
Specialized Housing Units for Veterans Incarcerated in United States Prisons and Jails

Elizabeth Goggin and Michele Roberts

> When you combine the two factors, the factor of service in the military of this country… with the problems that go with the removal from society for crimes of one sort or another, you have a very vulnerable population, a population which in my opinion deserves not to be forgotten.
>
> Statement of Hon. George E. Brown, Jr. of California during the hearings on *Incarcerated Veterans Rehabilitation and Readjustment Act* of 1989.

Manny is a 33-year-old Army veteran who deployed twice to Afghanistan over the course of 4 years in support of Operation Enduring Freedom (OEF). On his last deployment in 2012, he was "blown up" twice before he redeployed from theater to Walter Reed for recovery. Although Manny was recommended for extended treatment and enrollment in a Warrior Transition Unit (WTU) to focus on the Posttraumatic Stress Disorder (PTSD) and Traumatic Brain Injury (TBI) he sustained in Afghanistan, Manny's command hoped to return him to combat operations as quickly as possible given his specialized training and experience. Manny was placed on deployment orders to return to Afghanistan with his unit during the upcoming rotation in 2 months. Based on severe physical pain, Manny developed an opiate addiction. To sleep without memories of his combat experiences and lost comrades, Manny regularly consumed a case of beer each night until he slept due to fatigue and drunkenness. On the day of his scheduled deployment, Manny had overdosed on pain medications and alcohol and missed the movement of his unit. The command told him they were doing Manny a favor by urging him to accept an administrative discharge rather than court-martialing him. Manny was separated with an Other Than Honorable Discharge for Missing Movement, Disobeying an Order, and committing an act Prejudicial to Good Order and Discipline in the

E. Goggin (✉) · M. Roberts
VA Connecticut Healthcare System, West Haven, CT, USA
e-mail: Elizabeth.Goggin@va.gov; Michele.Roberts2@va.gov

J. Tsai, E. R. Seamone (eds.), *Intersections between Mental Health and Law among Veterans*, https://doi.org/10.1007/978-3-030-31664-8_7

Armed Forces. All of these were purely military offenses with no comparable civilian crimes.

As is the case with an estimated 20% of justice-involved veterans (Rosenthal & McGuire, 2013*), Manny's discharge characterization prevented him from obtaining disability compensation and comprehensive healthcare from the Department of Veterans Affairs (VA). Manny continued to experience severe symptoms, which began to affect his wife, Jasmine, and his toddler, Maxwell. In a moment of alcohol induced rage at his inability to obtain employment, Manny threw a bottle that shattered against the wall above Jasmine's head, permanently blinding her in her left eye. Manny was charged with felony domestic violence and, despite being considered for a local Veterans Treatment Court (VTC) where some of the treatment team members desired his participation, Manny was ultimately rejected from the program based on is discharge characterization. Although that VTC had in the past accepted felons and domestic violence perpetrators, the treatment team decided they did not want to violate the program's universal prohibition on enrolling participants who did not have discharges under honorable conditions.*

Manny was incarcerated in a prison nicknamed "Gladiator School" based on its reputation for brutality and rampant gang involvement. Manny's exposure to the confined setting and acts of extortion, forced prostitution, and gang violence among members of the general population reminded Manny of life in a combat zone in Afghanistan—a "second tour" in which Manny had a set period during which he had to be subject to these conditions, he faced the threat of death and danger at all times, he was forced to adhere to specific rules for survival including being at the lowest level of a hierarchy of power, etc. Manny also experienced various triggers for his PTSD symptoms, including the sounds of victims of violence crying at night in their nearby cells like wounded comrades in Afghanistan and the sound of the automatically locking cell doors, which was not so different than automatic machine-gun fire. At times, Manny wanted to ask for help or medication to rid himself of these symptoms, except he knew that knowledge of visits to mental health can draw unwanted attention and perceptions of weakness and vulnerability to inmates who had more power and influence. Manny began to feel that his only method of surviving incarceration would be to align himself with a gang, which seemed similar to a military unit, aside from the drug dealing, extortion, and other illegal acts.

This illustration of an incarcerated combat veteran and his backstory is a composite of many stories we heard while working on a veteran's dorm in a Connecticut prison where a number of consistent patterns emerged: drug and alcohol addiction following combat and noncombat military service; subsequent and, in some cases temporary, loss of family support; history of trauma at some point in the course of their lives; turbulent relationships; outbursts of violent or self-destructive behavior; and insufficient resources in prisons and jails to support the needs of those who are incarcerated. We are far from alone in realizing the complex set of problems and needs veterans face before, during, and after their involvement with the criminal justice system. At least 24 states around the country have opened all-veterans units in jails and prisons at the local, state, and federal level in order to address the unsettling social problem of incarcerating veterans whose military service to their country may have contributed to drug addiction, poverty, mental health problems, and social isolation, all of which increase the risk of involvement with the criminal justice system (Seamone, 2016).

There have been major challenges to providing needed mental health and substance abuse treatment for incarcerated veterans. Glynn et al. (2016) noted that less than 60% of treatment offered in prison for substance use disorders is evidence-based. Similarly, trauma treatment has been almost non-existent despite the extremely high levels of trauma exposure in the prison population. With growing concern regarding recidivism, prisons have become increasingly open to innovation in treatment (Miller & Najavits, 2012). In this chapter, we will provide a general overview of how these units came to be, the philosophical perspectives which have informed them, and the various forms they take in different facilities around the country. By looking at examples from existing units, we will discuss patterns that emerge among the units and prevalent themes in their designs. Readers will also gain an understanding of the population served by these units in terms of demographics, experiences, and needs following release from prison. In addition, we will address what is currently known about outcomes following veterans' participation in the dorms. Given the relatively recent development of specialized veterans units, we will identify areas of study which would benefit from further exploration over time.

Genesis and Underlying Principles

A Brief History of Veterans in Prison

The idea to gather incarcerated veterans together for the purpose of appropriate treatment and rehabilitation is not a new one, despite minimal attention to the issue in contemporary discourse. According to Seamone (2013), a legal scholar, practicing attorney, and major in the U.S. Army Reserve, efforts to address the specific needs of incarcerated veterans goes back to the period following World War I, when it became clear that veterans were suffering and having difficulty readjusting after returning from combat. In addition to a thorough history (2013), Seamone (2016) also summarized some important historical considerations for incarcerated veterans in an educational webinar. Seamone (2013, 2016) pointed to an article published in the American Legion (Casey, 1923), which directly addressed the issue and used the example of efforts in Wisconsin, where "fully 25% of all prisoners in the state prison system were former soldiers, and in 20% of the case the crime was attributable in some way to military life" (Severo, Miller, Milford, Sheehan-Miles, & Ebook Library, 2016, p. 192).

Casey (1923) wrote that Governor Blaine of Wisconsin was so perturbed by incidents of veterans being incarcerated, largely for petty property crimes committed for purposes of meeting basic needs (Severo et al., 2016, p. 192), that he commissioned a study by two veterans with expertise in psychiatric care, W. F. Lorenz and W. S. Middleton. The findings were clear:

> Nothing in war is uplifting, at least not for the humbler participants. Those who actually got into battle and witnessed or took part in the dreadfulness of war may later in civil life have committed some overt act which by comparison with compulsory military duty seemed inconsequential. That such cases might be regarded in the light of war experiences brought into civil life requires no great stretch of the imagination (Casey, 1923).

Given this, it was their position that specialized prison units for veterans would be essential to address the set of issues that brought them into the justice system and help them to secure employment opportunities.

Going back as far as the 1920s, veterans were struggling with very similar issues to those witnessed today, and it was also in the 20s that the first iteration of what we now know as the Department of Veterans Affairs (VA) was created. Many veterans were battling substance use problems with alcohol, which was an illicit substance at the time under the Volstead Act, as well as physical and mental health issues related to combat. According to Casey's article, the Wisconsin study concluded decisively that veterans who were incarcerated needed treatment and that their military experiences necessitated that this be done by keeping veterans together in a space or unit while they were completing their sentences and receiving the targeted assistance they required. It is not clear to what extent this vision was ever realized.

Following World War II (WWII), further efforts were made on this front. The VA, formally enacted by Herbert Hoover in 1930, began to provide outreach and counselors to incarcerated veterans for a period of time. In addition, Seamone (2016) described a program in an Indiana correctional institution, Indiana State Farm at Green Castle, where veterans were encouraged to become more fully engaged in civic life following their stark removal from it during war time (Virgil & Hawkins, 1946). The program encouraged veterans to process their reintegration to the community and even connected them with veterans who were not incarcerated to foster connection and mentorship. Peer support has continued to be an important aspect of healing the wounds of war and has been a component of all the veterans' programs prisons being developed today, which we will address that in more detail later in the chapter.

While the aftermath of WWII brought with it a deep respect for what came to be known as "the great generation" and, thus, some meaningful efforts to support and address the difficulties experienced by returning troops, things changed when it was time to confront the aftermath of the Vietnam War and the soldiers it so profoundly impacted. Returning soldiers, who experienced myriad psychosocial stressors and a largely hostile public, struggled considerably to adapt to civilian life (MacPherson, 1993). According to Severo et al. (2016), upwards of 100,000 Vietnam veterans were addicted to opiates or alcohol and 80% of them were receiving no treatment at all; most didn't even know they were entitled to benefits. Unemployment was rampant and, once again, poverty and drug addiction were factors in the lives of veterans who found themselves ensnared by the criminal justice system. During the 70s, benefits provided through the Veterans Benefits Administration (VBA) were not expanded to meet these emergent needs. Rather, Nixon prevented funding for more doctors and cut monies which had been allocated to vocational rehabilitation (Severo et al., 2016).

Troubles for incarcerated veterans continued. In 1977 hearings in congress on the *Veterans Education and Readjustment Act* addressed, in part, the provision of educational opportunities and services to veterans during prison sentences. One individual, Howard S. Steed, who was the president of a college interested in providing educational services, stated that he saw providing services to veterans in prison as one strategy for "attacking this high rate of recidivism" (United States Congress, 1977). Despite these efforts, educational resources and access to GI Bill and other student aid while incarcerated remained restricted at the time. Seamone (2016) referred to the commonly held belief that veterans who were incarcerated could not be trusted to use educational monies for their intended purpose, which could be one reason for why funding was denied again in 1991 when the *Incarcerated Veterans Rehabilitation and Readjustment Act*, which would have additionally held "the Federal Bureau of Prison… responsible for the psychological treatment of veterans incarcerated within their facilities," (Sigafoos, 1994, p. 118) failed to pass, in part due to opposition from the VA. That said, a number of important points were raised throughout hearings on this issue, including the idea that treating the "psychological readjustment" issues that led to incarceration would reduce recidivism.

The VA's role over time has not always been positive when it comes to the matter of incarcerated veterans. Seamone (2016) explained the timeline, beginning in the 50s, when some VHA medical centers refused to serve veterans with felony records. While this changed for a time, in 1986 the VHA's regulations shifted and they were no longer "required" to provide services to incarcerated veterans. Worse still, in 1999, the VHA was legally restricted from providing direct healthcare services to veterans due to duplication of services presumed to be the responsibility of departments of corrections (Glynn et al., 2016). This bar on providing services includes all healthcare and psychological services, which can mean that veterans, with their specific set of treatment needs, may not have access to adequately trained providers. Ultimately, Congress intervened to expand options for addressing incarcerated veterans' needs with attention to post-incarceration transition. According to Pinals (2010),

> Congress has recognized the critical importance of understanding the special needs of veterans in the criminal justice system and, in 2001, passed a law mandating the Veterans Health Administration (VHA) to develop a coordinated plan with the Under Secretary for Health for veterans at risk of homelessness who are released from incarceration. This mandate contributed to the development of the VHA Health Care for Re-entry Veterans (HCRV) program.

This program continues today and has provided incarcerated veterans with case management services toward the end of their sentences, such as linkages to medical, mental health, and financial resources, to aide in their re-entry to the community following incarceration.

All of this history is helpful to understanding contemporary efforts to support veterans while they are in prison through the development of specialized veterans units within local, state, and federal correctional institutions. Since New York Department of Corrections (NYDOC) began their program, the longest running, in 1987, upwards of 24 states have implemented these units in some form. Seamone (2016) stated that there is a strong connection to VTCs, which are the subject of a subsequent chapter in this book. VTCs were essential in raising awareness of the issues facing veterans who are now returning home from Operation Enduring Freedom (IEF) and Operation Iraqi Freedom (OIF). Like VTCs, these units emphasize rehabilitation over punishment; utilization staff who are familiar with military culture and, often times, who have served in the US Military; involvement of the VHA for care coordination; the development of partnerships with other non-governmental organizations, such as counseling centers, universities, and Veterans Service Organizations (VSOs) in order to connect veterans to services which will address underlying issues which brought them into the criminal justice system; and use of peer mentors (Seamone et al., 2014).

The distinction between prisons and jails is also notable and worth exploring to better understand how these programs function. Jails house individuals who are awaiting trial or transfer to other facilities for shorter periods of time and it is therefore difficult to address any long-standing concerns and long-term needs; on average, jail inmates are only there for a few weeks and usually not longer than a month. Given this, our research indicates there are fewer jail-based veterans units with inmates taking on defined leadership roles. Their function is really to stabilize acute emergencies and provide support in a stressful time rather than to address the impact of service-related trauma. Jails are, however, uniquely poised to more quickly make changes, like specialized dorms. This is because prisons, part of complex state and federal systems, often take a great deal of time to coordinate and gain permission from various levels of administration before implementing new programs and initiatives. It is in the prisons where the greatest opportunity to address issues and needs in a more meaningful way and, theoretically, to obtain more long-lasting results. Veterans units can focus on creating institutional knowledge through the ongoing participation of those with longer or even life sentences.

Philosophy and Objectives of Specialized Veterans Units

As discussed, efforts to address the intersection of military service and incarceration have been made going back to the aftermath of WWI. They've included the Indiana State Farm at Green Castle in the 1940s (Virgil & Hawkins, 1946), the Veterans in Prison (VIP) program, launched by the Southern California Brentwood VHA healthcare center in 1977 (Pentland & Scurfield, 1982), the Second Tour Program at the federal prison in Phoenix (Sigafoos, 1994), and the Veterans Residential Therapeutic Program at Groveland Correctional Facility run by the NYDOC (1994), among others outside of our knowledge. These programs, among others in jails and prisons, have been a way to gather people with a similar set of needs together in one place so that resources can be provided in the most efficient way in order to address underlying problems that may have led to incarceration in the first place. Prisons have not limited these types of programs to veterans alone. Rather, they have developed dorms for individuals who are committed to earning GEDs, have an interest in practicing a certain faith tradition while incarcerated, and for those who would benefit from support in developing fatherhood skills, among others. For veterans, supporters of this concept have suggested that the dorms may be able to meet any number of objectives and provide the unique, often only, opportunity to meaningfully engage with veteran-specific psychological and readjustment concerns.

First, it's important to note some unifying themes which exist in all or most units. Among the veterans dorms that we know of, certain common themes have emerged, many of which have been highlighted in the National Institute of Corrections' handbook (Vanek, Brown, Busby, Amos, & Crawford, 2018) on "veteran-specific housing units." Military culture is fostered in a number of ways: visually, units have murals on the walls; enforcement of strict rules with emphasis on good behavior; memorials and monuments to honor veterans; special uniforms to increase pride; or even through participation in military rituals, like color guard. The atmosphere in veterans units is consistently structured, as well, and veterans are encouraged to connect to one another and embrace the commonality of their experiences while holding a high standard for conduct, ideally by honoring confidentiality. Leadership training encourages personal responsibility and accountability, and veterans are given work duties, like service dog training, unit maintenance, peer support, and many more. Interaction with the community is also fairly consistent in terms of providing service and including veterans from the community, including placing staff with military experience on units, and inviting community members in to mentor and help with the transition out of prison. Units also aim to provide access to real resources to facilitate smoother and more productive transitions, hopefully permanent ones, back to the community and to offer programming that will be of particular benefit or interest to veterans.

Approaches to Veterans Units: Four Models

There are a variety of models which have been implemented around the country, so the attributes discussed thus far may not all come together in any given program due to some inherent contradictions. As an example, at the first and only veterans unit in Connecticut, many veterans reported feeling distressed by the military themes and emphasis on creating an environment reminiscent of the military. For those who expressed that opinion, it brought them back in the frame of mind they had during the military, which for many was traumatic. Randall Liberty, the sheriff who ran a veterans' dorm in Kennebec County, Maine, was sensitive to this tension in noting the inherent difficulty of creating a military environment while also expecting veterans to work through their trauma and difficulties when he said, "There is a culture of suffer in silence. You suck it up and take the pain. That's a behavior that serves us well in combat, but when you get out, that mentality unfortunately continues to be adopted" (Schroeder, 2013). Liberty has advocated for something he calls 'purpose-driven incarceration' (Vanek et al., 2018, p. 11), which incorporates the principle of acknowledging service but also tailoring interventions to help veterans cope with the impact of combat-related trauma. For instance, he implemented a fly-fishing course to help with concentration difficulties secondary to trauma.

Veterans may come with vastly different experiences and thus potentially divergent needs, and therefore institutions may adopt models which emphasize military culture on a spectrum ranging from very central to more of theme in the background. Sociologist William Brown has written about the possible harms of overdoing the military culture aspect of these dorms and pointed out that the most important thing should be to encourage assimilation to civilian life (Ferdman, 2018). While there may be some disagreement about this tension between military culture and trauma triggers, Rosenthal and McGuire (2013) noted, "Regardless of whether in combat or not, each incarcerated veteran carries with him or her a military history and a sense of service to the country" (p. 345). The models described in this section highlight the various ways in which prisons have taken this tension into consideration in working to address veterans' needs while incarcerated.

Readjustment Model: "Second Tour"

Dorms which have used this model have emphasized structure, organization, and reeducation on psychological impacts of military service and readjustment to civilian life. Seamone (2016) described the overarching objective of the model to be the development by veterans of an understanding of how the prison experience may overlap with experiences of confinement (taking orders, limited privacy, temporarily losing control of one's life, and being in the presence of danger and physical threat) and using that knowledge to prepare, in vivo, for community reintegration. Based on implementation at Indiana State Farm (Virgil & Hawkins, 1946) and the "Second Tour" program at FCI Phoenix (Sigafoos, 1994), the structure has been described as a "captive audience" and is thought to help retrain veterans to better understand how their military service impacted their psychology and behavior (Seamone, 2016). As Seamone notes elsewhere in this volume, one benefit of being a captive audience is "time to spare, [giving] incarcerated veterans … a competitive advantage over non-incarcerated veterans to effectively obtain discharge upgrades" (p. 30). Programs which have utilized this model differentiate between combat and non-combat veterans in order to tailor psychoeducational efforts to groups who may have been impacted differently while at the same time keeping the program open to veterans with any type of military service, including non-military contractors. The approach may vary for combat veterans given the understanding that they will need more assistance in understanding how extended time in fight or flight can cause significant legal and personal problems once out of the war zone. Readjustment-oriented units have also taken a longer-term vision, aiming to connect veterans with mentors in the community after their release. A last feature is the "squad orientation" through which veterans are offered mutual support and shared learning as they move through the program, in many ways replicating the brotherhood and comradery often associated with military service.

Trauma-Informed Approach: PTSD Model

Seamone (2016) outlined an approach which has focused on addressing combat trauma and PTSD in a more targeted way. For reference, this type of model was used by the FCI Phoenix and the Southern California VIP programs. Under this model, mental health providers offer trauma services in institutional settings, sometimes with the assistance of consultation from VHA. This consultation is important to note because it is the only way VHA can be involved given the 1999 bar on VHA services in prisons; it has meant that, despite the specialized training that VHA mental health providers receive, they are unable to directly assist with issues as they arise in a prison setting. For this reason, units which aim to tackle issues connected to trauma have collaborated extensively, at times, with VHA, even so far as to gain medical records, with the veteran's approval, to contextualize care. In addition, the VA may provide training to prison staff and providers on effective and evidence-based approaches to working with veterans (Seamone, 2016).

The PTSD treatment model, not surprisingly, is heavily reliant on the creation of therapeutic settings and both individual and group treatment. Stabilization of PTSD symptoms and the development coping skills are two objectives of the programs and veterans are encouraged to "make meaning" of their military service, in part through addressing beliefs about the campaigns in which they participated. Additionally, families are included where possible so that PTSD's impact on relationships can be explored and processed with the veteran's support system.

The PTSD model does not restrict access only to those who meet criterion outlined in DSM-5 for PTSD due to a need for flexibility and acknowledgement of the various ways trauma responses can manifest behaviorally and psychologically. Rosenthal and McGuire (2013) referred to an acronym, BATTLEMIND, to define some of the specific ways that veterans suffer in civilian life for having adapted to an entirely different context through their military training and service. What may have been adaptive and necessary during war time or military training can manifest quite differently in day-to-day life back home. For example, the ability and need to make split-second decisions about whether or not to act is something that would help a soldier in combat to maintain a protective stance but may appear more like impulsivity, anger, and disproportionate response outside of the conditions of war. Similarly, a soldier is trained to have a weapon at all times in combat, which may pose additional challenges when back home and struggling with hypervigilance and a reduced threshold for anger. Given this, specialized veterans' units have a role to play in acknowledging and providing additional services to those who may not have had effective reentry counseling, if any at all, especially as more and more soldiers return from OIF and OEF.

Community Re-entry

Reentry models purposefully select veterans who are near to the end of their sentences, generally 3 years or less, because appropriate time to prepare for transition and to make linkages to community resources. The transition from prison to the community is known to be rife with material and emotional pitfalls, which often contribute to recidivism. This model is also seen as valuable because veterans may have to wait to gain residence on such units while serving out their sentences in general population, which is seen as incentive for good behavior. Veterans in community re-entry dorms are not expected to be engaged in long term treatment or trained in leadership roles on the unit. Rather, this model is based on the incentive of obtaining mental and physical healthcare and potentially vocational or economic resources, including housing for homeless veterans (Seamone, 2016). This makes it an ideal setting for HCRV, the VHA's program for connecting incarcerated veterans to VHA services upon release from prison, to perform outreach and provide this type of case management. Given the short time frame of these programs, it can be difficult to apply and determine eligibility for VHA services and VBA benefits. Per Seamone (2016) reentry dorms could potentially be less useful for those who are not VA-eligible. Possible solutions could include prioritizing the connection to VSOs who work with those who aren't eligible; building and maintaining ongoing relationships non-profits to help with employment and housing; and utilization of prison staff to assist with applications for state benefits, like Medicaid and SNAP, along with Social Security.

"Espirit De Corps" Model

Seamone (2016) called the *espirit de corps* model the equivalent of "barracks behind bars." These units and those that run them foster discipline, reward for military experience, and tend to be friendlier to those that both had honorable discharges and who are not dealing with significant trauma issues, as this type of military environment can be triggering for many, as previously noted. In such dorms, like those in Florida and Virginia's state prisons, military murals are prominent, as they may be in other dorm styles, as well; special uniforms are worn; clear roles are assigned; and military ceremonies and rituals are enacted with regularity. The value of this model is in its capacity to energize, foster pride, and encourage a sense of purpose for those veterans who live there.

Possible benefits of participation in any of these units are hard to ignore and correctional systems around the country are increasingly seeing the potential they offer. Seamone (2016) cited cost-savings through the provision of resources in one place; the improvement behavior through therapeutic approach, which could increase officer safety and ultimately public safety should veterans improve the conditions that brought them to prison; a decrease in officer stress by fostering a more respectful environment; and the ability to observe behavioral changes more quickly in a communal atmosphere. Seamone and Albright (2017) also pointed out the intense experience of shame given that "Service members and veterans typically hold themselves to extremely high standards in recognition of the responsibility for safeguarding the nation" (p. 486). These units are able to address this shame by offering some sense of pride and belonging among veterans. While public sentiment toward those labeled criminals and felons has long been hardened in the United States, this notable interest in rehabilitation promises potentially different results as outcomes are studied. Veterans units are, for now, a test subject in uncovering improvements that may truly benefit both those that have served their country as well as the general public.

Existence of Specialized Veterans Units Nationally

While increasingly prevalent, there are relatively few veterans dorms considering the need and promise they present. Based on research by Jessica Blue-Howells and incorporated by Seamone (2016) there were 24 states with veterans units in either a local, state, or federal jail or prison in 2016 with only two in federal facilities, Florida and West Virginia. According to the National Institute of Corrections (2018), there are at least 84 units around the country. While they are sometimes called "specialized housing units," other times "pods," "wings," "blocks," "units," "dorms," and other labels, they have been developed at a steady pace as word has spread about their benefits. For our purposes, we will highlight a small percentage of programs around the country where many of the themes and practices described above are taking place in real time.

We want to first draw attention the program in Connecticut at Cybulski Correctional Institution because it is the basis for much of our interest in and knowledge of veterans dorms, having assisted with the development of the unit and ongoing implementation of programming and structure. The dorm, the product of collaboration among state and federal agencies, opened in the fall of 2015 and was developed in an effort to not only help veterans be successful following incarceration by streamlining and consolidating service. In line with the re-entry model described above, the Veterans Service Unit at Cybulski is made up primarily of veterans who are close to the end of their sentences or who had short sentences to begin with. This is partly because the unit is located in a minimum-security prison where individuals with more serious charges or intensive treatment needs are restricted entirely. The program itself, however, is largely based on the idea of providing community resources so that veterans can connect with the VHA, BVA, and other services in order to be more successful when they are released. It is the primary function of the unit to assist with and execute re-entry plans, which are facilitated by both VHA social workers and DOC staff, depending on whether or not the veteran is eligible for VHA benefits. The unit also has a strong emphasis on educational and vocational development and partnered with the Connecticut Department of Labor to provide employment services and with local schools to enroll veterans in training courses.

While the Cybulski program does offer ongoing group treatment, primarily for substance use disorders, it would not be considered a treatment-specific program. This is in part because the facility is not equipped to deal with complex and intensive mental health treatment for trauma or other disorders and in part because of the short-term nature of the program. A recent news report on a veterans dorm called HUMV in a county jail in Billerica, Massachusetts highlighted the two primary components of that program, which were described to be a "hyper-structured setting" and the provision of mandatory group and individual treatment for underlying mental health and substance use issues (Ferdman, 2018). The program, like Cybulski, is operated at very little cost with most additional services provided on a voluntary basis. For instance, it costs no additional money to have professionals from the VHA come in as a consultant or to provide case management services, nor would funding be required to integrate veteran mentors from the community. It should be remembered that VHA is barred by federal regulation from offering direct healthcare to incarcerated veterans, which imposes several limitations on service delivery.

Perhaps because of its early adoption of veterans prison units in 1987, the New York corrections system has a comprehensive system to address the needs of veterans tailored to meet veterans at a number of levels of need. Based on the DOC website, all New York State facilities coordinate with the VHA for connection to services and obtain copies of Certificates of Release or Discharges from Active Duty (DD 214s) for veteran inmates. At 14 prisons, there are veterans organizations that foster that "squad mentality" identified by Sigafoos (1994) as extremely helpful in adjusting to prison, treatment, and, ultimately, assimilation to civilian life. Veterans gather, participate in educational groups, and take part in military ceremonies and memorials. The system also has three prisons with veterans dorms, Veterans Residential Therapeutic Programs, in which veterans spend 6 months addressing readjustment issues and getting treatment for substance use, anger, aggression, and PTSD. Veterans are also connected with community providers to help counteract the inhibiting factor of power dynamics which exist in the prison setting and may preclude the "therapeutic" aspect of programming, at times. Of note, the Albany unit is known to avoid the use of military rituals and ceremonies in favor of a more assimilation-based model.

The task of describing the entire scope of operational veterans units is a large one, so we offer some final observations on noteworthy aspects of a smaller selection. For instance, the Stafford Creek Corrections Center Veteran Unit in Washington State has provided veterans an opportunity to train abandoned dogs so that they can become adoptable pets. The program has trained dozens of dogs and has been met with praise from veterans, the prison staff, and the families who are getting well-trained dogs. This is another example of a trauma-informed intervention given what is known about the therapeutic elements of animal therapy for individuals with PTSD. The San Bruno veterans unit in San Diego has provided veterans with extra perks, like the ability to obtain more comfortable bedding and the provision of televisions. There, veterans are able to take yoga classes, participate in a program to videotape themselves reading so they can connect with their children, and, like other units, mandates participation in treatment. Units in Erie, Pennsylvania, and Kennebec, Maine, among others, are connected directly with VTCs so that those whose treatment options don't adequately address the problem have a plan once incarcerated.

In all of the programs we have reached out to or read about in the process of researching this phenomenon, we have found a deep personal connection to the military among those who spent their time and energy advocating for incarcerated veterans to have a more treatment-focused experience. In Kennebec, Warden Randall Liberty, a veteran himself, experienced personal loss and sought to fulfill a "moral duty" to provide veterans with care after they have returned from deployments (Schroeder, 2013). In Connecticut, many of the staff, including a critically involved deputy warden, had personal ties to the military and had their own experiences with the grief and loss suffered by veterans and their families in the aftermath of war. In each unit, there are staff who have themselves served in the military and are now working to view veterans in the justice system in a more holistic, healing way.

Participant Characteristics and Preliminary Outcomes

While the percentage of veterans in prison has vastly declined since the Vietnam era along with the reduction in troops, the most recent reports estimated that 8% of inmates in state and federal prisons and local jails are veterans (Bronson, Carson, Noonan, & Berzofsky, 2015), many of whom have significant trauma histories; one study in two states found that 93% of their incarcerated veterans reported a history of trauma (Hartwell et al., 2014), and the Bureau of Justice Statistics has also reported that nearly all justice-involved veterans have experienced some type of trauma, including military and non-military related trauma (Noonan & Mumola, 2007). According to Bronson et al. (2015), in 2011–2012, nearly half of all incarcerated veterans reported that they were either told they had a mental health disorder by a professional or formally diagnosed with one, and nearly twice as many veterans, 23%, reported they had been told they had PTSD compared to non-veterans. In addition, 64% of incarcerated veterans were serving time for violent crimes compared to 48% in the nonveteran population (Bronson et al., 2015). Estimates of the prevalence of mental disorders have been far from exact. For example, one review estimated that 13–62% reported having a mental health problem of any kind, 21–71% for alcohol, and 26–65% for drug use (Blodgett et al., 2015).

Incarcerated veterans were "more likely… to be white, older, more educated, and to have been married" (Bronson et al., 2015). The majority were discharged between 1974 and 2000, had served in the army (55% compared to roughly 20% in Marine Corps and Navy), and had done so for less than 3 years. Most veterans reported that they had not experienced combat (75% in prison and 69% in jail) (Bronson et al., 2015). Records have also indicated that the vast majority of veterans in prison were discharged with honorable or general under honorable conditions military discharges, which has been surprising to some who assume deviant behavior in the military was a precursor to involvement in the criminal justice system. The minority of veterans with less-than-honorable conditions discharges is still substantial at 20% posing special considerations for discharge upgrading during the course of confinement (Seamone, this volume).

Additionally, it should be noted that veterans are often prepared with job training and skills during their time in the military, as well as the minimum requirement of a high school diploma or GED, which are strengths when considering opportunities for vocational development. With ever-changing statistics on who is impacted by PTSD and depression following service and with the wars in Iraq and Afghanistan still going on, it is essential to continue work to understand the complex set of issues that are related to combat exposure, PTSD, and the criminal justice system. Rosenthal and McGuire (2013) noted, according to the Institute for Operations Research and the Management Sciences in 2009, "it is estimated that veterans of the Iraq and Afghanistan wars will have a rate of PTSD as high as 35%." It has also been understood that veterans service longer prison sentences overall than their nonveteran counterparts (Rosenthal & McGuire, 2013).

It is more difficult to know the demographics of the veterans who have participated in veterans dorms, although, in 2017, Tsai and Goggin asked veterans living in the unit at Cybulski about their perceptions of needs and their particular challenges, as well as demographics. Compared to the national statistics, there were higher rates of substance use and mental health issues reported with 45% reporting a substance use disorder and 30% reporting PTSD. The Connecticut DOC's own numbers based on their intake assessments had the rates of mental health diagnosis at 63% and substance use diagnosis of any kind at 84% within months of administering the survey. While this data is far from generalizable, it does point to a least a very high prevalence of psychological issues in one veterans' unit. From this research a picture of individuals struggling under the weight of poverty also emerged. Out of the 87 who participated, 52% said they needed help with obtaining housing and 57% reported that they had needed help to pay utilities prior to incarceration. Even larger numbers (72% and 64%, respectively) reported that they needed access to healthcare and dental care. Perhaps most disturbing, roughly 70% of respondents said they had been unable to afford food and basic clothing. This snapshot of the impact of poverty on veterans is widely replicated among all prison populations nationally and here we can see veterans are no exception.

Again, because of our familiarity with the veterans unit in Connecticut, we believe it may be helpful to offer a brief overview of qualitative feedback, obtained from quality-improvement questionnaires completed by those residing in the unit. Individuals shared that they considered physical fitness and "fresh air" primary needs given the sedentary nature of prison life. In this particular program, veterans wanted to be able to have assurances that they would be able to get outside, even if the weather was not cooperative. On the survey, one veteran wrote, "Fitness has always been a big part of my life. It keeps me level-headed and balanced. Helps with combat related stress and PTSD. This is a must for future success. I would like to see more weight room implemented." Responses about fitness and activity frequently focused on the mental and physical challenges of inactivity, such as boredom, ill health, and possible negative impacts on mental health. Veterans also expressed strong desires to receive mental health and substance use treatment that they hadn't received on the outside and stressed the importance of vocation in their recoveries. With great frequency, veterans mentioned the cleanliness, order, and "brotherhood" that the dorm offered to them while numerous others reported feeling that the gathering of VA eligible and non-eligible, as well as combat and non-combat, veterans together was problematic because of resentments and ensuing divisions. This seemed to be an area of disagreement among respondents. Altogether, 60.5% of veterans said this unit was preferable to other units and over 50% said they felt safer and more prepared for reentry having participated in the program.

Early longitudinal data on recidivism points to successes among these fledgling veterans units, perhaps in large part due to the emphasis on connecting veterans to healthcare, housing, vocational training and other basic resources. Preliminary outcomes data revealed that out of the 117 veterans who had been released after spending at least a month in the program, only 5 were rearrested since 2016. For the rest of the state, the recidivism rate is closer to 70% over a 3-year period (Ferdman, 2018). Similarly, in Albany, in the first 2 years of the program, 195 veterans went through the unit and only 10 had returned. Back in 1994 when the Groveland unit was evaluated, it was determined that the recidivism rate among the veterans who completed the program was at 6.1% compared to 40.57% for veterans who didn't participate and 51.85% in the general population. We also know that the HCRV program run by the VHA, which is interactive with most veterans units in some form, has demonstrated its value; connecting veterans to VHA services post release "has been shown to be associated with a reduction in the risk of death for veterans when they are released from prison" (Blodgett et al., 2015). While this may seem dramatic, we believe it sets the stage for the high stakes nature of this endeavor with this population and the importance of bringing veterans together to best serve them and facilitate their healing. Anecdotally, those professionals, including ourselves, who have been engaged with veterans units have overwhelmingly been enthusiastic about the impact it has on veterans who engage with programming.

Topics for Further Exploration

There is much we still do not know about the outcomes and benefits of veterans units. Most importantly, longitudinal data is needed to track outcomes and rates of recidivism. If the goal is rehabilitation and improvement of the lives of participants, this is crucial information to gather. While all signs point to the effectiveness of the model, which prioritizes treatment, training, and resource gathering over punishment, it needs to be explored and documented in well-designed studies. It would also be essential to understand the experiences and needs of women veterans in prison since this has not been well-documented or studied. Seamone (2016) had posited that there may be cost-savings associated with this model and though that isn't the primary issue at hand, it may be a way to motivate policy-makers and bureaucratic institutions to embrace this model of incarceration all the more and to continue on the path toward better care and treatment for our veterans.

The limitations of the model could also be better understood. There seems to be some level of disagreement about whether or not to treat these units as replicas of military experience or to get away from that in favor of a more purely therapeutic approach. The question of who benefits from which approach will likely reveal that different veterans require different things. This is to be expected, given the diversity of veterans themselves as well as their roles in the military. In fact, tensions among DOC employees and veterans, as well as among veterans with such differing experiences, is another potential limitation or important aspect to understand. There is also the problem, which was raised in the 70s and again in the early 90s, about the way VBA benefits, especially for education, are withheld during incarceration and the 1999 decision that the VHA could not provide direct healthcare services, a problem given the concentration of expertise on veterans issues and trauma-informed treatment at VHA.

We are hopeful that the historical context of specialized veterans units, coupled with the philosophy behind them, will provide insight to those in positions to help incarcerated veterans and perhaps inspire similar programs for all of those who are likely to have a complex set of issues that the typical prison experience isn't able to meaningfully address. Units around the country are continuing to develop and those that have been in existence are demonstrating positive results in terms of recidivism and veterans' reports of satisfaction.

References

Blodgett, J. C., Avoundjian, T., Finlay, A. K., Rosenthal, J., Asch, S. M., Maisel, N. C., & Midboe, A. M. (2015). Prevalence of mental health disorders among justice-involved veterans. *Epidemiologic Reviews, 37*, 163–176. https://doi.org/10.1093/epirev/mxu003

Bronson, J., Carson, A., Noonan, M., & Berzofsky, M. (2015). Veterans in prison and jail, 2011–12. Retrieved from http://www.bjs.gov/index.cfm?ty=pbdetail&iid=5479

Casey, R. J. (1923, September 28). The lost legion. *The American Legion Weekly,* 5(39). Retrieved from https://www.archive.legion.org/bitstream/handle/123456789/3046/americanlegionwe539amer.pdf?sequence=1&isAllowed=y

Ferdman, R. (2018, February 22). Inside an experimental, veterans-only jail housing unit [video file]. *Vice News Tonight.* Retrieved from https://news.vice.com/en_us/article/a34488/what-its-like-inside-an-experimental-veterans-only-jail-housing-unit

Glynn, L. H., Kendra, M. S., Timko, C., Finlay, A. K., Blodgett, J. C., Maisel, N. C., & Blonigen, D. M. (2016). Facilitating treatment access and engagement for justice-involved veterans with substance use disorders. *Criminal Justice Policy Review, 27*(2), 138–163. https://doi.org/10.1177/0887403414560884

Hartwell, S. W., James, A., Chen, J., Pinals, D. A., Marin, M. C., & Smelson, D. (2014). Trauma among justice-involved veterans. *Professional Psychology: Research and Practice, 45*(6), 425–432. https://doi.org/10.1037/a0037725

MacPherson, M. (1993). Long time passing: Vietnam and the haunted generation. New York, NY: Doubleday.

Miller, N. A., & Najavits, L. M. (2012). Creating trauma-informed correctional care: A balance of goals and environment. *European Journal of Psychotraumatology, 2012*, 3. https://doi.org/10.3402/ejpt.v3i0.17246

National Institute of Corrections. (2018). Prisons and jails with dorms for veterans. Washington, DC: National Institute of Corrections. Retrieved from https://info.nicic.gov/jiv/node/27

New York State Department of Correctional Services. (1994). Veterans Residential Therapeutic Program, Groveland Correctional Facility, Sonyea, New York: Program overview. Retrieved from https://www.ncjrs.gov/pdffiles1/Digitization/149417NCJRS.pdf

Noonan, M. E., & Mumola, C. J. (2007). Veterans in state and federal prison, 2004. Bureau of Justice Statistics special report. Retrieved from https://www.bjs.gov/content/pub/pdf/vsfp04.pdf

Pentland, B., & Scurfield, R. (1982). Inreach counseling and advocacy with veterans in prison. *Federal Probation, 46*, 21–28.

Pinals, D. A. (2010). Veterans and the justice system: The next forensic frontier. *Journal of the American Academy of Psychiatry and the Law, 38*(2), 163–167. Retrieved from http://jaapl.org/content/38/2/163#sec-4

Rosenthal, J., & McGuire, J. (2013). Incarcerated veterans. In L. Gideon (Ed.), *Special needs offenders in correctional institutions* (pp. 345–376). Thousand Oaks, CA: SAGE Publications Ltd. https://doi.org/10.4135/9781452275444.n12

Schroeder, K. (2013, July 21). Kennebec County jail program aims to help inmates who are veterans. *Kennebec Journal and Morning Sentinel*. Retrieved from https://www.centralmaine.com/2013/07/21/kennebec-county-jail-program-aims-to-help-inmates-who-are-veterans/

Seamone, E. R. (2013, November/December). A historical touchstone for Nebraska in the mission to divert criminally-involved veterans from confinement. *Nebraska Lawyer, 16*(6), 7–15.

Seamone, E. R. [AmericanUnivJPO]. (2016, May 16). Specialized housing units for veterans in prisons and jails [video file]. Retrieved from https://www.youtube.com/watch?v=UW-MykVqN3s

Seamone, E. R., & Albright, D. L. (2017). Veterans in the criminal justice system. In L. Hicks, E. L. Weiss, & J. E. Coll (Eds.), *The civilian lives of veterans: Issues and identities* (pp. 481–507). Santa Barbara, CA: Praeger: ABC-CLIO, LLC.

Seamone, E. R., McGuire, J., Sreenivasan, S., Clark, S., Smee, D., & Dow, D. (2014). Moving upstream: Why rehabilitative justice in military discharge proceedings serves a public health interest. *American Journal of Public Health, 104*(10), 1805–1811. Retrieved from https://search.proquest.com/docview/1564433185?accountid=30097

Severo, R., Miller, M. C., Milford, L., Sheehan-Miles, C., & Ebook Library. (2016). *The wages of war: When America's soldiers came home: From Valley Forge to Vietnam*. New York, NY: Open Road Integrated Media, LLC.

Sigafoos, C. E. (1994). A PTSD treatment program for combat (Vietnam) veterans in prison. *International Journal of Offender Therapy and Comparative Criminology, 38*(2), 117–130.

Tsai, J., & Goggin, E. (2017). Characteristics, needs, and experiences of U.S. veterans on a specialized prison unit. *Evaluation and Program Planning, 64*, 44–48. https://doi.org/10.1016/j.evalprogplan.2017.05.016

United States. Congress. House. Committee on Veterans' Affairs. Subcommittee on Education and Training. (1977). *Veterans' education and readjustment legislation, 1977: Hearings before the Subcommittee on Education and Training of the Committee on Veterans' Affairs, House of Representatives, Ninety-fifth Congress, first session*. Washington, DC: U.S. G.P.O.

Vanek, S., Brown, R. M., Busby, H., Amos, S., & Crawford, G. (2018). Barracks behind bars: In veteran-specific housing units, veterans help veterans help themselves. Washington, DC: National Institute of Corrections. Retrieved from https://info.nicic.gov/jiv/sites/info.nicic.gov.jiv/files/Barracks-Behind-Bars-508.pdf

Virgil, A. E., & Hawkins, H. L. (1946, May–June). The short-term institution and the delinquent veteran. *Prison World, 8*(3), 16, 28, 29.

Chapter 8
Military Discipline and the Incarcerated Veteran

Evan R. Seamone

> *Evidence of misconduct, including any misconduct underlying a veteran's discharge, may be evidence of a mental health condition, including PTSD; TBI; or of behavior consistent with experiencing sexual assault or sexual harassment.*
>
> – A. M. Kurta (2017, ¶ 6)
> U.S. Department of Defense

Introduction

Since the origins of the naval and land forces, militaries have relied upon a unique system of discipline to keep troops in line (Winthrop, 1920). Severe penalties for breaches of order within the ranks—often including death—served as leverage to enforce command directives and overcome the powerful instinct of self-preservation impulses on the battlefield (Gabriel, 1987). When dispensing justice, these differences have stood in stark contrast to the traditional civilian justice system's objective to balance society's interests against the offender's interest (Seamone et al., 2014).

In a widely publicized court-martial, Army Sergeant Robert "Bowe" Bergdahl was sentenced by a military judge to a Dishonorable Discharge, reduction to the lowest rank, forfeiture of $1000 per month for 10 months, and no term of confinement for misbehavior before the enemy and desertion (Oppel, 2017). While some

The positions in this chapter are solely those of the author based upon his experience in the military and providing legal services for veterans. These positions do not represent and are not endorsed by any federal organization to include the Department of Defense or the Department of Veterans Affairs. The author extends special thanks to Dana Montal to of the Legal Services Center for reviewing and providing excellent suggestions on earlier versions of this chapter.

E. R. Seamone (✉)
Veterans Benefits Attorney, Loxley Services, and Major, U.S. Army Reserve, Gainesville, FL, USA

J. Tsai, E. R. Seamone (eds.), *Intersections between Mental Health and Law among Veterans*, https://doi.org/10.1007/978-3-030-31664-8_8

seasoned military veterans believed that Bergdahl should have been confined for many years or the maximum term of life given the deaths of soldiers on search parties (Oppel, 2017), others argued that he should be spared military punishment due to his severe Posttraumatic Stress Disorder (PTSD) from being held captive by the Taliban in deplorable conditions for many years (Cuthbert, 2017a, 2017b). This puzzling sentence underscores the isolated and incomparable nature of the military justice system.

One question that emerged was whether Mr. Bergdahl should be spared a punitive discharge from the court, which would likely bar him from receiving benefits and treatment from the Department of Veterans Affairs (VA), given that he would require such care for years to come (Cuthbert, 2017a). While the military judge's sentence included the worst type discharge Mr. Bergdahl could receive, cementing his ineligibility for future care (Brooker, Seamone, & Rogall, 2012), Mr. Bergdahl still left the courtroom as a free man.

Bergdahl's court-martial echoes some key themes that characterize the military justice system: First, military discipline operates with different considerations in mind. That is, while civilian justice requires the balance of the interests of society against the interest of the defendant, military justice considers preservation of good order and discipline within the ranks as a necessary third element. As the Court of Federal Claims confirmed long ago, "The power to command depends upon discipline, and discipline depends upon the power to punish" (*Swaim v. United States*, 1893, p. 221). Second, military sentencing authorities need to consider various factors in arriving at the appropriate punishment, including mental health conditions sustained during the course of one's service (Seamone, 2011; Seamone et al., 2014; Seamone et al., 2017). Finally, even with the exception of strict sentencing protocols for sex crimes, there is great variability and subjectivity in the outcome that is ultimately doled out at a court-martial or a separation board (Seamone, 2011, 2013).

This chapter explores the procedures and consequences of the military justice system and the manner in which it impacts incarcerated veterans, sometimes long after their service. Part II explores the different types of disciplinary proceedings and the range of punishments that can result from each one. Part III discusses the most severe form of military discipline through trial by court-martial. Part IV then describes the impact of less-than-honorable discharge characterizations ("bad paper"), to include consequences on veterans' benefits and in civilian life. This part also explores a growing body of research linking stigmatizing discharge characterizations to poor health outcomes, criminal justice involvement, and significant social consequences. Part IV further discusses standards for obtaining VA benefits or upgrading discharges through military review boards despite bad paper designations. Part V concludes by summarizing different measures within confined settings to assist veterans impacted by the military justice system in a manner that assists re-entry and reduces criminal recidivism.

Pathways to Military Discipline

Unlike the civilian criminal justice system, in which district attorneys are responsible for pursuing criminal charges and considering alternative disposition of cases, the military justice system reserves ultimate decision-making authority to military commanders at all stages of the process (Seamone, 2011). In this "command controlled" system, the same general officer who decides to send a case to court-martial also selects the members of the military jury and decides whether to approve the conviction and sentence (Seamone, 2011). While the general receives advice from a military lawyer throughout the process, the legal guidance is not binding. With the exception of sexual assault,[1] substantial command discretion still exists. Rule for Court-Martial 306(c)(1) explicitly states that a commander has the inherent authority to "decide to take no action on an offense" after a violation is known or suspected.

In practice, most military discipline never reaches the level of a court-martial. All military leaders are encouraged to resolve issues at the lowest level and they enjoy a wide arsenal to address minor misconduct (Seamone et al., 2014). Rule for Court-Martial 306(c)(2) describes a host of administrative actions that are supposed to be "corrective" in nature rather than punitive, including any combination of "counseling, admonition, reprimand, exhortation, disapproval, criticism, censure, rebuke, extra duty, military instruction, or the administrative withholding of privileges…. " The discussion to the Rule further includes administrative action authorized through the service secretaries, such as "efficiency reports, academic reports, and other reports; rehabilitation and reassignment; career field reclassification; administrative reduction for inefficiency; bar to reenlistment; personnel reliability program reclassification; security classification changes; pecuniary liability for negligence or misconduct; and administrative separation" (Rule for-Court-Martial 306, Discussion).

Because most recruits are young, have just graduated high school, and may face challenges adjusting to the transition from civilian to warrior, flexibility is required to deal with offenses like the failure to report for duty on time, underage drinking, a disrespectful comment, or the failure to be in the appropriate uniform. Minor misconduct does not normally lead to court-martial or even less formal administrative sanctions. The six command options below describe progressively severe forms of administrative action commonly used by commanders. Commanders can impose multiple options simultaneously.

[1] In 2013, through the 2014 National Defense Authorization Act, Congress fundamentally altered the commander's clemency powers in the face of outrage over an Air Force General's decision to reverse a military jury's conviction of an officer for the crime of rape (Simms, 2014). Scrutiny over command discretion led to new standards mandating special procedures in sexual assault cases and stripping commanders of post-conviction clemency in serious cases (National Defense Authorization Act of 2014, 2013).

Written Counseling

The first step along the continuum of military discipline is a written counseling statement in which a responsible leader gives the service member an opportunity to respond, identifies a plan to address the behavior, and warns the service member about the potential consequences of military misconduct (e.g., U.S. Department of Army, 2014, p. 1–2 ¶ 1–7). The language below is a representative counseling template, which may vary based upon the Service and the counselor:

> You are being counseled for the above indicated misconduct and/or unsatisfactory duty performance IAW AR 635-200, 1-16b. Continued behavior of this kind may result in initiation of separation action to eliminate you from the Army or non-judicial punishment. Any further acts of misconduct or unsatisfactory performance may cause you to be eliminated without further counseling. If you are administratively separated from the Army, you could receive an Honorable (HON), General Under Honorable (GEN) or an Other Than Honorable (OTH) Conditions Discharge. Any less than Honorable discharge could deprive you of many or all military and Veterans Administration (VA) benefits including loss of both education benefits and civil service retirement credit. A negative characterization of your service can have lasting negative impact on future civilian employment. Should you receive a discharge less favorable than Honorable you may apply to have your characterization of service upgraded by the Army Board for the Correction of Military Records and/or the Army Discharge Review Board (Army Writer, n.d.)

In some cases, such as the service member who has engaged in multiple instances of misconduct, regulations may require notice and the opportunity to correct one's deficiencies prior to involuntary separation. Commanders have different ways of documenting counseling, but such statements usually record the bases that later result in administrative or judicial action. Beyond the written counseling, leaders can require the service member to take corrective action at the individual level.

Corrective Training

Commanders can deter unwanted behavior by assigning corrective training. The classic example might be to assign push-ups or other physical exercises as an "on-the-spot" correction for an infraction. While this is common practice in basic training environments, regulations emphasize the importance of tailoring the corrective training to a specific deficiency. For example, a service member who fails to show up on time to morning training may be required to write an essay about the importance of showing up to work on time and then report to scheduled formations a half-hour early for a week. Whatever the form, corrective training aims "to correct a deficiency in the servicemember's ability to perform the mission" (Gilligan & Lederer, 2017, § 3-20.00).

Letters of Reprimand

Commanders can recommend or issue written reprimands, normally signed by a general officer. This officer can file the letter in the service member's official military personnel file, where it will follow the individual throughout his or her career, or in the local file, which is normally destroyed upon the service member's departure to a new command. The Manual for Court-Martial recognizes that such reprimands are "corrective," rather than "punitive" measures (Department of Defense, 2012, Part V, p. 1g). Issuance of a General Officer Memorandum/Letter of Reprimand ("GOMOR") usually marks the end of one's military career and may trigger administrative separation (Bojan, 2016). Commanders often have policies that mandate the issuance of a GOMOR, such as an arrest for driving under the influence on or off the military installation, or negligently discharging a firearm either in training or a combat setting. While service members may submit rebuttal matters prior to the filing determination in support of a request for local filing, governing standards will support official filing in all but the rarest of circumstances, such as demonstrably false statements in the memorandum (Bojan, 2016).

Nonjudicial Punishment

Commanders can also impose nonjudicial punishment (NJP) under Article 15 of the Uniform Code of Military Justice (10 U.S.C. § 815). In these more formal proceedings, the commander advises the service member that there is enough evidence to bring charges at a court-martial and the service member will agree to participate in the proceedings or reject the administrative punishment and demand a court-martial. During Article 15 proceedings, the imposing commander presides and holds a hearing to determine the issue of guilt and punishment, including reduction of rank, fines, and restrictions on one's liberty but nothing approaching a federal conviction or imprisonment (Gilligan & Lederer, 2017).[2] Many service members elect the administrative process to avoid the possibility of court-martial and a federal conviction. A service member electing NJP can ask for a hearing on the merits of the charges or plead guilty. While he or she may normally consult with a military attorney to review the strength of the case, there is no right to representation from a military lawyer at the NJP proceedings.

Even though the military generally considers NJP appropriate for minor offenses (Gilligan & Lederer, 2017), these proceedings can have lasting consequences. Officially filed NJP records often lead to non-selection for promotion or the initiation

[2] The severity of punishment depends on the level of NJP and the recipient's rank, with a summary court-martial imposing the least punishment and a General Officer Article 15 imposing the greatest punishment (Article 15, Uniform Code of Military Justice).

of involuntary separation proceedings. Very often, commanders will issue a punishment, such as rank reduction or a fine, and immediately suspend the punishment, providing an incentive for the NJP recipient to improve his or her performance. Suspensions can be removed (vacated) for future acts of misconduct, leaving the service member with the original punishment and exposure to additional NJP for the more recent misconduct.

Summary Courts-Martial

The Summary Court-Martial is the least severe form of court-martial (compared to the Special and General Court-Martial). A Summary Court-Martial does not result in a federal conviction, even if the hearing officer finds the service member guilty of certain offenses. The proceeding is administrative, as opposed to punitive, because the authorized punishment at this low level cannot include any type of discharge from the Service. A punitive discharge is only available when the law authorizes discharge as a lawful punishment for a conviction. Even with these limitations in mind, the Summary Court-Martial represents the most aggressive form of administrative discipline short of being kicked out of the military (10 U.S.C. § 820).[3] As one of several other limitations, lower ranking service members may be exposed to 30 days' confinement and reduction in rank, which exceed the maximum punishment authorized at NJP proceedings.

Because the stakes are lower than a punitive court-martial, the accused has fewer rights at a Summary Court-Martial. The service member is not eligible for representation from a military attorney during the hearing proceedings and he or she is not entitled to the fact-finding of a military judge. Instead, a non-lawyer officer is usually appointed to find facts and adjudge punishment with the aid of an advising attorney. This officer acts "as judge, factfinder, prosecutor, and defense counsel" (*Middendorf v. Henry*, 1976, p. 32). For a number of reasons, including conservation of time and resources, a commander might choose a summary court-martial followed by an administrative separation, rather than a court-martial. The commander may desire the deterrent effect of sending the offender to jail in shackles closer to the time of his or her offense, rather than waiting for many months of proceedings that are required for a special or general court-martial.

[3]The U.S. Supreme Court has observed that the Summary Court-Martial "occupies a position between informal nonjudicial disposition under Article 15 and the courtroom type procedure of the general and special courts-martial" (Middendorf v. Henry, 1976, p. 32).

Administrative Separation Proceedings

The administrative separation (ADSEP) proceeding is the military's method of terminating a service member's military status prior to the completion of a contractual term of enlistment. Although some service members request ADSEPs for a host of reasons, commanders can involuntarily separate a service member based upon civilian or military misconduct. Not all service members have the right to a hearing when the command initiates involuntary separation. Moreover, many who have the right to a hearing do not exercise the right.

Separation proceedings have evolved over time since their origin in the 1800s (Sandel, 1984). First, a board of leaders will hear the facts and circumstances and determine whether the service member committed the alleged misconduct. Second, the board members will determine whether the misconduct should result in involuntary separation and a specific type of discharge classification (e.g., Honorable, General, or Other-Than Honorable (OTH)). The administrative nature of these proceedings signifies that the discharge from such proceedings was not supposed to be considered as punishment.

Despite this purely administrative nature, any discharge prior to the completion of one's service brings some degree of stigma in society because it reveals that the military deemed the service member as unfit for military service (Sandel, 1984). The military's own standards recognize the gravity of this consequence by according service members the right to defend against an involuntary separation at an official hearing as long as the service member has 6 or more years of prior service in the military or has been recommended for a discharge that could lead to an OTH characterization.

Aside from recent requirements mandating OTH discharges at administrative separation proceedings related to sexual offenses, not all involuntary separations can or must lead to a bad paper discharge. For example, when the military discharges a service member solely on the basis of unsatisfactory performance or failing to meet the standards required of a soldier, sailor, airman, or marine, the service member will receive a fully honorable discharge if the board votes for separation. Presently, bad paper discharges are reserved for acts of misconduct or are given in lieu of trial by court-martial (U.S. Department of Defense, 2017).

Discharge Characterizations at Administrative Separation Proceedings

Honorable Discharge

Modernly, there are three types of administrative discharge: Honorable, General, and OTH (formerly known as Undesirable until the mid-70s). The Honorable Discharge represents the best characterization and the greatest number of discharges among veterans—usually over 90% (Legal Services Center, 2016). While this discharge does not indicate perfect performance, it means that "the quality of the ... Service member's service generally has met the standards of acceptable conduct and performance of duty for military personnel, or is otherwise so meritorious that any other characterization would be clearly inappropriate" (Department of Defense, 2017, Enclosure 4, p. 30 ¶ 3.b(2)(a)).

General Under Honorable Conditions Discharge

The General Discharge represents a discharge under honorable conditions, which is not as meritorious as an Honorable Discharge. The Department of Defense Directive on administrative separations explains that the General Discharge denotes "service that is honest and faithful ... when the positive aspects of the enlisted Service member's conduct or performance of duty outweigh negative aspects of the enlisted Service member's conduct or performance of duty as documented in their service record" (Department of Defense, 2017, Enclosure 4, p. 30 ¶ 3.b(2)(b)). The biggest consequence of a General Discharge is ineligibility for G.I. Bill educational benefits. Aside from this limitation, the General Discharge still permits a recipient to enjoy the same host of veterans' benefits that are available to the recipient of an Honorable Discharge. Despite eligibility for almost all veteran rights and privileges, anything besides Honorable brings stigma, as the District of Columbia Circuit Court of Appeals observed:

> Job application forms almost universally require a statement as to military service and the type of discharge received; since about ninety per cent of the discharges issued are honorable, disclosure of discharge in any other form is ordinarily certain to produce further inquiry with predicable results (*Bland v. Connally*, 1961, p. 858 n.10)

Courts have routinely declined to find the same type of stigma from a General Discharge as an OTH.

Undesirable and Other-Than-Honorable Discharges

The Other-Than-Honorable Discharge began with the name "Undesirable." The military changed the name and the corresponding certificate in 1977 (Editorial, 1977, p. 52; Egeland, 1977, p. 198). The current Department of Defense Directive on administrative separations authorizes an OTH under two circumstances: when (1) a pattern of behavior or (2) one or more acts or omissions "constitute a significant departure from the conduct expected of enlisted Service members of the Military Services" (Department of Defense, 2017, Enclosure 4, pp. 30–31 ¶¶ 2c(1)(a)–(b)). The Directive provides examples of specific factors surrounding conduct including,

> use of force or violence to produce bodily injury or death; abuse of a special position of trust; disregard by a superior of customary superior-subordinate relationships; acts or omissions that endanger the security of the United States or health and welfare of other Service members of the Military Services; and deliberate acts or omissions that seriously endanger the health and safety of other persons (Department of Defense, 2017, Enclosure 4, p. 31 ¶2c(1)(b))

In light of widespread decriminalization of possession of small amounts of marijuana, officials in the Department of Defense have questioned whether this offense should result in an OTH (e.g., Kurta, 2017).

Troubling studies reporting increased OTH discharges among veterans diagnosed with service-connected mental health conditions (Legal Services Center, 2016; U.S. Government Accountability Office, 2017) have led the DoD to revise the administrative discharge process because of post-service consequences. This seriousness is evident in the requirement that any service member who faces the possibility of an OTH discharge has the choice to demand that his or her case be heard by a separation board. Practical consequences of the OTH discharge is automatic reduction of the service member's rank to the lowest enlisted grade, E-1, eviscerating any benefits that would have accumulated due to seniority, elimination of all accrued leave, termination of the ability to have one's goods shipped home, and loss of the right to even wear the uniform on special occasions.

Additionally, the OTH will prevent a veteran from receiving veterans preference for public sector hiring determinations, could result in the loss of naturalization for immigrant veterans, and may prevent licensure or bonding in a given professional field. These significant consequences have remained relatively unchanged through the decades (Brooker et al., 2012; Doan, 1976; Effron, 1974; Jones, 1973). Given the potential consequences of an OTH, commanders can normally recommend an OTH only if the underlying offense would have made the service member eligible for a punitive discharge at a court-martial (Department of Defense, 2017). An exception to this rule is the cumulative effect of an ongoing pattern of minor misconduct over a period of time that would warrant an OTH.

The Service Member's Rights When Facing Involuntary Administrative Separation

Most service members recommended for involuntary separation have the right to consult with military attorneys in deciding whether to demand or waive board proceedings. Since Vietnam, the military has realized that administrative separations can be cost and time saving over pursuing charges at a court-martial (Brooker et al., 2012). Compared with courts-martial, administrative separation proceedings offer service members fewer rights and procedural protections. For example, the rules of evidence do not apply, permitting written statements without the need to bring witnesses. Also, the standard of proof is preponderance of the evidence—more likely than not—rather than beyond a reasonable doubt (Irwin, 2017). In many cases, evidence obtained in violation of one's rights may still be admissible at a separation proceeding even if it would have been barred by rules of evidence in a court-martial (Irwin, 2017).

After media and government investigations and reports, the military recognized that military misconduct may be related to a service member's military trauma (Seamone et al., 2017). Starting in 2009, Congress responded to significant numbers of service members separated with OTH discharges after having been diagnosed with PTSD. The legislation instituted a requirement to determine whether the service member had been diagnosed with PTSD or Traumatic Brain Injury (TBI) after having deployed in support of a contingency operation (deployed to a warzone) within the last 24 months prior to the separation proceedings (10 U.S.C. § 1177, P. L. 111–84). In such cases, commanders must evaluate whether there is a relationship between the mental health condition and the underlying misconduct that forms the basis of the discharge.

This provision does not divest commanders of their ample discretion. Even when a service member's PTSD or TBI did contribute to the misconduct, a commander may still elect to continue with the separation and the law requires only that he or she *consider* such information. However, it is an important difference. In 2016, Congress further imposed a new requirement to evaluate whether the subject of a proposed separation was a victim of Military Sexual Trauma (MST) and had made an unrestricted report of the assault within 24 months of the separation proceedings (10 U.S.C. § 1177, P. L. 114–328). Like a diagnosis of deployment-related PTSD, the commander is merely required to *consider* evidence of a nexus and is not prohibited from instituting a separation with an OTH.

Despite these standards, a comprehensive study published by the Government Accountability Office in 2017 revealed that, "the Army and Marine Corps may not have adhered to their own screening, training, and counseling policies relating to PTSD and TBI" (U.S. Government Accountability Office, 2017, Executive Summary). The same study described other significant shortfalls in Air Force and Navy practices.

Trial by Courts-Martial

Unlike administrative proceedings, courts-martial permit a military judge or military panel (jury) to make separation from the Service part of one's punishment for violating the law. The power to punish is limited by the type of court-martial ordered by the commander. Military courts-martial are unlike civilian criminal trials (Seamone, 2011). Not only does the military eschew distinctions between misdemeanors and felonies, military jury verdicts need not be unanimous. Unlike the civilian sector, military judges are not permanently sitting in a single place with the ability to revisit a given case. Instead, the court-martial is a temporary court that exists only long enough to determine guilt or innocence and then, once guilt is established, to determine a punishment (Seamone, 2011).

A service member facing a court-martial has the right to request a hearing by a military judge alone or by a military jury (a "panel"). If the service member elects a hearing by panel, the panel, and not the military judge, will determine the sentence for the service member. A service member cannot switch from jury to judge alone after guilt has been established. While civilian juries are drawn from a large pool of one's peers, military juries are made up of military members, usually assigned to the same base or installation, but not within one's immediate command. The general who ordered the court-martial into existence essentially picks the members of the jury based on a host of factors including the candidate's maturity and experience.

Military courts give accused service members special rights during jury selection based upon the unique manner in which a general selects the panel. The defense may strike one potential military juror for any reason and any number of jurors for cause. Beyond this, under the "liberal grant mandate," the defense may challenge juries for implied bias, i.e., where an outside observer would have reason to doubt the reliability of the proceedings (*United States v. Smart*, 1985). The military courts liberally apply this rule in recognition that the commander who convened the court-martial gets an unlimited number of challenges based on the members he or she eventually recommends for the venire. If the service member is enlisted, he or she has a right to request a panel composed of one-third enlisted members or to request a panel of all officer members.

Courts-martial are distinct from civilian trials in other important ways. Because the court-martial only exists for a limited time, military trials normally transition directly from the verdict on the merits to sentencing without the traditional delay present in civilian criminal cases (Seamone, 2011). Probation is not permitted as part of the sentence of a court-martial, even when a judge or panel members recommend suspension of an adjudged punishment (Seamone, 2011). The main reason why there is no military probation is the inability of a judge to revisit a case after sentencing. While military juries often ask if they can adjudge an administrative discharge rather than a punitive discharge, this too is not an option. A panel can either adjudge no punitive discharge, allowing the service member to be retained in the service, or the panel can adjudge a punitive discharge if permitted (Seamone, 2011). Judges routinely instruct military jurors that they should not attempt to anticipate what a commander or the military service might do following their verdict. So, for example, even if a commander plans to administratively separate the service member upon retention by the panel, the panel should not anticipate that the command will actually take these steps when fashioning its sentence (Seamone, 2011).

Punitive discharges generally bar many or *all* of the benefits administered by the VA. Like the administrative OTH, a punitive discharge can create substantial hardships in civilian life (Brooker et al., 2012). Accordingly, the military judge will advise the panel of the following information before they deliberate on a sentence: "This court may adjudge either a dishonorable discharge or a bad-conduct discharge. Such a discharge deprives one of substantially all benefits administered by the Department of Veterans Affairs and the Army establishment" (U.S. Department of Army, 2010, p. 99).

The Special Court-Martial and the more severe General Court-Martial are the only courts empowered to adjudge a punitive discharge. The Special Court-Martial has limitations on punishment with possible confinement capped at 12 months, a reduction to the lowest enlisted grade, and forfeiture of 2/3 pay per month for 12 months. While a Special Court-Martial can result in a Bad-Conduct Discharge, it cannot result in a Dishonorable Discharge. Military officers may not be discharged by a Special Court-Martial and must be tried by a General Court-Martial to be punitively separated. At a General Court-Martial, officers are subject to Dismissal, which is the equivalent of a Dishonorable Discharge (Brooker et al., 2012).

The Special Court-Martial does not require preliminary investigation of the charges and may proceed faster than a General Court-Martial. While there is lack of clarity on the difference between a Bad-Conduct Discharge and a Dishonorable Discharge, the Bad-Conduct Discharge is recognized as: "a severe punishment, although less severe than a dishonorable discharge, and may be adjudged for one who, in the discretion of the court, warrants severe punishment for bad conduct" (Department of Army, 2010, p. 1068 ¶ 8-3-25). The more severe Dishonorable Discharge is "reserved for those who, in the opinion of the court should be separated under conditions of dishonor after conviction of serious offenses of a civil or military nature warranting such punishment" (Department of Army, 2010, p. 1068 ¶ 8-3-24). Since June 24, 2014, as a result of efforts to increase the severity of punishments for sex offenses, any conviction relating to sex offense at a court-martial automatically results in a Dishonorable Discharge (2014 National Defense Authorization Act of 2014, 2013 §1705).

A General-Court Martial removes the sentencing limitation on Special Courts-Martial, exposing offenders to sentences greater than a year, a Dishonorable Discharge, and total forfeitures of pay and allowances. While there is no grand jury in the military, the Uniform Code of Military Justice requires a preliminary investigation of all charges before a General Court-Martial can take place (Gilligan & Lederer, 2017). Unless the accused service member waives such proceedings, an Article 32 Investigating Officer, who may be a military lawyer, will conduct an inquiry to determine whether there is evidence to support the charges and whether the charges accurately reflect the nature of the offenses. The Article 32 Investigating Officer may recommend that the charges be sent to a different, less severe, forum than a General Court-Martial. However, the general who ordered the court-martial is not obligated to adopt the Article 32 Investigating Officer's recommendations (Gilligan & Lederer, 2017).

When charges are serious, it may take months—or even years—before a court-martial takes place. During this time, the command is responsible for paying for experts out of the unit's operational funds. The command must also pay for production of witnesses, including travel from remote locations or combat zones to testify in person. Contemporary scholarship suggests that military defendants are often able to avoid court-martial in combat zones by making the process of investigating the charges and seating a panel too demanding to simultaneously meet mission requirements (Rosenblatt, 2010).

Whether it is the sheer expense of conducting a court-martial or the nuisance of removing senior leaders from their duties to serve as military jurors, the military has decreased its use of courts-martial as the Global War on Terror progressed. What trials do occur usually involve the prosecution of sexual offenses or homicides. Whereas the military services conducted 4350 courts-martial empowered to punitively discharge accused service members in Fiscal Year 2003 (U.S. Court of Appeals for the Armed Forces, 2003), by Fiscal Year 2011, they convened nearly half the number at 2351—just more than half (U.S. Court of Appeals for the Armed Forces, 2011). Meanwhile, the number of administrative discharges for misconduct has increased exponentially (Legal Services Center, 2016). Between 2011 and 2015 alone, the military branches 91,764 service members for misconduct (Government Accountability Office, 2017, Executive Summary).

Following the sentence of a court-martial, if the military member received a punitive discharge or 1 year or more of confinement, he or she is entitled to automatic appellate review by a military court, though a service member can waive review (Baker, 2014). Each Service has its own appellate courts, presided over by active duty military judges. Beyond that first level of appellate review, some cases may be suitable for review by the military's highest court, the Court of Appeals for the Armed Forces, which is presided over by civilian judges who are appointed to multi-year terms by the President. Final review is available at the U.S. Supreme Court, though rarely do military cases get heard there. Because a service member is permitted to have attorney representation at a court-martial, it is rare that a military review board will grant relief that was not provided through the military's own legal process.

Five Major Reasons to Identify Incarcerated Veterans with "Bad Paper" and Empower Them to Upgrade Discharges as Early as Possible

Five justifications support the identification of incarcerated veterans with bad paper and efforts to assist them in obtaining upgrades or benefits. First, a veteran may be incarcerated because a Veterans Treatment Court program deemed the veteran ineligible to participate specifically due to his or her bad paper. Second, an upgrade to one's discharge may open the door to the receipt of benefits that increase the chances of successful re-entry and decrease criminal recidivism. Third, the military discharge may have been a byproduct of the veteran's loyal and faithful military service rather than intentional decisions to violate the law. Fourth, new DoD guidance on discharge upgrading has improved the chances of upgrading success for those veterans most in need of continued mental health care. Finally, veterans with bad paper can use their confinement time to maximize the chances of discharge upgrading success.

Bad Paper as the Basis for Incarceration

Incarcerated veterans are more likely to have bad paper discharges than their non-incarcerated veteran peers (e.g., Brignone et al., 2017). This increased likelihood of incarceration is explained, in part, by the consequences of bad paper, which have limited recipients' success in the civilian community following discharge from the Armed Forces. Studies consistently reveal that bad paper increases the chances of mental health and substance use disorders, homelessness, criminal involvement and incarceration, and suicide (Brignone et al., 2017). On average, 20% of justice-involved veterans tracked by the VA are ineligible for VA benefits as a result of their military discharge characterization (Rosenthal & McGuire, 2013). In some incarcerated settings, the majority of inmates with military experience have bad paper discharges (Schwartz & Levitas, 2011, p. 53).

Benefit ineligibility as a result of bad paper can have a direct impact on eligibility for programs that divert veterans from confinement to treatment. The purpose of Veterans Treatment Courts is "*de*carceration"—to avoid incarceration and provide superior mental health treatment over community resources for non-veterans (McLoed, 2012, pp. 1590–1591). A major lesson from the development and growth of Veterans Treatment Courts is that they are built upon the foundation of VA treatment resources and entitlements (Blue-Howells, Clark, Berk-Clark, & McGuire, 2012). When veterans are ineligible for VA services, this impairs the ability to provide high quality services and may be the factor that results in a veteran's ineligibility.

While Veterans Treatment Courts have varied participation criteria depending upon a host of program-specific factors, in a recent study of 114 Veterans Treatment Courts, over 35% of programs excluded participants with dishonorable discharges. Further, nearly a quarter excluded recipients of BCDs, and 24.1% of the of the programs barred enrollment of veterans who did not qualify for VA benefits based on their discharges (Baldwin, 2016, p. 723). With these considerations in mind, it would be advantageous to identify incarcerated veterans with bad paper and enable them to obtain discharge upgrades as a method to broaden their eligibility for alternatives to incarceration.

In considering questions of eligibility, veterans often have multiple discharges from their time in service. The VA is required to honor prior periods of successfully completed service. If a veteran obtained an Honorable Discharge for the first term and an OTH for the second, the first discharge may qualify the veteran for VA services despite the later OTH (Brooker et al., 2012). The VA could grant treatment for any service-related conditions that occurred during the honorable period of service and then deny treatment for injuries that arose from the subsequent period of service. Thus, it is wise to review all prior periods of military service to determine eligibility for VA benefits and potential enrollment in diversion programs.

The VA's Character of Discharge Review Process

Veterans with bad paper are limited in receipt of various state and federal benefits, not simply VA benefits (Brooker et al., 2012). If a veteran desires eligibility for all types of benefits that depend upon discharge characterization, he or she may petition for a discharge upgrade with the secretary of his or her Service. An upgrade to General or Honorable Discharge will be binding on the VA for the purpose of benefit eligibility (Brooker et al., 2012).

Separate from the military review boards' upgrading process, the VA has its own process for evaluating bad paper discharges to determine VA benefit eligibility. Often, VA employees will recommend that veterans apply for secretarial upgrades prior to applying for VA benefits. Such advice is misleading to the extent that it ignores other procedures (Adams & Montalto, 2017; Legal Services Center, 2016). Discharge upgrades are not the exclusive avenue for obtaining VA benefits notwithstanding bad paper. It is possible for the VA to grant VA benefits to the recipient of bad paper who is unsuccessful in obtaining a discharge upgrade. In fact, some veterans with OTHs are receiving disability compensation because the VA deemed their service to be sufficiently honorable.

According to the VA, a veteran must have a discharge that is "under conditions other than dishonorable" (38 U.S.C. § 101(2)). Since 1944s passage of the Servicemen's Readjustment Act, the VA has operated a distinct "Character of Discharge" evaluation process to address this standard (Brooker et al., 2012). Notably, the VA uses different definitions and concepts than DoD and "conditions other than dishonorable" is not solely limited to a Dishonorable Discharge. When a former-service member with bad paper requests VA services or benefits, VA adjudicators should consider a number of vague regulations and statutes to determine whether he or she had a military term that can be characterized as conditions other than dishonorable.

The statute 38 U.S.C. § 5303(a) provides a number of *statutory bars* to VA benefits that will disqualify an ex-service member from benefits. One notable example of a statutory bar is the recipient of any punitive discharge resulting from a General Court-Martial. Beyond this, the Code of Federal Regulations also contains VA's own administrative guidance adding distinct *regulatory bars* to the analysis (38 C.F.R. § 3.12(d)). A common regulatory bar is the service member who accepts an Undesirable Discharge in lieu of a General Court-Martial. A detailed description of the COD process and its factors would require more pages than this entire volume. The major difficulty with VA's COD process is lack of consistent and uniform standards across regional offices with inconsistent outcomes for similarly situated applicants (Brooker et al., 2012). Although precise numbers are hard to find, it is generally the case that an applicant is more likely to be denied VA benefits through the COD process (Brooker et al., 2012; Legal Services Center, 2016). Corrections professionals should know that the VA process offers another opportunity for veterans to obtain VA benefits, even if they have been denied upgrades by the military review boards.

The VA's COD process may take months or years to complete, raising questions about the nature of services that these veterans can receive while they wait. The need for more immediate access to healthcare has resulted in special rules providing limited access to mental health treatment for purposes of emergency stabilization. In 2017, the VA Secretary liberalized eligibility rules after he learned of the VA's refusal to provide mental health services to veterans at risk of suicide based on OTH discharge characterizations. The new standard, effective June 5, 2017, permitted VA Medical Centers to provide emergency stabilization healthcare to OTH recipients in order to encourage these veterans to seek necessary services and to prevent suicide (U.S. Department of Veterans Affairs, 2017). The policy only applies to temporary care for mental health emergencies and may do little to impact chronic homelessness or physical health conditions among less-than-honorably discharged veterans.

Because the VA's emergency stabilization policy does not actually ensure long-term mental health recovery, in 2018, Congress passed the Honor Our Commitment Act to extend mental health care beyond 90 days in some cases (Press Release, 2018). Qualifying veterans must have experienced sexual victimization, served in a combat or hostile fire zone, been involved in drone operations in combat environments (Press Release, 2018). Similar to emergency stabilization benefits, the legislation is limited to mental health conditions and does not provide care for physical injuries or disability compensation.

Another alternative for OTH recipients is mental health treatment at Vet Centers for combat veterans, survivors of MST, those in need of bereavement services, and drone crew members (U.S. Department of Veterans Affairs, n.d.). Vet Centers operate in locations apart from VA Medical Centers. They were established by Congress to assist Vietnam Veterans and others with alternatives to traditional VA treatment. Vet Centers are unique in the way they also provide family counseling for family members of qualifying veterans.

Discharge Upgrades as the Means to Obtain VA Benefits

As an alternative to the VA COD process, military discharge review boards provide an additional method for bad paper veterans to upgrade their discharges. Beyond giving criminally-involved veterans better chances for diversion from incarceration, discharge upgrades can provide several other federal and state benefits that can increase the chances of successful re-entry and decrease criminal recidivism. Military review boards bring the benefit of more objective guidance. If the incarcerated veteran was discharged within 15 years, he or she can appeal to the appropriate discharge review board (10 U.S.C. § 1553). If more than 15 years have passed since the discharge, the veteran must apply to a different board of correction for records for that service (10 U.S.C. § 1552). These bodies exist to determine whether legal errors impacted the separation process or whether equitable considerations favor upgrading the discharge (Connecticut Veterans Legal Center, 2011). For veterans who had mental health conditions at the time of the commission of the underlying offenses that led to their discharges, the recent Kurta (2017), discussed below, offers new hope for upgrading success.

Discharges Due to Consequences of Faithful Military Service

To understand the impact of military discharges, it is necessary to appreciate the context from which they originate: military discipline, which has no analogue in civilian society or the civilian criminal justice system. It is also vital to understand the unique and disproportionate manner in which military discipline has criminalized the very symptoms of mental illness that can be expected as operational hazards of military service (Seamone, 2013; Seamone et al., 2014, 2017). Because military discipline is essential in the Armed Forces, there is a tendency to demonize those who detract from it. Service members who use narcotics are seen as selfish individuals who would rather serve themselves than their peers. Yet, not all military offenses have their genesis in willful misconduct by service members who decided to place their needs over the military's. In many cases, service members get caught up in the military justice and disciplinary system as a result of behavior that represents symptoms of untreated service-related mental health conditions (Seamone, 2011, 2013; Seamone et al., 2014, 2017). The American Psychiatric Association developed a diagram of the Veteran's Brain, below, to highlight the cumulative risks of mental health conditions facing today's military veterans:

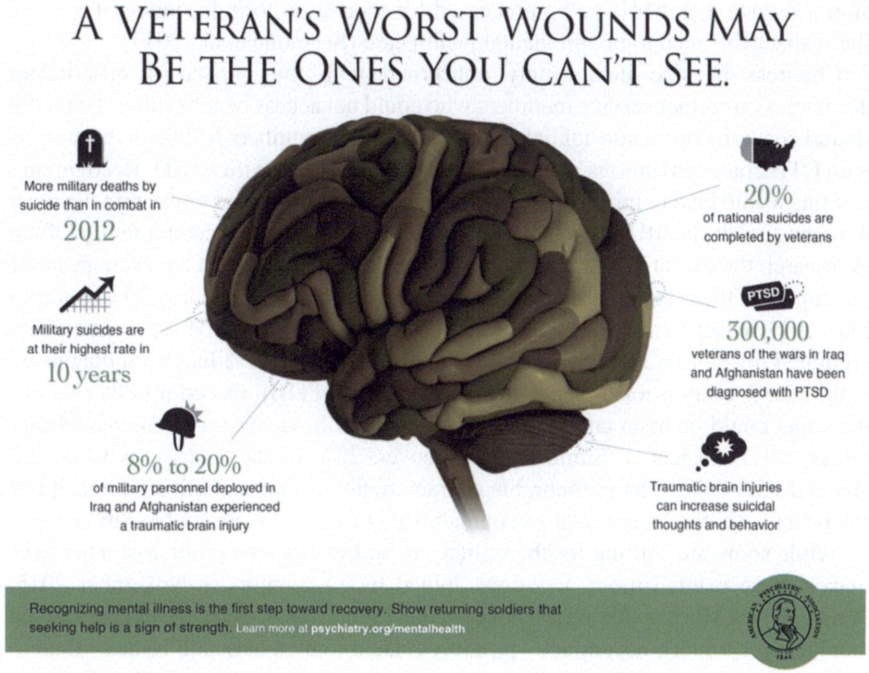

(American Psychiatric Association, 2013). As depicted above, combat trauma can result in a variety of conditions—aside from PTSD, TBI, and Major Depression—that result in maladaptive behaviors, including subthreshold PTSD and moral injury (Brooker et al., 2012; Seamone, 2011, 2013).

The military now formally acknowledges the impact of mental health conditions on behavior. In the current era, Army Manuals on combat stress began to identify a distinct form of "misconduct stress behaviors," which were acts of misconduct that are directly attributable to the stressful environments in combat (Brooker et al., 2012; Seamone, 2013). Interestingly, the same manuals acknowledged that service members could actually transport those behaviors home following combat and continue to engage in misconduct (Seamone, 2013). Misconduct stress is somewhat predictable as a result of experiences which may include the act of killing, feelings of tremendous guilt for wounded or killed comrades, or perceptions of having to violate one's own moral code (Brooker et al., 2012; Seamone, 2013). Strong and pervasive stigmas prevent those impacted by misconduct stress from requesting assistance (Seamone, 2013).

Military members are governed by a set of special rules that make them more likely to be considered criminal offenders when they experience such symptoms. Whereas a civilian employee might be fired for failing to come to work on time or having an angry outburst at a demanding boss, a military member could face significant penalties, including punitive discharge and years of confinement (Seamone, 2013; Seamone et al., 2014). Given the reluctance to seek help until it is too late, many describe a "military misconduct catch-22" phenomenon in which it is only after a service member is being processed for separation for misconduct that he or she realizes the need to obtain mental health care (Seamone et al., 2017).

Congress became increasingly concerned with the impact of misconduct discharges on former service members who could not access benefits after the media shared concerns that a substantial number of service members had been discharged with OTH characterizations after they had been diagnosed with PTSD. Recognizing that this would lead to initial exclusion from healthcare amongst those with the most desperate needs, in 2014, Congress requested the Government Accountability Office to research the extent of the problem and whether commanders were even aware of the impact of their disciplinary decisions on service members' futures. The resulting May 2017 report found that "62 percent, or 57,141 of the 91,764 servicemembers separated for misconduct from fiscal years 2011 through 2015 had been diagnosed within the 2 years prior to separation with [PTSD], [TBI], or certain other conditions that could be associated with misconduct" (U.S. Government Accountability Office, 2017, Executive Summary). Moreover, 23% of these veterans were discharged with Other-Than-Honorable characterizations that imperiled the receipt of VA benefits (U.S. Government Accountability Office, 2017, Executive Summary).

While some are waiting for the military to address its own problems, other lawmakers have exerted more pressures. Joined by 11 senators in November 2015, Senator Chris Murphy voiced the concern that "it may be easier to discharge service members for minor misconduct—possibly related to mental health issues—than to evaluate them for conditions that may warrant a medical discharge" (Murphy et al., 2015). Later, in February 2016, he and three other senators called for the Army to impose a moratorium on OTH discharges for military members with mental illness until more reliable standards could be established (Zwerdling & De Yoanna, 2016).

In June 2017, Defense Undersecretary Kurta provided the clearest guidance yet for the manner to evaluate discharges in cases involving underlying mental health conditions. On balance, the increasing recognition of the nexus between faithful military service, combat trauma, and misconduct stress raises the very real possibility that an incarcerated veteran's bad paper discharge may simply reflect the fact that he or she did not have the opportunity to obtain necessary or effective treatment for service-connected trauma. As emphasized elsewhere in this volume, many Veterans Treatment Courts and Specialized Housing Units for incarcerated veterans recognize the importance of diversion opportunities on the basis of treatment needs (see also Blue-Howells et al., 2012). The same rationale would support opportunities to upgrade discharges.

The Game-Changing Kurta Memorandum

August 2017 marked a watershed moment in discharge upgrading: the articulation of specific standards to upgrade discharges based on mitigating factors related to MST, sexual harassment, PTSD, TBI, and other "mental health conditions" (Kurta, 2017). The Kurta Memorandum would not exist without prior efforts to encourage discharge review boards and boards of correction to consider mitigating factors.

Most notably, in 2014, then-Defense Secretary Chuck Hagel issued a memorandum in response to widespread criticisms and a lawsuit highlighting how Vietnam veterans with PTSD were routinely denied discharge upgrades even when their discharges stemmed from the symptoms of untreated service-related trauma (Veterans Legal Services Clinic, 2015). For example, Secretary Hagel underscored how military records from periods before PTSD was officially recognized by the psychiatric profession often lack "substantive information concerning medical conditions" (Hagel, 2014, p. 1). Accordingly, he stressed that review boards should give "special consideration" to post-service diagnoses of PTSD by the VA and liberal consideration to any service-related records revealing "one or more symptoms" associated with a PTSD diagnosis (Hagel, 2014, Attachment p. 1). Despite this new guidance, the boards continued to deny upgrade requests, even in cases that appeared to be on all fours with the mitigating factors Secretary Hagel articulated.

In 2016, the Acting Principal Deputy Under Secretary of Defense, Brad Carson, issued guidance to supplement the Hagel Memorandum clarifying that Hagel's guidance "remaine[d] exceptionally important" and that the boards "must renew and re-double … efforts" to ensure that applicants received the benefits of such guidance. Carson's memorandum underscored that applicants whose petitions were denied without the benefit of such guidance should have the chance to reapply under the new standards and further that the Boards of Correction should waive bars to their consideration of such petitions (Carson, 2016, p. 1). Yet, widespread denial rates persisted.

In an unexpected but extremely helpful move, Undersecretary Kurta's memorandum provides new hope for veterans hoping to upgrade discharges, specifically for the purpose of obtaining needed healthcare benefits from the VA. The full five-page Kurta Memorandum is reprinted at Appendix 1. For the purposes of this chapter, six of its revelations provide guidance that can substantially increase the chances of success in discharge upgrading petitions. First, the Kurta Memorandum recognizes that:

> Invisible wounds … are some of the most difficult cases to review and there are frequently limited records for the boards to consider. [The boards] should rightfully consider the unique nature of these cases and afford each veteran a reasonable opportunity for relief even if the sexual assault or sexual harassment was unreported, or the mental health condition was not diagnosed until years later (Kurta, 2017, p. 1)

Second, consistent with the theory of misconduct stress behavior, the Kurta Memorandum highlights the fact that "[e]vidence of misconduct, including any misconduct underlying a veteran's discharge, may be evidence of a mental health condition, including PTSD; TBI; or of behavior consistent with experiencing sexual assault or sexual harassment" (Kurta, 2017, Attachment p. 1 ¶ 6). Third, the Memorandum explains that "[e]vidence that may reasonably support more than one diagnosis should be liberally considered as supporting a diagnosis, where applicable, that could excuse or mitigate the discharge" (Kurta, 2017, Attachment p. 2 ¶ 10).

Fourth, with regard to mental health conditions, those "that may reasonably have existed at the time of discharge will be liberally considered as excusing or mitigating the discharge" (Kurta, 2017, Attachment p. 2 ¶ 16). Fifth, in applying the concept of "liberal consideration," the Kurta Memorandum notes that "[i]t is unreasonable to expect the same level of proof for injustices committed years ago when TBI; mental health conditions, such as PTSD; and victimology were far less understood than they are today" (Kurta, 2017, Attachment p. 3 ¶ 26.b). Finally, the Memorandum clarifies the scope of an Honorable Discharge by explaining, "An Honorable discharge characterization does not require flawless military service. Many veterans are separated with an honorable characterization despite some relatively minor or infrequent misconduct" (Kurta, 2017, Attachment p. 4 ¶ 26.h.). In sum, by addressing these various heretofore unaddressed issues, the Kurta Memorandum offers the clearest guidance yet for those hoping to upgrade their military discharges. The Kurta Memorandum also offers incarcerated veterans a much-needed roadmap for supporting their applications with necessary and competent evidence.

The Kurta Memorandum, in clarifying multiple issues that impacted practice before the military review boards, also paved the way for subsequent clarifications. In July 2018, Robert Wilkie, acting in his capacity as a DoD official, issued separate guidance on the boards' standards for considering "equity, injustice, or clemency determinations." Although these factors apply to many forms of discharge upgrade, the clemency standards are appropriate for upgrading punitive discharges from courts-martial (Wilkie, 2018, p. 1). The Wilkie Memorandum articulates specific considerations that present a framework for evaluating a veteran's rehabilitation over the years since his or her discharge. The Wilkie Memorandum is reprinted in Appendix 2, and should be read in conjunction with the Kurta Memorandum.

Time as a Commodity in Developing Evidence

Commanders may have given less than a few moments to the consideration of the discharge to pursue and any mitigating evidence marshalled by the service member. Yet, it can take decades to undo errors in the process. Veterans often see the short discharge upgrade forms and believe that it is sufficient to use the small textbox provided to plead their case (see Appendices 3 and 4). It is often lost on veterans that the most successful applications contain written briefs/reports which cite standards for upgrading and explain how the evidence they have collected supports a given standard (Connecticut Veterans Legal Clinic, 2011). It can take months to obtain one's official military personnel records, and even more time to obtain separate mental health records or records related to criminal investigations.

Veterans who succeed in upgrading their discharges must understand the standards of review, where to obtain supporting information, and, most importantly, they must have the time to devote to the collection, evaluation, and assembly of the supporting evidence. As a captive audience with time to spare, incarcerated veterans have a competitive advantage over non-incarcerated veterans to effectively obtain discharge upgrades. Moreover, with the added benefits of Under Secretary Kurta's standards, incarcerated veterans can maximize their time with the greatest advantage that any applicants have ever enjoyed in discharge upgrading proceedings.

As a caveat, it is possible that the military review boards will consider post-discharge conduct, including the applicant's criminal history, when deciding on a discharge upgrade petition. In such cases, the veteran's confinement could be a factor that works against his or her chances of success. Veterans who wish to apply for a discharge upgrade from a confined setting should consider this risk. If they have mental health conditions from military service, inmates should address how criminal involvement may have resulted from the same mental health issues that surrounded the military discharge years ago. Input from a mental health provider is likely to make such observations more persuasive.

The possibility of a denial based on inmate status should not stop the veteran from requesting the necessary records, obtaining supporting evidence, and drafting the petition that he or she will ultimately file. Preparation or filing of the petition has a special, independent value. Bruce Pentland, who ran the Veterans Incarcerated Program throughout Los Angeles in the 1970s and 1980s, observed that the process of requesting benefits not only reiterates to veterans the importance of following rules and procedures, but also offers an opportunity for renewed faith in government systems (Pentland, 1979, p. 525; Pentland & Scurfield, 1982, p. 25). This observation also applies to contemporary times.

Conclusion

This chapter highlighted several reasons why it is vital to identify veterans with bad paper and support them with resources to upgrade their discharges as early as possible during the course of their incarceration. Discharge characterizations arise from a distinct system of military justice that is based upon the discretion of military commanders. Given their broad discretion in the exercise of discipline, it is nearly impossible to identify the aims of a specific commander in pursuing the discharge that an inmate ultimately received. While it is possible that the inmate acted in a reprehensible manner and fully deserved the bad paper designation, it is equally possible that this discharge type was the result of discrimination or the random determination to make this individual an example to others in the unit despite the fact that the underlying conduct was widespread. This chapter also explained how many veterans may have been punished for the untreated symptoms of mental health conditions that arose from their loyal and faithful service.

For these reasons, the veteran with bad paper deserves a presumption of worthiness for assistance in discharge upgrading. Given the immense value of time incarcerated in developing the evidence necessary to support discharge upgrading requests, corrections professionals should permit veterans to learn about the standards for upgrading and prepare their own applications as early as possible during their term of confinement. An investment of minimal resources may result in the opportunity for diversion they would have had but for their discharge characterization. Moreover, resulting receipt of benefits will assist those inmates in reentering society and abstaining from further criminal conduct based on the success of treatment for which they would now be eligible. Appendix 5 summarizes various resources that will benefit incarcerated veterans in preparing their discharge upgrading requests.

Appendix 1: A.M. Kurta Memorandum

OFFICE OF THE UNDER SECRETARY OF DEFENSE
4000 DEFENSE PENTAGON
WASHINGTON, DC 20301-4000

PERSONNEL AND READINESS

AUG 25 2017

MEMORANDUM FOR SECRETARIES OF THE MILITARY DEPARTMENTS

SUBJECT: Clarifying Guidance to Military Discharge Review Boards and Boards for Correction of Military/Naval Records Considering Requests by Veterans for Modification of their Discharge Due to Mental Health Conditions, Sexual Assault, or Sexual Harassment

In December 2016, the Department announced a renewed effort to ensure veterans were aware of the opportunity to have their discharges and military records reviewed. As part of that effort, we noted the Department was currently reviewing our policies for the Boards for Correction of Military/Naval Records (BCM/NRs) and Discharge Review Boards (DRBs) and considering whether further guidance was needed. We also invited feedback from the public on our policies and how we could improve the discharge review process.

As a result of that feedback and our internal review, we have determined that clarifications are needed regarding mental health conditions, sexual assault, and sexual harassment. To resolve lingering questions and potential ambiguities, clarifying guidance is attached to this memorandum. This guidance is not intended to interfere with or impede the Boards' statutory independence. Through this guidance, however, there should be greater uniformity amongst the review boards and veterans will be better informed about how to achieve relief in these types of cases.

To be sure, the BCM/NRs and DRBs are tasked with tremendous responsibility and they perform their tasks with remarkable professionalism. Invisible wounds, however, are some of the most difficult cases they review and there are frequently limited records for the boards to consider, often through no fault of the veteran, in resolving appeals for relief. Standards for review should rightly consider the unique nature of these cases and afford each veteran a reasonable opportunity for relief even if the sexual assault or sexual harassment was unreported, or the mental health condition was not diagnosed until years later. This clarifying guidance ensures fair and consistent standards of review for veterans with mental health conditions, or who experienced sexual assault or sexual harassment regardless of when they served or in which Military Department they served.

Military Department Secretaries shall direct immediate implementation of this guidance and report on compliance with this guidance within 45 days. My point of contact is Lieutenant Colonel Reggie Yager, Office of Legal Policy, (703) 571-9301 or reggie.d.yager.mil@mail.mil.

A. M. Kurta
Performing the Duties of the Under Secretary of Defense for Personnel and Readiness

Attachment:
As stated

cc:
Chairman of the Joint Chiefs of Staff
General Counsel of the Department of Defense
Assistant Secretary of Defense for Legislative Affairs
Assistant to the Secretary of Defense for Public Affairs

Attachment

Clarifying Guidance to Military Discharge Review Boards and Boards for Correction of Military/Naval Records Considering Requests by Veterans for Modification of their Discharge Due to Mental Health Conditions; Traumatic Brain Injury; Sexual Assault; or Sexual Harassment

Generally

1. This document provides clarifying guidance to Discharge Review Boards (DRBs) and Boards for Correction of Military/Naval Records (BCM/NRs) considering requests by veterans for modification of their discharges due in whole or in part to mental health conditions, including post-traumatic stress disorder (PTSD); Traumatic Brain Injury (TBI); sexual assault; or sexual harassment.

2. Requests for discharge relief typically involve four questions:

   a. Did the veteran have a condition or experience that may excuse or mitigate the discharge?
   b. Did that condition exist/ experience occur during military service?
   c. Does that condition or experience actually excuse or mitigate the discharge?
   d. Does that condition or experience outweigh the discharge?

3. Liberal consideration will be given to veterans petitioning for discharge relief when the application for relief is based in whole or in part on matters relating to mental health conditions, including PTSD; TBI; sexual assault; or sexual harassment.

4. Evidence may come from sources other than a veteran's service record and may include records from the DoD Sexual Assault Prevention and Response Program (DD Form 2910, *Victim Reporting Preference Statement*) and/or DD Form 2911, *DoD Sexual Assault Forensic Examination [SAFE] Report*), law enforcement authorities, rape crisis centers, mental health counseling centers, hospitals, physicians, pregnancy tests, tests for sexually transmitted diseases, and statements from family members, friends, roommates, co-workers, fellow servicemembers, or clergy.

5. Evidence may also include changes in behavior; requests for transfer to another military duty assignment; deterioration in work performance; inability of the individual to conform their behavior to the expectations of a military environment; substance abuse; episodes of depression, panic attacks, or anxiety without an identifiable cause; unexplained economic or social behavior changes; relationship issues; or sexual dysfunction.

6. Evidence of misconduct, including any misconduct underlying a veteran's discharge, may be evidence of a mental health condition, including PTSD; TBI; or of behavior consistent with experiencing sexual assault or sexual harassment.

7. The veteran's testimony alone, oral or written, may establish the existence of a condition or experience, that the condition or experience existed during or was aggravated by military service, and that the condition or experience excuses or mitigates the discharge.

8. Cases falling under this guidance will receive timely consideration consistent with statutory requirements.

Was there a condition or experience?

9. Absent clear evidence to the contrary, a diagnosis rendered by a licensed psychiatrist or psychologist is evidence the veteran had a condition that may excuse or mitigate the discharge.

10. Evidence that may reasonably support more than one diagnosis should be liberally considered as supporting a diagnosis, where applicable, that could excuse or mitigate the discharge.

11. A veteran asserting a mental health condition without a corresponding diagnosis of such condition from a licensed psychiatrist or psychologist, will receive liberal consideration of evidence that may support the existence of such a condition.

12. Review Boards are not required to find that a crime of sexual assault or an incident of sexual harassment occurred in order to grant liberal consideration to a veteran that the experience happened during military service, was aggravated by military service, or that it excuses or mitigates the discharge.

Did it exist/occur during military service?

13. A diagnosis made by a licensed psychiatrist or psychologist that the condition existed during military service will receive liberal consideration.

14. A determination made by the Department of Veterans Affairs (VA) that a veteran's mental health condition, including PTSD; TBI; sexual assault; or sexual harassment is connected to military service, while not binding on the Department of Defense, is persuasive evidence that the condition existed or experience occurred during military service.

15. Liberal consideration is not required for cases involving pre-existing conditions which are determined not to have been aggravated by military service.

Does the condition/experience excuse or mitigate the discharge?

16. Conditions or experiences that may reasonably have existed at the time of discharge will be liberally considered as excusing or mitigating the discharge.

17. Evidence that may reasonably support more than one diagnosis or a change in diagnosis, particularly where the diagnosis is listed as the narrative reason for discharge, will be liberally

construed as warranting a change in narrative reason to "Secretarial Authority," "Condition not a disability," or another appropriate basis.

Does the condition/experience outweigh the discharge?

18. In some cases, the severity of misconduct may outweigh any mitigation from mental health conditions, including PTSD; TBI; sexual assault; or sexual harassment.

19. Premeditated misconduct is not generally excused by mental health conditions, including PTSD; TBI; or by a sexual assault or sexual harassment experience. However, substance-seeking behavior and efforts to self-medicate symptoms of a mental health condition may warrant consideration. Review Boards will exercise caution in assessing the causal relationship between asserted conditions or experiences and premeditated misconduct.

Additional Clarifications

20. Unless otherwise indicated, the term "discharge" includes the characterization, narrative reason, separation code, and re-enlistment code.

21. This guidance applies to both the BCM/NRs and DRBs.

22. The supplemental guidance provided by then-Secretary Hagel on September 3, 2014, as clarified in this guidance, also applies to both BCM/NRs and DRBs.

23. The guidance memorandum provided by then-Acting Principal Deputy Under Secretary of Defense for Personnel and Readiness Brad Carson on February 24, 2016, applies in full to BCM/NRs but also applies to DRBs with regards to de novo reconsideration of petitions previously decided without the benefit of all applicable supplemental guidance.

24. These guidance documents are not limited to Under Other Than Honorable Condition discharge characterizations but rather apply to any petition seeking discharge relief including requests to change the narrative reason, re-enlistment codes, and upgrades from General to Honorable characterizations.

25. Unless otherwise indicated, liberal consideration applies to applications based in whole or in part on matters related to diagnosed conditions, undiagnosed conditions, and misdiagnosed TBI or mental health conditions, including PTSD, as well as reported and unreported sexual assault and sexual harassment experiences asserted as justification or supporting rationale for discharge relief.

26. Liberal consideration includes but is not limited to the following concepts:

a. Some circumstances require greater leniency and excusal from normal evidentiary burdens.

b. It is unreasonable to expect the same level of proof for injustices committed years ago when TBI; mental health conditions, such as PTSD; and victimology were far less understood than they are today.

c. It is unreasonable to expect the same level of proof for injustices committed years ago when there is now restricted reporting, heightened protections for victims, greater support available for victims and witnesses, and more extensive training on sexual assault and sexual harassment than ever before.

d. Mental health conditions, including PTSD; TBI; sexual assault; and sexual harassment impact veterans in many intimate ways, are often undiagnosed or diagnosed years afterwards, and are frequently unreported.

e. Mental health conditions, including PTSD; TBI; sexual assault; and sexual harassment inherently affect one's behaviors and choices causing veterans to think and behave differently than might otherwise be expected.

f. Reviews involving diagnosed, undiagnosed, or misdiagnosed TBI or mental health conditions, such as PTSD, or reported or unreported sexual assault or sexual harassment experiences should not condition relief on the existence of evidence that would be unreasonable or unlikely under the specific circumstances of the case.

g. Veterans with mental health conditions, including PTSD; TBI; or who experienced sexual assault or sexual harassment may have difficulty presenting a thorough appeal for relief because of how the asserted condition or experience has impacted the veteran's life.

h. An Honorable discharge characterization does not require flawless military service. Many veterans are separated with an honorable characterization despite some relatively minor or infrequent misconduct.

i. The relative severity of some misconduct can change over time, thereby changing the relative weight of the misconduct to the mitigating evidence in a case. For example, marijuana use is still unlawful in the military but it is now legal in some states and it may be viewed, in the context of mitigating evidence, as less severe today than it was decades ago.

j. Service members diagnosed with mental health conditions, including PTSD; TBI; or who reported sexual assault or sexual harassment receive heightened screening today to ensure the causal relationship of possible symptoms and discharge basis is fully considered, and characterization of service is appropriate. Veterans discharged under prior procedures, or before verifiable diagnosis, may not have suffered an error because the separation authority was unaware of their condition or experience at the time of discharge. However, when compared to similarly situated individuals under today's standards, they may be the victim of injustice because commanders fully informed of such conditions and causal relationships today may opt for a less prejudicial discharge to ensure the veteran retains certain benefits, such as medical care.

k. Liberal consideration does not mandate an upgrade. Relief may be appropriate, however, for minor misconduct commonly associated with mental health conditions, including PTSD; TBI; or behaviors commonly associated with sexual assault or sexual harassment; and some significant misconduct sufficiently justified or outweighed by the facts and circumstances.

Appendix 2: Robert L. Wilkie Memorandum

UNDER SECRETARY OF DEFENSE
4000 DEFENSE PENTAGON
WASHINGTON, D.C. 20301-4000

PERSONNEL AND READINESS

JUL 25 2018

MEMORANDUM FOR SECRETARIES OF THE MILITARY DEPARTMENTS

SUBJECT: Guidance to Military Discharge Review Boards and Boards for Correction of Military / Naval Records Regarding Equity, Injustice, or Clemency Determinations

The Department has evaluated numerous aspects of the Service Discharge Review Boards (DRBs) and Boards for Correction of Military / Naval Records (BCM/NRs) over the last two years. We have redoubled our efforts to ensure veterans are aware of their opportunities to request review of their discharges and other military records. We have initiated several outreach efforts to spread the word and invite feedback from veterans and organizations that assist veterans and active duty members, and issued substantive clarifying guidance on Board consideration of mental health conditions and sexual assault or sexual harassment experiences. And, we have partnered with the Department of Veterans Affairs to develop a web-based tool that provides customized guidance for veterans who want to upgrade their discharges. But our work is not yet done.

Increasing attention is being paid to pardons for criminal convictions and the circumstances under which citizens should be considered for second chances and the restoration of rights forfeited as a result of such convictions. Many states have developed processes for restoring basic civil rights to felons, such as the right to vote, hold office, or sit on a jury, and many states have developed veterans' courts to consider special circumstances associated with military service. States do not have authority, however, to correct military records or discharges.

The Military Departments, operating through DRBs and BCM/NRs, have the authority to upgrade discharges or correct military records to ensure fundamental fairness. DRBs and BCM/NRs have tremendous responsibility and perform their tasks with remarkable professionalism, but further guidance to inform Board decisions on applications based on pardons for criminal convictions is required.

The attached guidance closes this gap and sets clear standards. While not everyone should be pardoned, forgiven, or upgraded, in some cases, fairness dictates that relief should be granted. We trust our Boards to apply this guidance and give appropriate consideration to every application for relief.

Military Department Secretaries will ensure that Board members are familiar with and appropriately trained on this guidance within 90 days. My point of contact is Monica Trucco, Director, Office of Legal Policy, who may be reached at (703) 697-3387 or monica.a.trucco.civ@mail.mil.

Robert L. Wilkie

Attachment:
As stated

cc:
Chairman of the Joint Chiefs of Staff
General Counsel of the Department of Defense
Assistant Secretary of Defense for Legislative Affairs
Assistant Secretary to the Defense for Public Affairs

Attachment

Guidance to Military Discharge Review Boards and Boards for Correction of Military / Naval Records Regarding Equity, Injustice, or Clemency Determinations

Generally

1. This document provides standards for Discharge Review Boards (DRBs) and Boards for Correction of Military / Naval Records (BCM/NRs) in determining whether relief is warranted on the basis of equity, injustice, or clemency.

2. DRBs are authorized to grant relief on the basis of issues of equity or propriety. BCM/NRs are authorized to grant relief for errors or injustices. These standards, specifically equity for DRBs and relief for injustice for BCM/NRs, authorize both boards to grant relief in order to ensure fundamental fairness.

3. Clemency refers to relief specifically granted from a criminal sentence and is a part of the broad authority that DRBs and BCM/NRs have to ensure fundamental fairness. BCM/NRs may grant clemency regardless of the court-martial forum; however, DRBs are limited in their exercise of clemency in that they may not exercise clemency for discharges or dismissals issued at a general court-martial.

4. This guidance applies to more than clemency from sentencing in a court-martial; it also applies to any other corrections, including changes in a discharge, which may be warranted on equity or relief from injustice grounds.

5. This guidance does not mandate relief, but rather provides standards and principles to guide DRBs and BCM/NRs in application of their equitable relief authority. Each case will be assessed on its own merits. The relative weight of each principle and whether the principle supports relief in a particular case, are within the sound discretion of each board.

6. In determining whether to grant relief on the basis of equity, an injustice, or clemency grounds, DRBs and BCM/NRs shall consider the following:

a. It is consistent with military custom and practice to honor sacrifices and achievements, to punish only to the extent necessary, to rehabilitate to the greatest extent possible, and to favor second chances in situations in which individuals have paid for their misdeeds.

b. Relief should not be reserved only for those with exceptional aptitude; rather character and rehabilitation should weigh more heavily than achievement alone. An applicant need not, for example, attain high academic or professional achievement in order to demonstrate sufficient rehabilitation to support relief.

c. An honorable discharge characterization does not require flawless military service. Many veterans are separated with an honorable characterization despite some relatively minor or infrequent misconduct.

d. Evidence in support of relief may come from sources other than a veteran's service record.

e. A veteran or Service member's sworn testimony alone, oral or written, may establish the existence of a fact supportive of relief.

f. Changes in policy, whereby a Service member under the same circumstances today would reasonably be expected to receive a more favorable outcome than the applicant received, may be grounds for relief.

g. The relative severity of some misconduct can change over time, thereby changing the relative weight of the misconduct in the case of the mitigating evidence in a case. For example, marijuana use is still unlawful in the military, but it is now legal under state law in some states and it may be viewed, in the context of mitigating evidence, as less severe today than it was decades ago.

h. Requests for relief based in whole or in part on a mental health condition, including post-traumatic stress disorder (PTSD); Traumatic Brain Injury (TBI); or a sexual assault or sexual harassment experience, should be considered for relief on equitable, injustice, or clemency grounds whenever there is insufficient evidence to warrant relief for an error or impropriety.

i. Evidence submitted by a government official with oversight or responsibility for the matter at issue and that acknowledges a relevant error or injustice was committed, provided that it is submitted in his or her official capacity, should be favorably considered as establishing a grounds for relief.

j. Similarly situated Service members sometimes receive disparate punishments. A Service member in one location could face court-martial for an offense that routinely is handled administratively across the Service. This can happen for a variety of lawful reasons, for example, when a unit or command finds it necessary to step up disciplinary efforts to address a string of alcohol- or drug-related incidents, or because attitudes about a particular offense vary between different career fields, units, installations, or organizations. While a court-martial or a command would be within its authority to choose a specific disposition forum or issue a certain punishment, DRBs and BCM/NRs should nevertheless consider uniformity and unfair disparities in punishments as a basis for relief.

k. Relief is generally more appropriate for nonviolent offenses than for violent offenses.

l. Changes to the narrative reason for a discharge and/or an upgraded character of discharge granted solely on equity, injustice, or clemency grounds normally should not result in separation pay, retroactive promotions, the payment of past medical expenses, or similar benefits that might have been received if the original discharge had been for the revised reason or had the upgraded character.

7. In determining whether to grant relief on the basis of equity, an injustice, or clemency grounds, DRBs and BCM/NRs should also consider the following, as applicable:

a. An applicant's candor

b. Whether the punishment, including any collateral consequences, was too harsh

c. The aggravating and mitigating facts related to the record or punishment from which the veteran or Service member wants relief

d. Positive or negative post-conviction conduct, including any arrests, criminal charges, or any convictions since the incident at issue

e. Severity of misconduct

f. Length of time since misconduct

g. Acceptance of responsibility, remorse, or atonement for misconduct

h. The degree to which the requested relief is necessary for the applicant

i. Character and reputation of applicant

j. Critical illness or old age

k. Meritorious service in government or other endeavors

l. Evidence of rehabilitation

m. Availability of other remedies

n. Job history

o. Whether misconduct may have been youthful indiscretion

p. Character references

q. Letters of recommendation

r. Victim support for, or opposition to relief, and any reasons provided

Appendix 3: DD Form 293

APPLICATION FOR THE REVIEW OF DISCHARGE OR DISMISSAL FROM THE ARMED FORCES OF THE UNITED STATES
(Please read instructions on Pages 3 and 4 BEFORE completing this application.)

Form Approved
OMB No. 0704-0004
Expires Aug 31, 2006

The public reporting burden for this collection of information is estimated to average 30 minutes per response, including the time for reviewing instructions, searching existing data sources, gathering and maintaining the data needed, and completing and reviewing the collection of information. Send comments regarding this burden estimate or any other aspect of this collection of information, including suggestions for reducing the burden, to Department of Defense, Washington Headquarters Services, Directorate for Information Operations and Reports (0704-0004), 1215 Jefferson Davis Highway, Suite 1204, Arlington, VA 22202-4302. Respondents should be aware that notwithstanding any other provision of law, no person shall be subject to any penalty for failing to comply with a collection of information if it does not display a currently valid OMB control number.

PLEASE DO NOT RETURN YOUR FORM TO THE ABOVE ADDRESS. RETURN COMPLETED FORM TO THE APPROPRIATE ADDRESS ON BACK OF THIS PAGE.

PRIVACY ACT STATEMENT

AUTHORITY: 10 U.S.C. 1553; E.O. 9397.
PRINCIPAL PURPOSE(S): To apply for a change in the characterization or reason for military discharge issued to an individual.
ROUTINE USE(S): None.
DISCLOSURE: Voluntary; however, failure to provide identifying information may impede processing of this application. The request for Social Security Number is strictly to assure proper identification of the individual and appropriate records.

1. APPLICANT DATA *(The person whose discharge is to be reviewed).* **PLEASE PRINT OR TYPE INFORMATION.**

a. BRANCH OF SERVICE *(X one)* ☐ ARMY ☐ MARINE CORPS ☐ NAVY ☐ AIR FORCE ☐ COAST GUARD

b. NAME *(Last, First, Middle Initial)* | c. GRADE/RANK AT DISCHARGE | d. SOCIAL SECURITY NUMBER

2. DATE OF DISCHARGE OR SEPARATION *(YYYYMMDD) (If date is more than 15 years ago, submit a DD Form 149)*

3. UNIT AND LOCATION AT DISCHARGE OR SEPARATION

4. DISCHARGE CHARACTERIZATION RECEIVED *(X one)*
- ☐ HONORABLE
- ☐ GENERAL/UNDER HONORABLE CONDITIONS
- ☐ UNDER OTHER THAN HONORABLE CONDITIONS
- ☐ BAD CONDUCT *(Special court-martial only)*
- ☐ UNCHARACTERIZED
- ☐ OTHER *(Explain)*

5. BOARD ACTION REQUESTED *(X one)*
- ☐ CHANGE TO HONORABLE
- ☐ CHANGE TO GENERAL/UNDER HONORABLE CONDITIONS
- ☐ CHANGE TO UNCHARACTERIZED *(Not applicable for Air Force)*
- ☐ CHANGE NARRATIVE REASON FOR SEPARATION TO:

6. ISSUES: WHY AN UPGRADE OR CHANGE IS REQUESTED AND JUSTIFICATION FOR THE REQUEST *(Continue in Item 14. See instructions on Page 3.)*

☐ **7.** *(X if applicable)* **AN APPLICATION WAS PREVIOUSLY SUBMITTED ON** *(YYYYMMDD)* ____________ **AND THIS FORM IS SUBMITTED TO ADD ADDITIONAL ISSUES, JUSTIFICATION, OR EVIDENCE.**

8. IN SUPPORT OF THIS APPLICATION, THE FOLLOWING ATTACHED DOCUMENTS ARE SUBMITTED AS EVIDENCE: *(Continue in Item 17. If military documents or medical records are relevant to your case, please send copies.)*

9. TYPE OF REVIEW REQUESTED *(X one)*
- ☐ CONDUCT A RECORD REVIEW OF MY DISCHARGE BASED ON MY MILITARY PERSONNEL FILE AND ANY ADDITIONAL DOCUMENTATION SUBMITTED BY ME. I AND/OR *(counsel/representative)* WILL NOT APPEAR BEFORE THE BOARD.
- ☐ I AND/OR *(counsel/representative)* WISH TO APPEAR AT A HEARING AT NO EXPENSE TO THE GOVERNMENT BEFORE THE BOARD IN THE WASHINGTON, D.C. METROPOLITAN AREA.
- ☐ I AND/OR *(counsel/representative)* WISH TO APPEAR AT A HEARING AT NO EXPENSE TO THE GOVERNMENT BEFORE A TRAVELING PANEL CLOSEST TO *(enter city and state)* ____________ *(NOTE: The Navy Discharge Review Board does not have a traveling panel.)*

10.a. COUNSEL/REPRESENTATIVE *(If any)* **NAME** *(Last, First, Middle Initial)* **AND ADDRESS** *(See Item 10 of the instructions about counsel/representative.)*
b. TELEPHONE NUMBER *(Include Area Code)*
c. E-MAIL
d. FAX NUMBER *(Include Area Code)*

11. APPLICANT MUST SIGN IN ITEM 13.a. BELOW. If the record in question is that of a deceased or incompetent person, LEGAL PROOF OF DEATH OR INCOMPETENCY MUST ACCOMPANY THE APPLICATION. If the application is signed by other than the applicant, indicate the name *(print)* ____________ **and relationship by marking a box below.**
☐ SPOUSE ☐ WIDOW ☐ WIDOWER ☐ NEXT OF KIN ☐ LEGAL REPRESENTATIVE ☐ OTHER *(Specify)*

12.a. CURRENT MAILING ADDRESS OF APPLICANT OR PERSON ABOVE *(Forward notification of any change in address.)*
b. TELEPHONE NUMBER *(Include Area Code)*
c. E-MAIL
d. FAX NUMBER *(Include Area Code)*

13. CERTIFICATION. I make the foregoing statements, as part of my claim, with full knowledge of the penalties involved for willfully making a false statement or claim. *(U.S. Code, Title 18, Sections 287 and 1001, provide that an individual shall be fined under this title or imprisoned not more than 5 years, or both.)*

a. SIGNATURE - REQUIRED *(Applicant or person in Item 11 above)* | b. DATE SIGNED - REQUIRED *(YYYYMMDD)*

CASE NUMBER *(Do not write in this space.)*

DD FORM 293, AUG 2003 PREVIOUS EDITIONS ARE OBSOLETE. Reset Page 1 of 4 Pages

14. CONTINUATION OF ITEM 6, ISSUES *(If applicable)*

15. CONTINUATION OF ITEM 8, SUPPORTING DOCUMENTS *(If applicable)*

16. REMARKS *(If applicable)*

MAIL COMPLETED APPLICATIONS TO APPROPRIATE ADDRESS BELOW.

ARMY	NAVY AND MARINE CORPS
Army Review Boards Agency Support Division, St. Louis 9700 Page Avenue St. Louis, MO 63132-5200 (See http://arba.army.pentagon.mil)	Naval Council of Personnel Boards 720 Kennon Street, S.E. Room 309 (NDRB) Washington Navy Yard, DC 20374-5023
AIR FORCE	**COAST GUARD**
Air Force Review Boards Agency SAF/MRBR 550-C Street West, Suite 40 Randolph AFB, TX 78150-4742	U.S. Coast Guard Commandant (G-WPM) 2100 Second Street, S.W. Room 5500 Washington, DC 20593

DD FORM 293, AUG 2003

Reset

Page 2 of 4 Pages

INSTRUCTIONS FOR COMPLETION OF DD FORM 293

REQUESTING COPIES OF YOUR OFFICIAL MILITARY PERSONNEL FILE

Information on how to obtain military or health records is available at the National Personnel Records Center website at www.nara.gov/regional/mpr.html or at your local Veterans Administration office.

Applicants are strongly encouraged to submit any request for their military records prior to applying for a discharge review rather than after submitting a DD Form 293 in order to avoid substantial delays in processing of the application and scheduling of review. Applicants and their counsel may also examine their military personnel records at the site of their scheduled review prior to the review. The Board shall notify applicants of the date of availability of the records for examination in their standard scheduling information.

Submission of a request for an applicant's military records (including a request pursuant to the Freedom of Information Act or Privacy Act) after the DD Form 293 has been submitted will automatically result in the suspension of processing of the application for discharge review until the requested records are sent to an appropriate location for copying, are copied, and are returned to the possession of the headquarters of the Discharge Review Board. Processing of the application shall then be resumed at whatever stage of the discharge review process is practicable.

DD FORM 293 - PLEASE PRINT OR TYPE INFORMATION. (Items on the form are self-explanatory unless otherwise noted below.)

ITEM 1b. Use the name which you served under while in the Armed Forces. If your name has since changed, then also include your current name after adding the abbreviation "AKA". If the former member is deceased or incompetent, see Item 11.

ITEM 2. If you received more than one discharge, the information in this item should refer to the discharge that you want changed. **Discharge Review Boards cannot consider any type of discharge resulting from a sentence given by a general court-martial.**

ITEM 3. If the discharge you want reviewed was issued over 15 years ago, instead of applying on a DD Form 293, you must petition the appropriate Board for Correction of Military Record using DD Form 149, *Application for Correction of Military Record Under the Provisions of Title 10, U.S. Code, Section 1552.*

ITEM 5. If you request a change of narrative reason for separation, you must list the specific reason for discharge that you believe to be appropriate, otherwise the Board will presume that you do not want a change in reason for discharge. If you do not request a change of discharge characterization in this item, the Board will presume you want to change discharge to Honorable.

If you were separated on or after 1 October 1982 while in an entry level status with an under other than honorable conditions discharge and less than 180 days of active service, you can request a change of discharge characterization to "Uncharacterized" and discharge reason to "Entry Level Separation".

ITEM 6. "Issues" are the reasons why you think your discharge should be changed. You are not required to submit any issues with your application. However, if you want the Board to respond in writing to the issues of concern, you must list your specific issues in accordance with those instructions and regulations governing the Board. Issues must be stated clearly and specifically. Your issues should address the reasons why you believe that the discharge received was improper or inequitable. It is important to focus on matters that occurred while you served in the Armed Forces.

The following examples demonstrate one way in which issues may be stated (the example issues do not indicate, in any way, the only type of issues that should be submitted to the Board):

Example 1. My discharge was inequitable because it was based on one isolated incident in 28 months of service with no other adverse action.

Example 2. The discharge is improper because the applicant's pre-service civilian conviction, properly listed on his enlistment documents, was used in the discharge proceedings.

In Item 6 list each of your issues that you want the Board to address. There is no limit to the number of issues that you may submit. If you need additional space, continue in Item 14 or on a plain sheet of paper and attach it to this application.

NOTE: If an issue is not listed in Item 6, it may result in the Board not addressing the issue even if the issue is discussed in a legal brief or other written submissions or at the hearing. Changes or additions to the list may be made on the DD Form 293 anytime before the Discharge Review Board closes the review process for deliberation. Please be sure that your issues are consistent with the Board Action Requested (Item 5). If there is a conflict between what you say in your issues and what you requested in Item 5, the Board will respond to your issue in the context of the action requested in Item 5. For example, if you request a General Discharge in Item 5 but your issue in Item 6 indicated you want an Honorable Discharge, the Board will respond to the issue in terms of your request for a General Discharge. Therefore, if you are submitting issues for the purpose of obtaining an Honorable Discharge, be sure to mark the box for an Honorable Discharge in Item 5.

Incorporation by Reference. Issues that are listed on a legal brief or other written submissions may be incorporated by reference in Item 6. The reference must be specific enough for the Board to clearly identify the matter being submitted as an issue. At a minimum, it shall identify the page, paragraph, and sentence incorporated. Example: Issue 1. Brief, page 2, paragraph 1, sentences one and two.

Applicants should be as specific as possible with all references so the Board can clearly distinguish the scope of the issue. Because it is to your benefit to bring such issues to the Board's attention as early as possible in the review, if you submit a brief, you are strongly urged to set forth all such issues as a separate item at the beginning of the brief.

INSTRUCTIONS FOR COMPLETION OF DD FORM 293 *(Continued)*

ITEM 8. Evidence not in your official records should be submitted to the Board before the review date. It is to your advantage to submit such documentation with this application. This also applies to legal briefs or counsel submissions. However, you have the right to submit evidence until the time the Discharge Review Board closes the review process for deliberation. Documents that are of the most benefit are those which substantiate or relate directly to your issues in Item 6. Other documents that may be helpful are character references, educational achievements, exemplary post-service conduct, and medical reports. You should add your name and Social Security Number to each document submitted. The Board will consider all documents submitted in your behalf, but will respond in writing only to those issues set forth in Item 6.

ITEM 9. TYPE OF REVIEW REQUESTED

A Discharge Review is conducted in two basic ways: (1) Records Review or (2) Hearing.

1. Records Review. You may have the Board conduct a discharge review based solely on military records and any additional documentation that you provide. This review is conducted without personal appearance by you and/or your counsel appearing.

2. Hearing. You may appear personally (alone or assisted by a representative/counsel) before the Board in the Washington, D.C. Metro Area or before a Traveling Panel of the Board in selected locations throughout the U.S., if appropriate. The Department of Defense is not responsible for, nor will it pay for, any costs incurred by the applicant or representative/counsel for appearance or providing testimony or documentation. Detailed notification and/or scheduling information for all personal appearances will be provided after the application has been processed. In addition, without appearing yourself, you may have your case presented by a representative/counsel of your choice.

Applicants participating in a personal appearance or hearing examination may make sworn or unsworn state- ments, introduce witnesses, documents, or other information on their behalf. Applicants may make oral or written arguments personally and/or through representative/ counsel. Applicants and witnesses who present sworn or unsworn statements may be questioned by the Board.

FAILURE TO APPEAR AT A HEARING OR RESPOND TO A SCHEDULING NOTICE. If you do not appear at a scheduled hearing or respond as required to a scheduling notice, and you did not make a prior, timely request for a continuance, postponement, or withdrawal of the application, you will forfeit the right to a personal appearance and the Board shall complete its review of the discharge based upon the evidence of record.

ITEM 10.a - d. Omit if you do not have a representative/ counsel. If you later obtain the services of either, inform the Board immediately.

The military services do not provide counsel representation or evidence for you, nor do they pay the cost of such representation under any circumstance. The following organizations regularly furnish representation at no charge to you. Representatives may or may not be lawyers.

1. American Legion
2. Disabled American Veterans
3. Veterans of Foreign Wars
4. State or Regional Veterans Offices

In addition, there are other organizations willing to assist you in completing this application and to provide representation at no cost. It is to your advantage to coordinate with your counsel prior to submitting this application. This will insure that your counsel is able to appear at the location you listed in Item 9. Please note that some of the organizations listed above only represent applicants who appear before the Board in the Washington, D.C. Metro Area. Contact your local veterans affairs office, Veterans Administration Office or veterans service organization for further information.

ITEM 11. If the former member is deceased or incompetent, the application may be submitted by the next of kin, a surviving spouse or a legal representative. Legal proof of death or incompetency and satisfactory evidence of the relationship to the former member must accompany this application.

ITEM 12.a. Indicate the address to be used for all future correspondence regarding this application. If you change this address while this application is pending, you must notify the Discharge Review Board immediately. Failure to attend a hearing as a result of an unreported change in address may result in a waiver of your right to a hearing.

ITEM 13.a. and b. A signature and date entered by the applicant or person identified in Item 11 are required.

DD FORM 293, AUG 2003 Page 4 of 4 Pages

Appendix 4: DD Form 149

APPLICATION FOR CORRECTION OF MILITARY RECORD UNDER THE PROVISIONS OF TITLE 10, U.S. CODE, SECTION 1552
(Please read Privacy Act Statement and instructions on back BEFORE completing this application.)

OMB No. 0704-0003
OMB approval expires
Dec 31, 2017

The public reporting burden for this collection of information is estimated to average 30 minutes per response, including the time for reviewing instructions, searching existing data sources, gathering and maintaining the data needed, and completing and reviewing the collection of information. Send comments regarding this burden estimate or any other aspect of this collection of information, including suggestions for reducing the burden, to the Department of Defense, Washington Headquarters Services, Executive Services Directorate, Directives Division, 4800 Mark Center Drive, Alexandria, VA 22350-3100 (0704-0003). Respondents should be aware that notwithstanding any other provision of law, no person shall be subject to any penalty for failing to comply with a collection of information if it does not display a currently valid OMB control number.

RETURN COMPLETED FORM TO THE APPROPRIATE ADDRESS ON THE BACK OF THIS PAGE.

1. APPLICANT DATA *(The person whose record you are requesting to be corrected.)*

a. BRANCH OF SERVICE *(X one)* ☐ ARMY ☐ NAVY ☐ AIR FORCE ☐ MARINE CORPS ☐ COAST GUARD

b. NAME *(Print - Last, First, Middle Initial)* | **c. PRESENT OR LAST PAY GRADE** | **d. SERVICE NUMBER** *(If applicable)* | **e. SSN**

2. PRESENT STATUS WITH RESPECT TO THE ARMED SERVICES *(Active Duty, Reserve, National Guard, Retired, Discharged, Deceased)* | **3. TYPE OF DISCHARGE** *(If by court-martial, state the type of court.)* | **4. DATE OF DISCHARGE OR RELEASE FROM ACTIVE DUTY** *(YYYYMMDD)*

5. I REQUEST THE FOLLOWING ERROR OR INJUSTICE IN THE RECORD BE CORRECTED AS FOLLOWS: *(Entry required)*

6. I BELIEVE THE RECORD TO BE IN ERROR OR UNJUST FOR THE FOLLOWING REASONS: *(Entry required)*

a. IS THIS A REQUEST FOR RECONSIDERATION OF A PRIOR APPEAL? ☐ YES ☐ NO | **b. IF YES, WHAT WAS THE DOCKET NUMBER?** | **c. DATE OF THE DECISION**

7. ORGANIZATION AND APPROXIMATE DATE *(YYYYMMDD)* **AT THE TIME THE ALLEGED ERROR OR INJUSTICE IN THE RECORD OCCURRED** *(Entry required)*

8. DISCOVERY OF ALLEGED ERROR OR INJUSTICE

a. DATE OF DISCOVERY *(YYYYMMDD)* | **b. IF MORE THAN THREE YEARS SINCE THE ALLEGED ERROR OR INJUSTICE WAS DISCOVERED, STATE WHY THE BOARD SHOULD FIND IT IN THE INTEREST OF JUSTICE TO CONSIDER THE APPLICATION.**

9. IN SUPPORT OF THIS APPLICATION, I SUBMIT AS EVIDENCE THE FOLLOWING ATTACHED DOCUMENTS: *(If military documents or medical records are pertinent to your case, please send copies. If Veterans Affairs records are pertinent, give regional office location and claim number.)*

10. I DESIRE TO APPEAR BEFORE THE BOARD IN WASHINGTON, D.C. *(At no expense to the Government) (X one)* ☐ **YES. THE BOARD WILL DETERMINE IF WARRANTED.** ☐ **NO. CONSIDER MY APPLICATION BASED ON RECORDS AND EVIDENCE.**

11.a. COUNSEL *(If any)* **NAME** *(Last, First, Middle Initial)* **and ADDRESS** *(Include ZIP Code)* | **b. TELEPHONE** *(Include Area Code)* | **c. E-MAIL ADDRESS** | **d. FAX NUMBER** *(Include Area Code)*

e. I WOULD LIKE ALL CORRESPONDENCE/DOCUMENTS SENT TO ME ELECTRONICALLY. ☐ YES ☐ NO

12. APPLICANT MUST SIGN IN ITEM 15 BELOW. If the record in question is that of a deceased or incompetent person, LEGAL PROOF OF DEATH OR INCOMPETENCY MUST ACCOMPANY THE APPLICATION. If the application is signed by other than the applicant, indicate the name *(print)* ______ **and relationship by marking one box below.**

☐ SPOUSE ☐ WIDOW ☐ WIDOWER ☐ NEXT OF KIN ☐ LEGAL REPRESENTATIVE ☐ OTHER *(Specify)*

13.a. COMPLETE CURRENT ADDRESS *(Include ZIP Code)* **OF APPLICANT OR PERSON IN ITEM 12 ABOVE** *(Forward notification of all changes of address.)* | **b. TELEPHONE** *(Include Area Code)* | **c. E-MAIL ADDRESS** | **d. FAX NUMBER** *(Include Area Code)*

14. I MAKE THE FOREGOING STATEMENTS, AS PART OF MY CLAIM, WITH FULL KNOWLEDGE OF THE PENALTIES INVOLVED FOR WILLFULLY MAKING A FALSE STATEMENT OR CLAIM. *(U.S. Code, Title 18, Sections 287 and 1001, provide that an individual shall be fined under this title or imprisoned not more than 5 years, or both.)*

CASE NUMBER *(Do not write in this space.)*

15. SIGNATURE *(Applicant must sign here.)* | **16. DATE SIGNED** *(YYYYMMDD)*

DD FORM 149, DEC 2014 PREVIOUS EDITION IS OBSOLETE. Adobe Designer 9.0

PRIVACY ACT STATEMENT

AUTHORITY: 10 U.S.C. 1552 and E.O. 9397, as amended (SSN).

PRINCIPAL PURPOSE(S): To initiate an application for correction of military record. The form is used by Board members for review of pertinent information in making a determination of relief through correction of a military record. Completed forms are covered by correction of military records SORNs maintained by each of the Services or the Defense Finance and Accounting Service. The DoD Systems of Records Notices can be located at: http://dpclo.defense.gov/Privacy/SORNsIndex/DODComponentNotices.aspx.

ROUTINE USE(S): The DoD Blanket Routine Uses at http://dpclo.defense.gov/Privacy/SORNsIndex/BlanketRoutineUses.aspx may apply to this collection.

DISCLOSURE: Voluntary. However, failure by an applicant to provide the information not annotated as "optional" may result in a denial of your application. An applicant's SSN is used to retrieve these records and links to the member's official military personnel file and pay record.

Applicable SORNs:
Army (http://dpclo.defense.gov/Privacy/SORNsIndex/DODComponentArticleView/tabid/7489/Article/6000/a0015-185-sfmr.aspx)
Navy and Marine Corps (http://dpclo.defense.gov/Privacy/SORNsIndex/DODwideSORNArticleView/tabid/6797/Article/6510/nm01000-1.aspx)
Air Force (http://dpclo.defense.gov/Privacy/SORNsIndex/DODwideSORNArticleView/tabid/6797/Article/5904/f036-safpc-d.aspx)
Defense Finance and Accounting Service (http://privacy.defense.gov/notices/dfas/T5015a.shtml)
Coast Guard (http://www.gpo.gov/fdsys/pkg/FR-2011-10-28/html/2011-27881.htm)

Official Military Personnel Files:
Army (http://dpclo.defense.gov/Privacy/SORNsIndex/DODwideSORNArticleView/tabid/6797/Article/6131/a0600-8-104-ahrc.aspx)
Navy (http://dpclo.defense.gov/Privacy/SORNsIndex/DODwideSORNArticleView/tabid/6797/Article/6405/n01070-3.aspx)
Marine Corps (http://dpclo.defense.gov/Privacy/SORNsIndex/DODComponentArticleView/tabid/7489/Article/6775/m01070-6.aspx)
Air Force (http://dpclo.defense.gov/Privacy/SORNsIndex/DODwideSORNArticleView/tabid/6797/Article/5876/f036-af-pc-c.aspx)
Coast Guard (http://www.gpo.gov/fdsys/pkg/FR-2011-10-28/html/2011-27881.htm)

INSTRUCTIONS

Under Title 10 United States Code Section 1552, Active Duty and Reserve Component Service members, Coast Guard, former Service members, their lawful or legal representatives, spouses of former Service members on issues of Survivor Benefit Program (SBP) benefits, and civilian employees with respect to military records other than those related to civilian employment, who feel that they have suffered an injustice as a result of error or injustice in military records may apply to their respective Boards for Correction of Military Records (BCMR) for a correction of their military records. These Boards are the highest level appellate review authority in the military. The information collected is needed to provide the Boards the basic data needed to process and act on the request.

1. All information should be typed or printed. Complete all applicable items. If the item is not applicable, enter "None."
2. If space is insufficient on the front of the form, use the "Remarks" box below for additional information or attach an additional sheet.
3. List all attachments and enclosures in item 9. Do not send original documents. Send clear, legible copies. Send copies of military documents and orders related to your request, if you have them available. Do not assume that they are all in your military record.
4. The applicant must exhaust all administrative remedies, such as corrective procedures and appeals provided in regulations, before applying to the Board of Corrections.
5. ITEM 5. State the specific correction of record desired. If possible, identify exactly what document or information in your record you believe to be erroneous or unjust and indicate what correction you want made to the document or information.
6. ITEM 6. In order to justify correction of a military record, it is necessary for you to show to the satisfaction of the Board by the evidence that you supply, or it must otherwise satisfactorily appear in the record, that the alleged entry or omission in the record was in error or unjust. Evidence, in addition to documents, may include affidavits or signed testimony of witnesses, executed under oath, and a brief of arguments supporting the application. All evidence not already included in your record must be submitted by you. The responsibility of securing evidence rests with you.
7. ITEM 8. U.S. Code, Title 10, Section 1552b, provides that no correction may be made unless a request is made within three years after the discovery of the error or injustice, but that the Board may excuse failure to file within three years after discovery if it finds it to be in the interest of justice.
8. ITEM 10. Personal appearance before the Board by you and your witnesses or representation by counsel is not required to ensure full and impartial consideration of your application. If the Board determines that a personal appearance is warranted and grants approval, appearance and representation are permitted before the Board at no expense to the government.
9. ITEM 11. Various veterans and service organizations furnish counsel without charge. These organizations prefer that arrangements for representation be made through local posts or chapters.
10. ITEM 12. The person whose record correction is being requested must sign the application. If that person is deceased or incompetent to sign, the application may be signed by a spouse, widow, widower, next of kin (son, daughter, mother, father, brother, or sister), or a legal representative that has been given power of attorney. Other persons may be authorized to sign for the applicant. Proof of death, incompetency, or power of attorney must accompany the application. Former spouses may apply in cases of Survivor Benefit Plan (SBP) issues.
11. For detailed information on application and Board procedures, see: Army Regulation 15-185 and www.arba.army.pentagon.mil; Navy - SECNAVINST.5420.193 and www.hq.navy.mil/bcnr/bcnr.htm; Air Force Instruction 36-2603, Air Force Pamphlet 36-2607, and www.afpc.randolph.af.mil/safmrbr; Coast Guard - Code of Federal Regulations, Title 33, Part 52.

MAIL COMPLETED APPLICATIONS TO APPROPRIATE ADDRESS BELOW

ARMY	NAVY AND MARINE CORPS	AIR FORCE	COAST GUARD
Army Review Boards Agency 251 18th Street South, Suite 385 Arlington, VA 22202-3531	Board for Correction of Naval Records 701 S. Courthouse Road, Suite 1001 Arlington, VA 22204-2490	Board for Correction of Air Force Records SAF/MRBR 550-C Street West, Suite 40 Randolph AFB, TX 78150-4742	Department of Homeland Security Office of the General Counsel Board for Correction of Military Records 245 Murray Lane, Stop 0485 Washington, DC 20528-0485

17. REMARKS

DD FORM 149 (BACK), DEC 2014

Appendix 5: Resources for Discharge Upgrading Assistance

1. Connecticut Veterans Legal Center (2011). *Veterans Discharge Upgrade Manual*. Retrieved from https://law.yale.edu/system/files/documents/pdf/Clinics/wirac_CTdischargeUpgradeManual.pdf
2. Connecticut Veterans Legal Center (2014). *Applying for a Discharge Upgrade When you Have PTSD: A Supplemental Guide to the Connecticut Veterans Legal Center's Veterans Discharge Upgrade Manual*. Retrieved from https://ctveteranslegal.org/wp-content/uploads/2014/12/DU-Manual-Supplement.pdf
3. Yale Law School Veterans Legal Services Clinic (2017). *Discharge Upgrade Application Guide*. Retrieved from https://www.vetsprobono.org/library/attachment.312763
4. Swords to Plowshares (n.d.). *Upgrading Your Discharge AND Changing the Reason for Your Discharge*. Retrieved on March 19, 2018 from https://www.swords-to-plowshares.org/guides/upgrading-your-military-discharge-and-changing-the-reason-for-your-discharge/
5. Military Law Task Force of the National Lawyers Guild (2017). *Discharge Upgrades: Introductory Material and Resources for Attorneys and Counselors*. Retrieved from http://nlgmltf.org/military-law-library/publications/memos/discharge-upgrades/
6. Michael Ettlinger & David F. Addlestone (1990). *Military Discharge Upgrading and Introduction to Veterans Administration Law*. Washington, DC: National Veterans Legal Services Project). Retrieved from https://ctveteranslegal.org/wp-content/uploads/2012/12/MilitaryDischargeUpgrading_lr.pdf
7. Boston Bar Association (2015, June 2). *Representing Veterans in Discharge Upgrade Cases*. Boston, MA: Boston Bar Association Continuing Legal Education. Retrieved from http://www.legalservicescenter.org/wp-content/uploads/2012/10/Resource-Binder-Materials.pdf
8. John W. Brooker, Evan R. Seamone & Leslie C. Rogall (2012). Beyond "T.B.D.": Understanding VA's evaluation of a former servicemember's benefit eligibility following involuntary or punitive discharge from the armed forces. *Military Law Review*, *214*, 1–328.

References

Adams, B., & Montalto, D. (2017). With malice toward none: Revisiting the historical and legal basis for excluding veterans from "veterans" services. *Penn State Law Review, 122*(1), 69–139.

American Psychiatric Association. (2013, November 11). Military mental health infographic. Reprinted in Veterans Day and military mental health: The startling facts. *Psychiatric Times*. Retrieved from http://www.psychiatrictimes.com/military-mental-health/veterans-day-and-military-mental-health-startling-facts

Army Writer. (n.d.). Magic bullet counseling. Retrieved March 7, 2018 from http://www.armywriter.com/magic-statement.htm

Baker, J. E. (2014). Is military justice sentencing on the march? Should it be? And if so, where should it head? Court-martial sentencing process, practice, and issues. *Federal Sentencing Reporter, 27*(2), 72–87.

Baldwin, J. M. (2016). Investigating the programmatic attack: A national survey of veterans treatment courts. *Journal of Criminal Law and Criminology, 105*(3), 705–752.

Bland v. Connally, 293 F.2d 852 (D.C. Cir. 1961).

Blue-Howells, J. H., Clark, S. C., van den Berk-Clark, C., & McGuire, J. F. (2012). The U.S. Department of Veterans Affairs Veterans Justice Programs and the sequential intercept model: Case examples in national dissemination of intervention for justice-involved veterans. *Psychological Services, 10*(1), 48–53.

Bojan, M. E. (2016). Bad paper: Reforming the Army reprimand process. *Military Law Review, 224*, 1149–1209.

Brignone, E., Fargo, J. D., Blais, R. K., Carter, M., Samore, M., & Gundlapalli, A. (2017). Non-routine discharge from military service: Mental illness, substance use disorders, and suicidality. *American Journal of Preventive Medicine, 52*(5), 557–565.

Brooker, J. W., Seamone, E. R., & Rogall, L. C. (2012). Beyond "T.B.D.": Understanding VA's evaluation of a former servicemember's benefit eligibility following involuntary or punitive discharge from the armed forces. *Military Law Review, 214*, 1–328.

Carson, B. (2016, February 4). Memorandum for secretaries of the military departments, Subject: Consideration of discharge upgrade requests pursuant to supplemental guidance to military boards for correction of military/naval records (BCMRs/BCNR) by veterans claiming Post Traumatic Stress Disorder (PTSD) or Traumatic Brain Injury (TBI). Washington, DC: Office of Principal Deputy Under Secretary of Defense.

Connecticut Veterans Legal Center. (2011). *Veterans discharge upgrade manual*. Retrieved from https://law.yale.edu/system/files/documents/pdf/Clinics/wirac_CTdischargeUpgradeManual.pdf

Cuthbert, R. (2017a, November 3). An injustice in the Berghdal sentence. *New York Times*.

Cuthbert, R. (2017b, November 11). Mental health help for all who serve. *New York Daily News*.

Department of Defense. (2012). *Manual for courts-martial*. Washington, DC: Government Printing Office.

Doan, R. (1976). Civilian conviction—Basis of administrative military discharge. *Capital University Law Review, 5*, 33–61.

Editorial. (1977, January–February). Undesirable discharge dead. *Infantry Magazine, 67*(1), 52.

Effron, A. (1974). Comment, Punishment of enlisted personnel outside the UCMJ: A statutory and equal protection analysis of military discharge certificates. *Harvard Civil Rights-Civil Liberties Law Review, 9*, 227–324.

Egeland, A. M. (1977). Developments in airman administrative separations. *Air Force Law Review, 18*, 166–198.

Gabriel, R. A. (1987). *No more heroes: Madness and psychiatry in war*. New York, NY: Hill and Wang.

Gilligan, F. A., & Lederer, F. (2017). *Court-martial procedure*. New York, NY: LexisNexis Matthew Bender.

Hagel, C. (2014, September 3). Memorandum for secretaries of the military departments, Subject: Supplemental guidance to military boards for correction of military/naval records considering discharge upgrade requests by veterans claiming Post Traumatic Stress Disorder. Washington, DC: Office of Secretary of Defense.

Irwin, L. (2017). Justice in enlisted administrative separations. *Military Law Review, 225*, 35–83.

Jones, B. K. (1973). The gravity of administrative discharges: A legal and empirical investigation. *Military Law Review, 59*, 1–25.

Kurta, A. M. (2017, August 25). Memorandum for secretaries of the military departments, Subject: Clarifying guidance to military discharge review boards and boards of correction of military/naval records concerning requests by veterans for modification of their discharge due to mental health conditions, sexual assault, or sexual harassment. Washington, DC: Office of the Undersecretary of Defense.

McLoed, A. M. (2012). Decarceration courts: Possibilities and perils of a shifting criminal law. *Georgetown Law Journal, 100*, 1587–1674.

Middendorf v. Henry, 425 U.S. 25 (1976).

Murphy, C. S., Kane, T., Markey, E. J., Boxer, B., Tester, T., Baldwin, T., …, Wyden, R. (2015, November 4). Letter to Secretary of the Army Eric Fanning and General Mark A. Milley. Retrieved from https://www.npr.org/sections/thetwo-way/2015/11/04/454675053/lawmakers-call-for-army-to-investigate-misconduct-discharges-of-service-members

National Defense Authorization Act of 2014. (2013). Public Law No. 113-66 § 1702, 127 Stat. 672, 954-58 (amending 10 U.S.C. § 860).

Oppel, R. A., Jr. (2017, November 3). Bowe Bergdahl avoids prison for desertion; Trump calls sentence "disgrace". *New York Times*.

Pentland, B. (1979, July 11). Prepared statement as Coordinator, Veterans in Prison Project, Veterans Administration Medical Center (Brentwood), Los Angeles, CA. *Oversight on Issues Related to Incarcerated Veterans. Hearing Before the Comm. on Veterans' Affairs, United States Senate* (pp. 523–528). 96th Cong. 1st Sess. Washington, DC: Government Printing Office.

Pentland, B., & Scurfield, R. (1982). Inreach counseling and advocacy with veterans in prison. *Federal Probation, 46*, 21–28.

Press Release. (2018, March 22). Murphy's "Honor Our Commitment Act" included in FY18 Omnibus Appropriations Bill. Retrieved from https://www.murphy.senate.gov/newsroom/press-releases/murphys-honor-our-commitment-act-included-in-fy18-omnibus-appropriations-bill

Rosenblatt, F. D. (2010, September). Non-deployable: The court-martial system in combat from 2001-2009. *Army Lawyer*, 12–34.

Rosenthal, J., & McGuire, J. F. (2013). Incarcerated veterans. In L. Gideon (Ed.), *Special needs offenders in correctional institutions* (pp. 345–376). Thousand Oaks, CA: Sage.

Sandel, C. P. (1984). Other-than-honorable military administrative discharges: Time for confrontation. *San Diego Law Review, 21*, 839–859.

Schwartz, S., & Levitas, L. (2011). Restorative justice for veterans: The San Francisco Sheriff's Department's Community of Veterans Engaged in Restoration (COVER). *Washington University Journal of Law and Policy, 36*, 47–63.

Seamone, E. R. (2011). Reclaiming the rehabilitative ethic in military justice: The suspended punitive discharge as a method to treat military offenders with PTSD and TBI and reduce recidivism. *Military Law Review, 208*, 1–212.

Seamone, E. R. (2013). Dismantling America's largest sleeper cell: The imperative to treat, rather than merely punish, active duty offenders with PTSD prior to discharge from the armed forces. *Nova Law Review, 37*, 479–522.

Seamone, E. R., Mcguire, J. F., Sreenivasan, S., Clark, S., Smee, D., & Dow, D. (2014). Moving upstream: Why rehabilitative justice in military discharge proceedings serves a public health interest. *American Journal of Public Health, 104*(10), 1805–1811.

Seamone, E. R., Sreenivasan, S., McGuire, J. F., Smee, D., Clark, S., & Dow, D. (2017). A rehabilitative justice pathway for war-traumatized offenders caught in the military misconduct Catch-22. *Armed Forces & Society, 44*(1), 1–17.

Simms, S. (2014). Comment, Revision of Article 60 and the military clemency authority's clemency power: An alternative to enacted Legislation. *National Security Law Journal, 2*, 301–330.

U.S. Court of Appeals for the Armed Forces. (2003). *Annual report submitted to the Committees on Armed Services of the United States Senate and the House of Representatives and to the Secretary of Defense, Secretary of Homeland Security, and Secretaries of the Army, Navy, and Air Force Pursuant to the Uniform Code of Military Justice for the Period October 1, 2002 to September 30, 2003*. Washington, DC: U.S. Court of Appeals for the Armed Forces.

U.S. Court of Appeals for the Armed Forces. (2011). *Annual report submitted to the Committees on Armed Services of the United States Senate and the House of Representatives and to the Secretary of Defense, Secretary of Homeland Security, and Secretaries of the Army, Navy, and Air Force Pursuant to the Uniform Code of Military Justice for the Period October 1, 2010 to September 30, 2011*. Washington, DC: U.S. Court of Appeals for the Armed Forces.

U.S. Department of Army. (2010, January 1). *Department of the Army Pamphlet 27-9: Legal services, military judges' benchbook*. Washington, DC: Headquarters, Department of the Army.
U.S. Department of Army. (2014, July). *Army Technical Publication 6-22.1: The counseling process*. Washington, DC: Headquarters, Department of the Army.
U.S. Department of Defense. (2017, February 27). Directive No. 1332.14, Subject: Enlisted administrative separation. Washington, DC: Government Printing Office.
U.S. Department of Veterans Affairs. (2017, June 27). VA Secretary formalizes expansion of emergency mental health care to former service members with Other-Than-Honorable discharges. Retrieved from https://www.va.gov/opa/pressrel/pressrelease.cfm?id=2923
U.S. Department of Veterans Affairs. (n.d.). Vet Centers, eligibility. Retrieved June 25, 2018 from https://www.vetcenter.va.gov/eligibility.asp
U.S. Government Accountability Office. (2017, May). *Report to congressional committees: DoD health, actions needed to ensure Post-Traumatic Stress Disorder and Traumatic Brain Injury are considered in misconduct separations* (GAO-17-260). Washington, DC: Government Printing Office.
United States v. Smart, 21 M.J. 15 (C.M.A. 1985).
Veterans Legal Services Clinic. (2015). *Unfinished business: Correcting "bad paper" for veterans with PTSD: The Defense Department's adjudication of discharge upgrade applications one year since its September 2014 PTSD directive*. New Haven, CT: Yale Law School.
Veterans Legal Clinic. (2016). *Underserved: How the VA wrongfully excludes veterans with bad paper*. Jamaica Plain, MA: Harvard Legal Services Center.
Wilkie, R. L. (2018, July 25). Memorandum for secretaries of the military departments, Subject: Guidance to military discharge review boards and boards for correction of military/naval records regarding equity, injustice, or clemency determinations. Washington, DC: Office of the Undersecretary of Defense.
Winthrop, W. (1920). *Military law and precedents* (2nd ed.). Washington, DC: U.S. Government Printing Office.
Zwerdling, D., & De Yoanna, M. (2016, February 1). Senators want moratorium on dismissing soldiers during investigation. *National Public Radio*. Retrieved from https://www.npr.org/2016/02/01/464907342/senators-want-moratorium-on-dismissing-soldiers-during-investigation

Chapter 9
Military Veterans Who Are Sexual Offenders: What We Know and What We Don't Know

Shoba Sreenivasan, Stephanie Brooks Holliday, Allen Azizian, and James McGuire

Introduction

Although a recent nationwide justice survey found that veterans were incarcerated at a lower rate (855 per 100,000) than U.S. residents (968 per 100,000), military veterans were incarcerated at a proportionately higher rate for sexual offenses than other offenses when compared to criminal histories of non-veterans. Specifically, 35% of veterans were incarcerated in prison for a sexual offense as opposed to 23% of non-veterans; and 11.8% of veterans were incarcerated in jail for a sexual offense versus 5.3% of non-veterans (Bronson, Carson, Noonan, & Berzofsky, 2015). The reasons for such over-representation remain unclear; what we know about military veterans who are sexual offenders is limited; what we don't know encompasses a large field: whether military sexual offenders are described by the similar risk

The views expressed in this article are those of the authors and do not reflect the views of the Department of Veterans Affairs, RAND, California Department of State Hospitals or other governmental, academic or public institutions with which the authors are affiliated.

S. Sreenivasan (✉)
Department of Clinical Psychiatry and the Behavioral Sciences, Keck School of Medicine
University of Southern California, Los Angeles, CA, USA

Department of State Hospitals, Forensic Services Division, Sacramento, CA, USA

S. Brooks Holliday
RAND Corporation, Santa Monica, CA, USA
e-mail: holliday@rand.org

A. Azizian
Department of Criminology, California State University Fresno, Fresno, CA, USA

Department of State Hospitals, Sacramento, CA, USA
e-mail: aazizian@mail.fresnostate.edu

J. McGuire
Veterans Health Administration Justice Program (Retired), Washington, DC, USA

J. Tsai, E. R. Seamone (eds.), *Intersections between Mental Health and Law among Veterans*, https://doi.org/10.1007/978-3-030-31664-8_9

characteristics as civilian sexual offenders; the rates of sexual recidivism are; and what treatments and risk management strategies would work best.

This chapter will review the limited existing literature on military veterans who are sexual offenders and focus on three areas: (1) Does the military culture increase the risk of sexual offending? (2) Are risk factors for sexual offending in military veterans similar or dissimilar to civilians? (3) What community re-entry challenges are unique to military veterans with sexual offenses?

Does the Military Culture Increase Risk of Sexual Offending?

Military masculinity has been suggested by some as creating a culture that condones or facilitates sexual aggression (Karner, 1998). Supporting this view are statistics, i.e., higher rates of sexual assault, at times twice the rates, in the military as in the civilian arena; that the overwhelming majority of the victims are female and their assailants as male (Schmid, 2010); and that sexual assault in the military is greatly underreported (Turchik & Wilson, 2010). Military masculinity is characterized by an emphasis on strength, aggression, emotional detachment, and possible objectification of women. Moreover, some suggest that military male socialization for war-zone deployments may foster "hypermasculinity" essential to prepare for, to complete, and most importantly survive combat missions (Arkin & Dobrofsky, 1978; Dunivin, 1994; Higate, 2003; Seamone, Brooks Holliday, & Sreenivasan, 2018). Male experiences of trauma may be avoided due to hypermasculinity. It has also been argued that traditional masculine gender role socialization such as not showing weakness, developing tolerance for pain, keeping close control on all emotions except anger, emphasizing strength, obedience, and aggression is highly valued in the military. Emotionality triggered by trauma may be perceived as a lack of manliness or failure in masculinity (Fox & Pease, 2012). Avoidance of troubling emotions and in turn avoidance of mental health assistance (Lorber & Garcia, 2010) may serve to deepen trauma-related symptoms (e.g., irritability and anger) and lead to the use of maladaptive coping mechanisms (e.g., aggression or sexual aggression).

Recently, researchers from RAND studied themes that emerged from Office of Special Investigation and Judge Advocate Corps reports involving 196 Air Force sexual assault suspects with the goal of using such data to develop sexual assault preventive measures (Miller et al., 2018). The themes of hypermasculinity, peer attitudes, as well as the sexual assault reporting process itself were suggested to be potential contributors to higher levels of military offenders. Another aspect of military culture is the impact of rank; notably, an argument that low ranking military personnel are prosecuted, while those with higher ranks are able to exert power and authority to both perpetrate sexual assault and escape punishment. Durham (2014), using systematic sampling of 233 active duty military cases from the Department of Defense Annual Report on Sexual Assault in the Military for years 2008–2012, found no difference in punishment for sexual assault offenders with regard to military rank. The Durham (2014) and Miller et al. (2018) reports are notable because they describe in detail both military culture factors and the important differences and nuances of the military justice system in relation to civilian justice. Moreover, in response to concerns that sexual assault was rising in the military, the Department of Defense has taken steps to promote a culture that does not tolerate sexual assault (e.g., programs that encourage reporting and combat retaliation against those who report) (DoD, 2017). DoD (2017) reported statistically significant reduction in sexual assaults from Fiscal Year (FY) 2014 to FY 2016. In FY 2014, 20,300 service members were sexually assaulted while in FY 2016 there were 14,900 such reports. Of note, both Durham (2014) and Miller et al. (2018) studies were quite limited due to type of records available for the research, as data was not available on traditional risk factors and most offender characteristics. Nonetheless, such research offers a future research agenda for scope and methodology in identifying risk factors as they operate within the military, and subsequent carryover into the community as active duty service members are discharged and become veterans.

As a caution to concluding that military culture promotes sexual assault, it bears emphasizing that an exceedingly small minority of military members commit sexual assault; in fact, most military members adhere to strong core values that respect the rights of others. As well, the term "military masculinity" is not confined to negative traits or behaviors. Military culture can encompass positive attributes of a warrior such as strength, endurance, toughness, stoicism, service to others, camaraderie, commitment to value of protection of our nation and its values of democracy, and forward a mission focus. As such, it would be erroneous to conclude that military training creates sexual predators. In the military arena, as in the civilian arena, the factors that are related to the expression of sexual aggression are complex and reflect an interaction between traits and environment.

One area of exploration has been that of the rates of compulsive sexual behavior (CSB) as a post-deployment effect. CSB has been characterized as hypersexual behavior that encompasses inappropriate or excessive urges or fantasies. It has variously been described as "sexual addiction" or "sexual compulsivity" or "hypersexuality" (Kraus, Voon, & Potenza, 2016; Potenza, Gola, Voon, Kor, & Kraus, 2017; Krueger, 2016). Some draw a distinction between paraphilic (non-normative sexual behavior) and non-paraphilic (normative) compulsive sexual disorder (Coleman, 1991). Others have raised concerns that non-paraphilic CSB pathologizes individuals with high sexual drive (Moser, 2013). Still others suggest that hypersexuality may be a symptom of existing mental disorders and not a diagnostic entity of its own (Winters, 2010). In the most recent Diagnostic and Statistical Manual of Mental Disorders (DSM) revision, CSB or hypersexual disorder was proposed as a mental disorder (Kafka, 2010; Reid et al., 2012), but ultimately was not included in the DSM-5 (American Psychiatric Association, 2013). Nonetheless, whether a diagnostic entity or not, CSB can cause subjective distress or impairment in social functioning. Frequent comorbidities in CSB include mood, anxiety, substance abuse, or personality disorders.

Two studies have examined the incidence of CSB among military veterans using the Survey of the Experiences of Returning Veterans (SERV), a methodology designed to describe the post-deployment experiences of Operation Enduring

Freedom (OEF), Operation Iraqi Freedom (OIF), or Operation New Dawn (OND) veterans. In the first study, Smith et al. (2014) examined the prevalence of compulsive sexual behavior among 258 male veterans. Smith et al. (2014) examined the rates of response to two items: "Do you or others that you know think that you have a problem with being overly preoccupied with some aspect of your sexuality or being overly sexually active?" or "Do you have frequent sexual fantasies, urges, or repetitive behaviors which you feel are out of your control or cause you distress?" Though neither of these questions directly address criminal sexual behavior, such as pedophilia, exhibitionism, or rape, the prevalence of compulsive sexual behavior provides some data regarding hypersexuality that can be a precursor for sexual offending. Smith et al. (2014) found the prevalence of CSB in their sample to be 16.7% at the initial interview, dropping to 15.5% at the 3-month follow-up and to 8.8% at 6-months. However, military veteran endorsement of these items was still substantially higher than the estimated rate of 3–6% in the general population. Demographically, those with CSB tended to be older (mean age of 37.2 years) than those without CSB (mean age of 33.3 years), of a minority race or ethnicity, and had reported more post-deployment stressors and poor relationship quality. Smith et al. (2014), theorized that veterans may use sexual behaviors as a tension-reducing mechanism to cope with trauma symptoms. Indeed, 97.7% of those with CSB had a diagnosis of PTSD, and those with CSB had significantly more severe PTSD symptoms than those without CSB (as measured by PTSD Checklist scores). Moreover, the re-experiencing symptom cluster in particular significantly increased the odds of CSB. This is an important consideration, given rates of PTSD in veteran populations. That said, other risk factors for CSB in military veterans were not necessarily unique to the military experience, as there was no association with deployment/post-deployment experiences. Rather, as with the general population, childhood sexual trauma was a core risk factor for CSB in veterans.

In the second study, Kraus et al. (2017), using SERV data, examined the incidence of non-paraphilic CBS in an expanded sample of 820 of military veterans post-deployment (OEF/OIF/OND). Their study included male and female veterans, as well as medical and mental health variables. Demographically, males represented the majority of the sample (60%), though females were over-represented in this study (40% v. 14.8%) compared to their rate among active duty military personnel. The average age was 35.1, and non-Hispanic White/Caucasian males represented the majority of the sample (78%). Approximately half of those sampled were married (51%) and had children (53.8%) and with representation across the five branches of military service. The incidence of CSB was low among female veterans, at 4.8% (14 of the 327 sampled). Among male veterans, Kraus et al. (2016), found a high prevalence rate of CSB (13.8%, or 82 of the 493 sampled) relative to civilian samples (estimated at 3–5%) but cautioned that the rate may have been inflated by the use of only two questions to identify CSB. Sociodemographic associations of CSB among male veterans included a higher incidence among White/Caucasian and Black/African American, higher rates of religious attendance, and a history of arrest. There was no significant association with number of deployments overseas. CSB was significantly associated with suicidality, gambling, and sexually transmitted diseases. CSB was not associated with PTSD symptom severity or substance use disorders. Kraus et al. (2016), concluded that CSB may reflect underlying impulsivity given the significant association with gambling and suicidality, and an unmet treatment need among returning male veterans.

Are Risk Factors for Sexual Offending in Military Veterans Similar or Dissimilar to Civilians?

Researchers have just begun to examine the relationship between individual service member offender characteristics, risk factors and military sexual assault (Durham, 2014; Miller et al., 2018; Turchik & Wilson, 2010). This research is grounded in reviews of what is known about civilian offender risk, theories that might explain higher levels of military sex offending, and in the complexities and differences of military culture and military criminal justice proceedings. There is a large body of literature related to risk factors for sexual recidivism in civilian populations (Hanson & Morton-Bourgon, 2005, 2009; Mann, Hanson, & Thornton, 2010). Low risk sex offenders tend to be older, have female victims, do not have extensive criminal histories, and have engaged in incestual abuse or have victims to whom they are related. By contrast, high risk sexual offenders tend to have male victims who are unrelated, strangers, have prior sexual offense histories, have failures while on supervised community release, and harbor deviant sexual preoccupation.

Researchers agree that several civilian and military offender risk factors are likely similar: for example, childhood abuse, history of sexual assault, alcohol use during offense, attitudes and perceptions hostile to women, belief in stereotypical rape myths, and traditional attitudes regarding sex roles. For example, Turchik and Wilson (2010) cites three Navy studies that indicated that twice the percentage of Navy recruits reported perpetrating a rape prior to entry compared to a similar aged college entry population, and that Navy service member offenders had four times the rates of childhood abuse compared to the civilian offender sample. In an unpublished master's thesis, Sankaram (2010) examined whether there were differences in the personality characteristics of outpatient sexual offenders with and without military backgrounds. Sankaram (2010) found that not only were there no significant differences in the age of offenders or age of victims for participants with and without military backgrounds, but there were also no differences in antisociality and aggression scores between these groups. These studies suggest that there may be shared characteristics between civilian and veteran sexual offenders.

However, empirical research examining characteristics of offenders and risk factors for sexual recidivism among military veterans is limited. A handful of studies have examined the characteristics of veterans who commit sexual offenses in an effort to identify potential risk factors. These studies have highlighted high rates of psychosocial problems in military veterans who commit sexual offenses. One small descriptive study conducted by Bradley Schaffer (2011) described the characteristics of 42 male veterans with sexual offenses who were seeking care at the Cincinnati VA Medical Center between 2004 and 2008. The type of sexual offense was only broadly described as either "sexual assault" (80% of offenders) or "rape" (20% of offenders). Most of the veterans were older (mean age of 50.2), white (68.5%) or black (28.5%), and unemployed (81%). Only 14.2% of the sample were married. Over 90% were either discharged under honorable or general conditions, with Vietnam as the most frequent period of service (54.2%) and the Army as the most common branch of service (54.2%), and only 17.1% were service connected. A large percentage of the sample had been psychiatrically hospitalized (49%), with 21% reporting a history of hallucinations, 18% with reports of violent behavior, and 16% with suicidal ideations. The most common diagnoses were depression (54%) and anxiety (50%). Drug abuse was more common (65%) than alcohol abuse (35%).

In another study, again with a small sample of convenience, Schaffer and Zarilla (2018) described the psychosocial characteristics of 29 military veterans who were incarcerated in jail for a sexual offense and so identified by the VA's Veterans Justice Outreach (VJO) and Healthcare for Reentry Veterans (HCRV). Most were white (90%), male (97%) and older (average age was 48), almost 50% were estimated to be at risk for homelessness at release, with 38% reporting a prior history of homelessness. Drug problems were reported in 24% of the sample and alcohol in 38%. The most common psychiatric diagnosis was major depression or anxiety (79%), with PTSD at 14%. Ten percent of the Schaffer and Zarilla (2018) sample reported military sexual trauma and pre-service trauma. The majority were honorably discharged (76%).

In a paper in submission, Paden et al. (2019) examined characteristics of military veterans detained or civilly committed to a California state forensic hospital under the Sexually Violent Predator (SVP) law and discharged between 1996 and 2017. By way of background, the SVP law was first initiated in the State of Washington in 1990 as a civil commitment option post-prison incarceration and reserved for a small group of highly dangerous sexual offenders. Currently, 20 states and the Federal Government have such laws. Three criteria must be met in order for a sex offender to be deemed an SVP: (1) conviction of sexually violent offense, (2) current diagnosed mental disorder, and (3) risk to public safety as a result of the mental disorder. Demographic-clinical characteristics of veterans (n = 134) to nonveterans (n = 243) were examined. Veterans tended to be Caucasian (63.4%) when compared to civilians (46.5%). African-American veterans represented 20.1% of the sample when compared to 38.7% of the civilian sample. The rates for Hispanic, Native-American, and those who identified as other were similar across the groups. The mean (standard deviation) age of the veterans group at the time of hospital admission was 53.9 (*SD* = 11.6), whereas the mean age of the nonveterans group was 45.2 (*SD* = 9.78). The mean length of hospitalization in years for the veterans group was 6.77 (*SD* = 4.36), whereas the mean length of hospitalization for the nonveterans group was 7.46 (*SD* = 4.64). Within the overall sample, 62.7% of veterans met the diagnostic criteria for pedophilia compared to 39.9% of nonveterans. Further analysis of the data revealed that veterans had a two-fold higher prevalence of pedophilia diagnosis and higher rates of targeting minor males (under the age of 13) than their civilian counterparts. Civilians had a two-fold higher rate of antisocial personality disorder than military veterans and tended to target females over the age of 13. Rates of PTSD and combat exposure were not available.

Although these studies provide some insight into the characteristics of veteran sexual offenders, they are largely descriptive in nature, limiting conclusions about the factors that may actually serve to increase sexual recidivism risk. In a paper under submission, Brooks Holliday, Sreenivasan, Thornton, Elbogen, and McGuire (2018) sought to address this gap in research by examining differences in the characteristics of military veterans who committed a single documented sexual offense and had a single victim to those who had a history of multiple sexual offenses/or victims. These characteristics (number of offenses, number of victims) are associated with persistence of deviant sexual behavior (Hanson & Morton-Bourgon, 2005, 2009), and were therefore used as a proxy for severity of sexual offending behavior. This analysis used data from the Survey of Inmates in State and Federal Facilities (U.S. Department of Justice, 2004), which conducted comprehensive interviews of inmates between October 2003 and May 2004. A total of 1668 identified themselves as military veterans, and 287 had a sexual offense as their controlling case. Within this subsample of veteran sexual offenders, 28.9% (n = 83) were classified as having multiple sexual offenses and/or victims. Among veteran sexual offenders, approximately 49% had an index offense classified as sexual assault–other (e.g., fondling, sexual misconduct, gross sexual imposition by force); 34% had an index offense that was classified as rape–force (e.g., aggravated rape, assault with intent to commit rape); 14% were incarcerated for lewd act with children (e.g., molestation of a child, indecent behavior with a juvenile); and the remaining 4% committed rape–statutory–no force (e.g., statutory rape, violation of a child–no force). In contrast to the findings of Schaffer (2011), nearly 80% had been employed full-time prior to incarceration; however, consistent with his findings, 83% received an honorable discharge.

In this study, analyses were conducted to compare the multiple offenses/victims with the single offense/victim group with respect to sociodemographic, military, clinical, and criminal justice/offense-related characteristics. Specific characteristics were selected to reflect risk factors for sexual offending in civilian populations and common psychosocial concerns in veteran populations (e.g., PTSD, alcohol dependence). Veterans with single offense/victim were younger but did not differ from those with multiple offenses/victims with respect to rates of combat exposure (approximately 21% and 17%, respectively). Though combat exposure did not differentiate these groups, these data were collected at the beginning of the Iraq and Afghanistan engagements, and it is unclear if this trend would remain. Both groups had low rates of PTSD (approximately 9–10%) and moderate rates of alcohol dependence (34% for single offense/victim, 45% for multiple offenses/victims). Regarding offense history, both groups had a similar proportion of victims who were strangers, but those with multiple offenses and/or victims were more likely to have a male victim (24% vs. 10% of those with a single offense/victim)—a risk factor for recidivism in civilian populations. To the extent that individuals with multiple offenses/victims represent a more severe group of sexual offenders, these preliminary data provide insight into the characteristics associated with this more severe group. However, there are important limitations, especially that there was no comparison group of veterans who have not committed sexual offenses.

Though these studies described here provide initial insight into the factors that may increase the risk of sexual offending among military veterans, it is important to acknowledge the limitations. These studies relied on cross-sectional data, and, in the case of the analysis by Brooks Holliday et al. (2018), used a proxy measure for risk. In addition, there are some variables that these studies have not considered that may be relevant to sexual offending behavior. For example, it is unknown whether there is any link between male military personnel who experience military sexual trauma as a risk factor for future sexual offending. In the general sexual recidivism literature, there is a high level of reporting of childhood sexual trauma among sex offenders, though it is not a factor that predicts sexual recidivism (Hanson & Morton-Bourgon, 2005).

In addition, these studies leave open questions as to whether PTSD or combat exposure increases the risk for sexual violence; or what (if any) is the link of war-zone experiences or military culture on pedophilic behavior. We do know that there is an increased risk for general violence among veterans as associated with a combination of factors: severity of combat exposure, PTSD, anger, and alcohol abuse (Blonigen et al., 2016; Elbogen et al., 2010, 2012, 2014).

Though the previously described studies suggest that rates of combat exposure, PTSD, and alcohol abuse may be high in certain groups of veteran sexual offenders, there is no clear evidence that these factors contribute to sexual offending or risk of recidivism in this population. In addition, whether protective factors such as having housing and social support can reduce the recidivism risk for sexual violence, as they have been found to do so for general violence among military veterans (Elbogen et al., 2012) remains unknown.

Unlike the civilian arena, there are no prospective studies of what risk factors contribute to sexual recidivism among military veterans who are sexual offenders. It will be important for future research to examine the associations between these demographic, clinical, and criminogenic factors and offending behavior longitudinally; however, given the paucity of research on this topic, these studies are an important step toward understanding the factors that are important to consider in future investigations.

Are There Community Re-entry Challenges Unique to Military Veterans?

Sex offenders face a number of critical community re-entry challenges. One of the most notorious challenges is housing. Sex offender registry requirements can be an obstacle to obtaining stable housing, as can residency restrictions (i.e., laws preventing sex offenders from living near places where children congregate, such as schools or parks) (Levenson & Cotter, 2005; Zandbergen & Hart, 2006). Tsai, Blue-Howells, and Nakashima (2019) identified among the top three unmet needs, were that of housing for veterans who were registered sexual offenders. Tsai et al. (2019) note that there is virtually no research on the needs and challenges faced by veterans who are registered sexual offenders. The analyses by Brooks Holliday et al. (2018) highlighted that homelessness is a potential issue among military veterans with sexual offense. Though very few veterans in both the single offense/victim or multiple offenses/victims had been homeless prior to incarceration (less than 4%), this study also examined veterans at risk for homelessness, defined as individuals who were homeless or in unstable/temporary housing arrangements prior to incarceration and/or lack of stable housing plans upon release. Nearly 15% of each group met these criteria for homelessness risk. Moreover, this point-in-time definition of homelessness is likely a gross underestimate of the true risk for homelessness. In Schaffer's (2011) sample of veteran sex offenders, 59.4% had one episode of homelessness and 56.7% had two or more episodes. Limited access to housing was also identified as the top barrier to reentry in a recent qualitative study of veteran sex offenders (Simmons et al., 2018), further highlighting how critical this issue can be.

These challenges in obtaining housing are compounded by the lack of housing services available to veterans with sexual offenses. As noted, there are restrictions as to where they can reside, as well as the potential for opposition by neighbors who discover their sexual offense status through Internet sex offender registries. Moreover, though the VA specifically offers programs designed to target homelessness and has a suite of services available to veterans involved in the criminal justice system, there are limitations on what the VA can provide. For example, Veterans Affairs Supportive Housing (HUD-VASH), a program that substantially subsidizes rents for veterans, excludes those with sexual offenses. In addition, VA Grant and Per Diem (GPD) programs that pay for up to 2 years of transitional residence through community partnerships (such as the Salvation Army or Volunteers of America) also frequently exclude veterans with sexual offenses, in part due to resistance by the community partners.

Housing is not the only challenge that veteran sex offenders face when reentering the community; there is also the impact of stigma. Seamone et al. (2018) termed the stigma created by being a sexual offender as "veteran *non grata*." Veterans who are sexual offenders are excluded from Veterans Treatment Courts, a rehabilitative justice process that diverts veterans from the criminal justice system to treatment venues (largely VA) (Seamone et al., 2018). In addition to housing challenges, military sexual offenders face barriers to employment, and ability to re-integrate into society as a result of this stigma. For example, a qualitative study by Simmons et al. (2018) explored barriers and facilitators to reentry experienced by a sample of veteran sex offenders that had left incarceration. Stigma—both external and internal—was identified as a barrier that affected all aspects of the sex offender reentry experience. Participants described the way that external stigma affected their own safety (e.g., as the target of vandalism), as well as their prospects for employment (e.g., by having a job rescinded).

Participants in this study noted several other obstacles to community reintegration, including limited access to sex offender-specific treatment that would help to address their sexual impulses, stating that having access to sex offender treatment—as well as access to substance use disorder treatment—were important facilitators to reentry (Simmons et al., 2018). Participants also noted that having formal support through reentry classes, as well as informal support from family or other offenders, were key to successful reentry. This highlights the importance of services targeting clinical and psychosocial needs to facilitate reentry for veterans who are sexual offenders.

Conclusion

This review highlights the significant lack of information regarding sexual offending among veterans. Despite the disproportionate rate of sexual offending among veterans involved in the criminal justice system, there remain more questions than answers. However, there are several key areas in which further research has the potential to inform clinical practice and policy.

First, there is a need to better understand risk factors for sex offending in veteran populations. There are two logical starting points for the identification of these factors, as described previously: first, risk factors for sexual offending in civilian populations, and second, risk factors for other violent and offending behavior in veterans. A better understanding of risk factors in this population is important for decision-makers within the justice system (e.g., in guiding placement and classification decisions). It also has important implications for developing interventions to reduce recidivism risk—for example, interventions consistent with the risk-need-responsivity model, which indicates that the most effective interventions are those that target an individual's dynamic risk factors (Bonta & Andrews, 2017) and which has demonstrated effectiveness in sex offenders (Hanson & Morton-Bourgon, 2009).

Second, there is a growing movement in the criminal justice system to not only understand risk factors for sexual offending, but also to identify protective factors (de Vries Robbé, Mann, Maruna, & Thornton, 2015). Some work in this area has focused on veterans; for example, Elbogen et al. (2012) identified a number of factors that were protective against risk of violence in military veterans, including stable living situation, perception of control over one's life, positive social support, and having money to cover basic needs (Elbogen et al., 2012). Understanding protective factors among veterans who commit sexual offenses will be critical to mitigating risk—for example, by finding ways to address psychosocial needs and promote wellbeing.

In turn, research in these areas has the potential to affect policies related to veterans who are sex offenders. For example, if stable housing does indeed reduce risk of recidivism, this information could be used to renegotiate the eligibility criteria for the HUD-VASH program. Also, many veterans involved in the criminal justice system receive diversion services via veterans treatment courts (VTCs); however, those with sexual offenses are largely excluded from VTCs. A better understanding of what types of interventions reduce risk of sexual offending in this population might help jurisdictions feel more comfortable and capable of serving veterans who commit sex offenses through VTCs (Seamone et al., 2018). In these ways, future research related to this population is the critical next step.

References

American Psychiatric Association. (2013). *Diagnostic and statistical manual of mental disorders* (5th ed.). Arlington, VA: American Psychiatric Publishing.

Arkin, W., & Dobrofsky, L. R. (1978). Military socialization and masculinity. *Journal of Social Issues, 34*(1), 151–168. https://doi.org/10.1111/j.1540-4560.1978.tb02546.x

Blonigen, D. M., Bui, L., Elbogen, E. B., Blodgett, J. C., Maisel, N. C., Midboe, A. M., … Timko, C. (2016). Risk of recidivism among justice-involved veterans. *Criminal Justice Policy Review, 27*(8), 812–837. https://doi.org/10.1177/0887403414562602

Bonta, J., & Andrews, D. A. (2017). *The psychology of criminal conduct* (6th ed.). New York, NY: Routledge.

Bronson, J., Carson, E. A., Noonan, M., & Berzofsky, M. (2015). Veterans in prison and jail, 2011–12. *Bureau of Justice Statistics special report* (NCJ 249144, pp. 1–22). Washington, DC: U.S. Department of Justice, Office of Justice Programs.

Brooks Holliday, S., Sreenivasan, S., Thornton, D., Elbogen, E., & McGuire, J. (2018). Characteristics of veterans who are sex offenders: A preliminary study. Under review, *Sexual Abuse*, 08/09/2019.

Coleman, E. (1991). Compulsive sexual behavior: New concepts and treatments. *Journal of Psychology & Human Sexuality, 4*(2), 37–52. https://doi.org/10.1300/J056v04n02_04

de Vries Robbé, M., Mann, R. E., Maruna, S., & Thornton, D. (2015). An exploration of protective factors supporting desistance from sexual offending. *Sexual Abuse: A Journal of Research & Treatment, 27*(1), 16–33. https://doi.org/10.1177/1079063214547582

Dunivin, K. O. (1994). Military culture: Change and continuity. *Armed Forces & Society (0095327X), 20*(4), 531–547.

Durham, C. (2014). *An analysis of military sexual assault and subsequent punishment* (Master's thesis). Retrieved from https://uta-ir.tdl.org/uta-ir/handle/10106/24929

Elbogen, E. B., Cueva, M., Wagner, H. R., Sreenivasan, S., Brancu, M., Beckham, J. C., & Van Male, L. (2014). Screening for violence risk in military veterans: Predictive validity of a brief clinical tool. *American Journal of Psychiatry, 171*(7), 749–757. https://doi.org/10.1176/appi.ajp.2014.13101316

Elbogen, E. B., Fuller, S., Johnson, S. C., Brooks, S., Kinneer, P., Calhoun, P. S., & Beckham, J. C. (2010). Improving risk assessment of violence among military veterans: An evidence-based approach for clinical decision-making. *Clinical Psychology Review, 30*(6), 595–607. https://doi.org/10.1016/j.cpr.2010.03.009

Elbogen, E. B., Johnson, S. C., Wagner, R., Newton, V. M., Timko, C., Vasterling, J. J., & Beckham, J. C. (2012). Protective factors and risk modification of violence in Iraq and Afghanistan war veterans. *The Journal of Clinical Psychiatry, 73*(6), 767–773. https://doi.org/10.4088/JCP.11m07593

Fox, J., & Pease, B. (2012). Military deployment, masculinity and trauma: Reviewing the connections. *Journal of Men's Studies, 20*(1), 16–31.

Hanson, R. K., & Morton-Bourgon, K. E. (2005). The characteristics of persistent sexual offenders: A meta-analysis of recidivism studies. *Journal of Consulting & Clinical Psychology, 73*(6), 1154–1163. https://doi.org/10.1037/0022-006X.73.6.1154

Hanson, R. K., & Morton-Bourgon, K. E. (2009). The accuracy of recidivism risk assessments for sexual offenders: A meta-analysis of 118 prediction studies. *Psychological Assessment, 21*(1), 1–21. https://doi.org/10.1037/a0014421

Higate, P. R., (Ed.) (2003). Military Masculinities: Identity and the State. Westport, Connecticut: Praeger

Kafka, M. P. (2010). Hypersexual disorder: A proposed diagnosis for DSM-V. *Archives of Sexual Behavior, 39*(2), 377–400. https://doi.org/10.1007/s10508-009-9574-7

Karner, T. X. (1998). Engendering violent men: Oral histories of military masculinity. In L. H. Bowker & L. H. Bowker (Eds.), *Masculinities and violence* (pp. 197–232). Thousand Oaks, CA: Sage Publications, Inc. https://doi.org/10.4135/9781483328010.n11

Kraus, S., Voon, V., & Potenza, M. N. (2016). Should compulsive sexual behavior be considered an addiction? Addiction, 111, 2097–2106. https://doi.org/10.1111/add.13297

Kraus, S. W., Martino, S., Potenza, M. N., Park, C., Merrel, J. D., & Hoff, R. A. (2017). Examining compulsive sexual behavior and psychopathology among a sample of postdeployment U.S. male and female military veterans. *Military Psychology, 29*(2), 143–156. https://doi.org/10.1037/mil0000147

Krueger, R. B. (2016). Diagnosis of hypersexual or compulsive sexual behavior can be made using ICD-10 and DSM-5 despite rejection of this diagnosis by the American Psychiatric Association. *Addiction, 111*(12), 2110–2111. https://doi.org/10.1111/add.13366

Levenson, J. S., & Cotter, L. P. (2005). The effect of Megan's law on sex offender reintegration. *Journal of Contemporary Criminal Justice, 21*(1), 49–66. https://doi.org/10.1177/1043986204271676

Lorber, W., & Garcia, H. A. (2010). Not supposed to feel this: Traditional masculinity in psychotherapy with male veterans returning from Afghanistan and Iraq. *Psychotherapy Theory, Research, Practice, Training, 47*(3), 296–305.

Mann, R. E., Hanson, R. K., & Thornton, D. (2010). Assessing risk for sexual recidivism: Some proposals on the nature of psychologically meaningful risk factors. *Sexual Abuse: A Journal of Research & Treatment, 22*(2), 191–217. https://doi.org/10.1177/1079063210366039

Miller, L. L., Keller, K. M., Wagner, L., Marcellino, W., Donohue, A. G., Greathouse, S. M., … Ayer, L. (2018). *Air force sexual assault situations, settings, and offender behaviors*. Santa Monica, CA: RAND Corporation.

Moser, C. (2013). Hypersexual disorder: Searching for clarity. *Sexual Addiction & Compulsivity, 20*(1/2), 48–58. https://doi.org/10.1080/10720162.2013.775631

Paden, S., Azizian, A., Sreenivasan, S., Brooks Holliday, S., McGuire, J., & Seto, M. (2019). A comparison of risk factors among released military veterans committed under California's Sexually Violent Predator statute. *Sexual Abuse,* 08/01/2019.

Potenza, M. N., Gola, M., Voon, V., Kor, A., & Kraus, S. W. (2017). Is excessive sexual behaviour an addictive disorder? *The Lancet Psychiatry, 4*(9), 663–664. https://doi.org/10.1016/S2215-0366(17)30316-4

Reid, R. C., Carpenter, B. N., Hook, J. N., Garos, S., Manning, J. C., Gilliland, R., … Fong, T. (2012). Report of findings in a DSM-5 field trial for hypersexual disorder. *Journal of Sexual Medicine, 9*(11), 2868–2877. https://doi.org/10.1111/j.1743-6109.2012.02936.x

Sankaram, U. R. (2010). *Military influences on personality characteristics of sexual offenders: An examination of PAI scale scores* (Master's thesis). Retrieved from: http://commons.pacificu.edu/spp/123

Schaffer, B. (2011). Veteran sex offenders and reentry problems. *Journal of Correctional Health Care, 17*(3), 266–270. https://doi.org/10.1177/1078345811401355

Schaffer, B. J., & Zarilla, L. (2018). Military veteran sex offenders: Visible and on the radar. *Journal of Human Behavior in the Social Environment, 28*(1), 109–124. https://doi.org/10.1080/10911359.2017.1377135

Schmid, M. N. (2010). Combating a different enemy: Proposals to change the culture of sexual assault in the military. *Villanova Law Review, 55*(2), 475–508. Retrieved from http://digitalcommons.law.villanova.edu/vlr/vol55/iss2/6

Seamone, E., Brooks Holliday, S., & Sreenivasan, S. (2018). Veteran non grata: Veteran sex offenders with service-related mental health conditions and the need to mitigate risk. *Virginia Journal of Criminal Law, 6*(1), 182–237.

Simmons, M., McInnes, K., Kim, B., Hyde, J., Lemon, T., & Resnick, K. (2018, February). *Veteran sex offender access to housing and health services after release from incarceration: Best practices and obstacles*. Webinar presentation as part of the VA National Center on Homelessness among Veterans "Connecting Research to Practice" series.

Smith, P. H., Potenza, M. N., Mazure, C. M., Mckee, S. A., Park, C. L., & Hoff, R. A. (2014). Compulsive sexual behavior among male military veterans: Prevalence and associated clinical factors. *Journal of Behavioral Addictions, 3*(4), 214–222. https://doi.org/10.1556/JBA.3.2014.4.2

Tsai, J., Blue-Howells, J., & Nakashima, J. (2019). Needs of homeless veterans: 5 year of the CHAENG Survey 2012-16. *Journal of Public Health, 41*, e16–e24. https://doi.org/10.1093/pubmed/fdy076

Turchik, J. A., & Wilson, S. M. (2010). Sexual assault in the U.S. military: A review of the literature and recommendations for the future. *Aggression and Violent Behavior, 15*(4), 267–277. https://doi.org/10.1016/j.avb.2010.01.005

United States Department of Defense (DoD). (2017). Department of Defense annual report on sexual assault in the military, fiscal year 2016. Retrieved February 26, 2018 from www.sapr.mil/public/docs/reports/FY16_Annual/FY16_SAPRO_Annual_Report.pdf

United States Department of Justice, Office of Justice Programs, Bureau of Justice Statistics, Survey of Inmates in State and Federal Correctional Facilities. (2004). ICPSR04572-v2. Ann Arbor, MI: Inter-university Consortium for Political and Social Research [distributor]. https://doi.org/10.3886/ICPSR04572.v2. Retrieved April 27, 2016.

Winters, J. (2010). Hypersexual disorder: A more cautious approach. *Archives of Sexual Behavior, 39*(3), 594–596. https://doi.org/10.1007/s10508-010-9607-2

Zandbergen, P. A., & Hart, T. C. (2006). Reducing housing options for convicted sex offenders: Investigating the impact of residency restriction laws using GIS. *Justice Research & Policy, 8*(2), 1.

Chapter 10
The Critical Importance of Time, Place, and Type of Discharge from the Military

Elspeth Cameron Ritchie

Introduction

This chapter was first conceived by the editors as one on special populations "to include women, homeless, and Iraq and Afghanistan veterans". However, each service era and cohort of veterans is its own special population, often defined by where and when they served.

Thus, another way to conceptualize the veteran population is by either the time and place in which they served, conflicts in which they fought, or the period of service during peacetime.

For convenience these conflicts and/or wars are called by their most commonly used name, which is often the country in which they take place. These are summarized further below. The chapter also focuses on the "special populations" of female veterans and homeless veterans.

The chapter opens with a discussion of types of discharges veterans receive when they leave the military, as that discharge may be critically important to their future trajectory.

The chapter seeks to broaden the discussion by using a series of composite case examples. These are drawn from the authors' clinical experience, to illustrate particular points. Clinical treatment is not covered in this chapter but may be found in

E. C. Ritchie (✉)
Department of Psychiatry, Medstar Washington Hospital Center, Washington, DC, USA

Department of Psychiatry, Georgetown University School of Medicine, Washington, DC, USA

Department of Psychiatry, Uniformed Services University of the Health Sciences, Bethesda, MD, USA

Department of Psychiatry, George Washington University School of Medicine, Washington, DC, USA
e-mail: Elspeth.C.Ritchie@gunet.georgetown.edu

J. Tsai, E. R. Seamone (eds.), *Intersections between Mental Health and Law among Veterans*, https://doi.org/10.1007/978-3-030-31664-8_10

other venues (Ritchie, 2015). A limitation of this chapter is the lack of robust data to support some of the hypotheses. For example there is little to no known data on legal issues facing female veterans from any conflicts.

Discharges: Honorable, Other than Honorable, and Dishonorable Discharges

There are several ways that a military member may leave the Armed Forces. The preferred way is with an honorable discharge, either a routine administrative separation or with retirement. Administrative separations may be for a variety of reasons from a scheduled ETS (end of time in service), for pregnancy, for psychiatric reasons, and for misconduct. The administrative separations are classified as honorable, other than honorable or dishonorable. In general, honorable discharges offer access to the Veterans Health Administration (VHA) health care and may offer other financial benefits. Other-than-honorable or dishonorable discharges usually do not offer benefits. There have been some recent changes as noted below.

Retirement may occur after 20 years or more of military service, or for medical reasons. Retirement from the military usually offers both VA care and access to the military health care system, known as TRICARE. Access to the military health care system is prioritized, with active duty first, and then to dependents and retirees. There is also a priority list for the VA, with priority given to recent veterans, those with service connected disabilities and those below a certain income level. The determinations is a complex subject, covered further in other sources such as the Veterans Benefit Administration website (U.S. Department of Veterans Affairs, 2018).

Other service members may be discharged for a variety of less favorable conditions. In the past, many service members were discharged for personality disorders (Department of the Army, 2005). In the Army these were termed "5-13s", for the applicable governing regulations. Although these are technically honorable discharges, they usually did not bring VA benefits, as the condition was considered existing prior to services (EPTS) (Department of the Army, 2005).

There are other forms of other-than-honorable or dishonorable conditions. Until relatively recently (2011) service members could be discharged for being homosexual. Other service members have been discharged under a variety of chapter separations leading to "other than honorable conditions" or OTH. Often these discharges are related to drug offenses. Until recently these "OTH" veterans have had no access to VA care. Recently this has been changed to allowing them to have emergency mental health care for up to 6 months (Tsai & Rosenheck, 2018; U.S. Department of Veterans Affairs, 2017a).

Dishonorable discharges often followed allegations of misconduct, with or without judicial proceedings, such as courts martials. These are more punitive discharges as Veterans discharged this way have no VA benefits. The stain remains to follow them into the civilian word, making employment much harder to find, especially in fields like law enforcement.

All of those with the above negative discharges are at higher risk for problems with employment, homelessness, drug issues and legal problems. Studies have shown that they are far more expensive to society as well because of the tremendous medical costs related to homelessness (Rog & Buckner, 2007).

President Trump has recently mandated in an executive order that all transitioning veterans should have access to VA care following military service for 1 year (White House, 2018). Full details of implementation of this policy are still being developed.

The Importance of Military Time Served: Legal Issues Vary

The Wars of Our Fathers: WWI and II and Korea (1918–1953)

The major combat theaters in the past century include World Wars I and II, Korea, Vietnam, the first Gulf War, and the recent wars in Afghanistan and Iraq (also known as Operation Enduring Freedom (OEF), Operation Iraqi Freedom (OIF) and by other names). In general, large cohorts of men and women have gone to war during these periods, and often define themselves by these wartime experiences.

In the case of the first wars listed, each one has a different age group, a different cultural context and their own stressors. For example, surviving WWI vets are in their 90s, Korean vets in their 80s, and Vietnam vets in their 70s. Since the latter wars since 9/1/2001 have lasted almost 18 years, the ages of affected service members are more variable. Sometimes fathers and sons, and mothers and daughters, have served in the "Long War" which has been used to refer to the conflicts in Iraq and Afghanistan.

There have been numerous other deployments and combat operations over the last 30 years, which are not technically called "wars". These conflicts have been termed Operations Other Than War (OOTW). These include those in Panama, Haiti, Bosnia, Kosovo, Somalia and other theaters in Africa and the Middle East.

Humanitarian assistance and disaster relief may also be central to the military and mission. Although not technically wars between nations they have often been very dangerous operations, with both combat and other violence. For example, "Operation Restore Hope" in Somalia transitioned from a humanitarian mission into armed conflict. Many service members have served in multiple OOTWs during their military career.

Whether the veteran was drafted or enlisted voluntarily affects their views of their service. In World Wars I and II, Korea and Vietnam, most service members either volunteered or were drafted. In the World Wars serving was seen as a patriotic duty. Units were deployed together, in formations such as battalions or companies. They stayed together until the wars ended, perhaps for 3 or more years. They also returned home from overseas together by ship, to a welcoming United States (Ritchie, 2002).

In the Korean War (1950–1953) and the Vietnam War (1964–1972) service members usually deployed to the theater as individuals for 1 year, rather than as a unit. Thus, they had less unit cohesion. “Old timers” who were looking forward to heading home did not find much point in getting to know the new Soldiers.

The Korean War has often been called the “Forgotten War”, coming so soon after World War II. In many ways it was a proxy war between the superpowers during the Cold War. The return home of American veterans from Korea was further tainted by fears about “brainwashing”, especially among those taken Prisoner of War (POW) by the Chinese. Thus, many veterans slipped quietly back in US society, without highlighting their veteran status (Ritchie, 2002).

There is little known data about criminal activity from veterans in World War I and II, and other conflicts prior to Vietnam. Whether that was due to an actual lack of problems or a lack of data collection is not clear. However, those veterans, now generally dead or in their nineties, will not further be discussed here.

The Vietnam War and Aftermath

The Vietnam War is usually considered to have lasted between 1964 and 1972 although both the beginning and ending had murky dates. Many soldiers and other service members were drafted or enlisted to avoid the draft.

The Tet Offensive in 1968 led to both major offensives by the North Vietnamese and a rejection of the war back in the United States. Especially after 1968 many Service members had mixed feelings about serving—or were decidedly negative. Large protests against the war escalated throughout the country. The US received Soldiers back by spitting in their faces and calling them “baby killers” (Camp, 2011).

Veterans from the 8 years of war in Vietnam—until recently, the longest one in our history—are a very large cohort. They currently are mainly in their 70s. Thus, they are an aging but still vigorous population. However, the wear and tear of aging— no longer working, failing bodies, losing spouses—is taking its toll.

As mentioned above, veterans who served in Vietnam came home to a changing and often hostile United States (Camp, 2011). Many “dropped out” of conventional society. They often shunned the Veterans Affairs hospitals (Camp, 2011).

There was little mental health support back home for the veterans on their return. Importantly the formal concept of post-traumatic stress disorder (PTSD) had yet to be developed. Over time, however, many more mental health services were developed. In the VA system, veteran centers (“Vet centers”) were fielded to provide “store front counselors”.

PTSD emerged as a diagnosis in 1980, mainly based on the psychological sequelae of combat from Vietnam. PTSD was characterized by flashbacks, numbness and avoidance, and hypervigilance (8, DSM III). Along with the emergence of this new diagnosis, grew fears of “ticking time bombs” who were feared to be prone to unprovoked violence.

A far more common problem was and is unemployment and homelessness. Of course, homelessness is a ubiquitous problem, both among veterans and the civilian population. However, it was with Vietnam veterans that their homelessness really claimed public attention.

In the author's experience in working with both Vietnam and other veterans, in many cases the slide into homelessness is gradual. Musculoskeletal problems or other disorders may prevent working. Problems with relationships lead to the end of a relationship and moving out of a wife or girlfriend's house. Coach surfing yields to sleeping in a car, and then to the shelter or street.

In regards to the legal system, homeless individuals are far more likely to commit so called "nuisance crimes", e.g., trespassing or urinating in public places. They often rotate between the streets, the jails and psychiatric hospitals. Where they end up depends more on the customs and culture of the native police force and the judiciary than on the actual crimes.

It has long been known that jails are now where most mentally ill are housed. It is generally estimated that about 10% of the inmates in jails are veterans. (These issues are covered in more detail in other chapters in this volume.)

The Veterans Administration has made heroic efforts to minimize homelessness. If a veteran is eligible for services, they may receive a variety of benefits (please see other chapters for details).

Case Example

Mike is a 75-year-old veteran who presented to the homeless center of the VA for clearance for a housing voucher. He was not interested in treatment for his alcohol use or PTSD symptoms.

He had been housed until a break-up with his girlfriend 5 years earlier. He stayed with friends and family for a while, but wore out his welcome there, so he slept in his car. He refused to go to a shelter.

He had been in and out of jail, mainly for trespassing and public drunkenness. His jail stays were typically brief.

He eventually got housing through the VA and the "Housing First" program, which did not require sobriety. A public defender worked with him to get him into a veteran's court.

He finally decided to seek help for his PTSD and heavy alcohol use. Although he did not achieve complete sobriety, his symptoms dramatically improved and his quality of live was much better, once he was off the streets.

1990 Onwards

After Vietnam, the draft essentially ended. Since then, service members in the US military have been voluntary enlistees.

The first Gulf War (1990–1991) was relatively very brief, with few casualties, and considered a victory. PTSD and other psychological consequences of war were relatively rare. However, there was the emergence of mysterious physical illnesses, known then as "Gulf War syndrome". In general, this syndrome is believed to be related to a combination of toxic exposures, to include nerve agents, sand, petroleum products and other stressors.

There were numerous operations other than war (OOTW) before and after the first Gulf War. This author deployed to Somalia in 1993. Although Operations Restore Hope started as a humanitarian mission it turned into a combat one. The events depicted in "Black Hawk Down" lead to the cessation of American involvement in Africa for many years. However, allies served in Rwanda, the Congo and other bloody scenarios.

There is little hard data in the legal system available for these conflicts between Vietnam and the wars before 9/11. There does appears to be a connection between the use of an antimalarial medication, mefloquine, and suicide and violence. Mefloquine was used by in Somalia in 1992–1993, numerous other African nations throughout the last thirst years, the first year in the Iraq War, and the first 10 years of war in Afghanistan. There have been anecdotal reports of major psychiatric problems in Soldiers and Marines (Nevin & Ritchie, 2015).

Peacetime Veterans

There are many millions of veterans who served in times of relative peace, or who served in non-conflicts during wartime and other conflicts. Again, data is not available as to what their rate of criminal offenses are compared to other combat veterans.

Anecdotally, however, these veterans do not do as well as those who have served in combat (personal communication, Dr. Maria Llorente, March 2018). Why is that? There are several reasons. Non-combat veterans are less likely to receive benefits from the VA. These benefits are both financial (e.g., service connection disability, pensions, etc.) and health care related.

In addition, they probably have less of a social connection to other veterans. They are also less likely to receive a "hero's welcome" home or to get other services offered to combat veterans.

9/11 and the Aftermath

Troops deployed into Afghanistan shortly after 9/11/2001. They invaded Iraq in March of 2003. Veterans from these conflicts will be considered together, since many deployed repeatedly to one or both theaters of war. There were some differences and some similarities.

For many years after the initial invasion in 2001, the Afghanistan war was slower paced. On the other hand, the fighting in Iraq was especially intense during 2004–2008. Troops mainly withdrew from Iraq in 2010, but there is a continued military presence in Afghanistan.

Soldiers were usually sent for a year, although some were extended up to 15 months during the "surge" in 2005–2006. Marines usually went for 6–7 months. All services faced frequent deployments with short "dwell times" (times back in garrison).

Troops faced improvised explosive devices (IEDs) and other forms of bombs, initially mainly in Iraq and then in both conflicts. As a result, many suffered from a wide variety of injuries, to include facial burns, amputations and traumatic brain injury (TBI).

The most recent wars in the Middle East have produced robust advances in screening, detection and treatment of both PTSD and TBI. Research both in the theater of war and back home has been extraordinary (Gallaway, Millikan, Bell, & Ritchie, 2014). With awareness of the prevalence of PTSD and TBI have come monies for reintegration and treatment.

PTSD and TBI became the "signature wounds" of the war. Both were often due to the "signature weapon" of the war, the blast. Soldiers suffered multiple other severe and mild injuries, to include amputations and genital injuries. Both PTSD and TBI can contribute to increased irritability and impulsivity. Pain is another trigger.

While it is unclear as to the exact contributing factors of PTSD, TBI, pain and other injuries, there is an increase in several types of charges in recent veterans. These include domestic violence and weapons charges. There is not much published research on this topic. Research has shown increased violence associated with younger age, lower ranks and more exposure to combat (Gallaway et al., 2014).

There have also been about 50,000 wounded in these last wars. Many survived severe injuries which would have killed them in other years, such as multiple amputations and head wounds. Along with injury comes pain, disabilities, and addiction to opiates.

Many veterans also use marijuana to counter act their post-traumatic stress symptoms. With the decriminalization and/or use of medical marijuana common trends in America, it is hoped that this will not lead to a new wave of incarceration.

After 9/11/2001, with the conflicts in Afghanistan and Iraq, there was a tremendously positive attitude towards the military members, which persists today. There is tremendous support for the recent veterans.

Case Example

Sean was a 34 year old veteran of both Afghanistan and Iraq who had been honorably discharged 5 years prior to being arrested for breaking and entering. He was working as a contractor doing security when he gathered with fellow veterans from his Army unit. One night they mourned the loss of one of their colleagues who had killed himself recently.

Sean got very drunk, and apparently had a flashback. He entered a neighboring bar and moved through it room by room, apparently clearing the rooms. He was apprehended by local police but fought with them, kicking one in the kneecap.

The next morning he awoke in jail. He did not remember any of the prior nights events. However a video camera had recorded his strange movements.

After learning of his service and numerous medals the judge sentenced him to time served and probation.

Female Veterans

Although there is a lot of information about clinical issues for female service members and veterans, there is a dearth of published information about legal and forensic issues. That is likely because women commit crimes less often, in general and in particular for female veterans. Having said that there is no data known to this author on the relationship between female veterans and the criminal justice system. Therefore, this section will attempt to discuss what is known and to speculate how these issues may intersect with legal issues in the coming years.

We do know that the suicide rate among female veterans is about 4 times as high as their civilian counterparts. This is likely reflective of their increased familiarity and possession of firearms (Ghahramanlou-Holloway, George, Careno-Ponce, & Garrick, 2015; Price, 2018; U.S. Department of Veterans Affairs, 2017b).

The prevalence of sexual trauma in the military has been widely reported on. The combination of sexual trauma and trauma from combat leads to higher rates of PTSD, depression, substance abuse. For a summary see (Bell & McCutcheon, 2015).

Women in the military are of reproductive age. There is a high rate of unintended pregnancy, often cited as twice the civilian rate for matched cohorts (Grindlay & Grossman, 2013; Lindberg, 2011; Robbins, Chao, Frost, & Fonseca, 2005). This is probably due to a number of factors: in deployed environments birth control may or may not be easily accessible. In many countries where service women are stationed, such as Korea and Japan, abortion is illegal. TRICARE, the military health care system, does not cover abortion, except in the case of rape or incest. There is also a high rate of divorce for enlisted female service members compared to their civilian counterparts (Karney, Loughran, & Pollard, 2012). So, many young women find themselves as single mothers. They may or may not be able to sustain both a military career and motherhood, often depending on what family support is available.

So, they often decide to leave the military, planning to get a job or go back to school. But the cost of childcare may make those goals difficult. Thus, like their male counterparts they may end up staying with family or friends or otherwise couch surfing. Shelters are primarily available to men without families.

In the authors' experiences, but not yet in the literature, the legal difficulties female veterans get into are related to drug abuse, and domestic violence. Perhaps they may remain in a relationship with someone who is sexually trafficking them, because they are dependent on heroin or other substances.

Case Example
Ashley is a 28 year old single mother of 2 children, ages 2 and 4. She had done well in the military, raising quickly to the rank of sergeant. However when she became pregnant for the second time, she decided she could not maintain a military career and deploy, while being a mother.

She thought she would go back to school and get a business degree. However, despite some help from her mother, she could not afford rent and child care. She accumulated debt and was evicted from her apartment.

She lived with her mother and her children for a while, but it was cramped quarters. Her mother's boyfriend insisted that she leave by the end of the month. She left her children off at child care, penned a note, saying she loved them, then went to a park and shot herself with her mother's boyfriends' Glock.

Conclusion

Veterans are a varied group, ranging from their early 20s to centenarians. While drawn from many segments of the American population, they often define themselves depending on the time and war in which they served. These include both major conflicts, such World War II, Korea and Vietnam and the recent wars, and smaller scale missions such as in Bosnia, Somalia and humanitarian missions.

Depending on the time in service, their homecoming, and numerous other factors, they thrive—or do not—in US society. Those who do not thrive and become homeless are often entangled in the legal system often for relatively minor crimes Rarely, serious crimes occur, often dealing with domestic violence and gun charges (Gallaway et al., 2014). Other risk factors for legal problems include the physical and psychological effects of war. These include, but are not limited to, PTSD, TBI, and addiction to narcotics.

The wars in Iraq and Afghanistan have dragged on, without clear victories. At the time of writing of this chapter, the United States has been in Afghanistan for almost 18 years. Patriotic support for the military persists, but the funding for various military and veterans health and addiction programs is less clear. We believe that funding is essential to decrease entanglement in the criminal justice system.

References

Bell, M. E., & McCutcheon, S. J. (2015). The Veterans Health Administration response to military sexual trauma. In E. C. Ritchie & A. L. Naclerio (Eds.), *Women at war* (pp. 321–328). New York, NY: Oxford University Press.

Camp, N. M. (2011). US army psychiatry legacies of the Vietnam War. In E. C. Ritchie (Ed), *Combat and operational behavioral health* (pp. 9–42), Borden Institute, Washington DC.

Department of the Army. (2005). *Active duty enlisted administrative separations* (AR 635-200). Washington, DC: U.S. Headquarters.

Gallaway, M. S., Millikan, A. M., Bell, M. R., & Ritchie, E. C. (2014). Epidemiological consultation team findings. In E. C. Ritchie (Ed.), *Forensic and ethical issues in military behavioral health* (pp. 135–150). Houston, TX: Borden Institute.

Ghahramanlou-Holloway, M., George, B., Careno-Ponce, J. T., & Garrick, J. (2015). Suicide-related ideation and behaviors in military women. In Ritchie EC, Naclerio A (Eds), (PP. 243–265) *Women at war*, Oxford University Press, New York City.

Grindlay, K., & Grossman, D. (2013). Unintended pregnancy among active-duty women in the United States military, 2008. *Obstetrics & Gynecology, 121*(2), 241–246.

Karney, B. R., Loughran, D. S., & Pollard, M. S. (2012). Comparing marital status and divorce status in civilian and military populations. *Journal of Family Issues, 33*(12), 1572–1594.

Lindberg, L. D. (2011). Unintended pregnancy among women in the US military. *Contraception, 84*(3), 249–251.

Nevin, R. L., & Ritchie, E. C. (2015). The mefloquine intoxication syndrome: A significant potential confounder in the diagnosis and management of PTSD and other chronic deployment-related neuropsychiatric disorders. In *Posttraumatic stress disorder and related diseases in combat veterans* (pp. 257–278). Cham: Springer.

Price, J. (2018). Battling depression and suicide among female veterans. *NPR News*. Retrieved from https://www.npr.org/2018/05/29/614011243/battling-depression-and-suicide-among-female-veterans

Ritchie, E. C. (2002). Psychiatry in the Korean War: Perils, PIES, and prisoners of war. *Military Medicine, 167*(11), 898–903.

Ritchie, E. C. (Ed.). (2015). *Posttraumatic stress disorder and related diseases in combat veterans*. Cham: Springer International Publishing.

Robbins, A. S., Chao, S. Y., Frost, L. Z., & Fonseca, V. P. (2005). Unplanned pregnancy among active duty servicewomen, US Air Force, 2001. *Military Medicine, 170*(1), 38–43.

Rog, D. J., & Buckner, J. C. (2007). *Toward understanding homelessness: the 2007 national symposium on homelessness research*. Washington, DC: Department of Health and Human Services.

Tsai, J., & Rosenheck, R. A. (2018). Characteristics and health needs of veterans with other-than-honorable discharges: expanding eligibility in the veterans health administration. *Military Medicine, 183*(5–6), e153–e157.

U.S. Department of Veterans Affairs. (2017a, June 27). VA secretary formalizes expansion of emergency mental health care to former service members with other-than-honorable discharges. Retrieved from https://www.blogs.va.gov/VAntage/39092/va-secretary-formalizes-expansion-emergency-mental-health-care-former-service-members-honorable-discharges/

U.S. Department of Veterans Affairs. (2017b, August). Facts about suicide among women veterans: August 2017. Retrieved from https://www.mentalhealth.va.gov/docs/VA-Women-Veterans-Fact-Sheet.pdf

U.S. Department of Veterans Affairs. (2018, July 23). Health benefits. Retrieved from https://www.va.gov/healthbenefits/apply/

White House. (2018, January 9). President Donald J. Trump takes care of veterans from the battlefront to the home front. Retrieved from https://www.whitehouse.gov/briefings-statements/president-donald-j-trump-takes-care-veterans-battlefront-home-front/

Index

J. Tsai, E. R. Seamone (eds.), *Intersections between Mental Health and Law among Veterans*, https://doi.org/10.1007/978-3-030-31664-8

The manufacturer's authorised representative in the EU is Springer Nature Customer Service Centre GmbH, Europaplatz 3, 69115 Heidelberg, Germany. If you have any concerns regarding our products, please contact ProductSafety@springernature.com

Printed and bound by CPI Group (UK) Ltd, Croydon, CR0 4YY
05/10/2026
02228145-0004